Paul Hattaway, a native New Z[illegible]
for most of his life. He is an ex[illegible]
of *The Heavenly Man*; *An Asia*[illegible]
Chronicles series: *Shandong*, *G*[illegible], [illegible]*ejiang*, and *Tibet*; and many
other books. He and his wife Joy are the founders of Asia Harvest
(www.asiaharvest.org), which supports thousands of indigenous missionaries and has provided millions of Bibles to spiritually hungry
Christians throughout Asia.

Also by Paul Hattaway:

The Heavenly Man

An Asian Harvest

Operation China

China's Book of Martyrs

The China Chronicles: Shandong (Volume 1)

The China Chronicles: Guizhou (Volume 2)

The China Chronicles: Zhejiang (Volume 3)

The China Chronicles: Tibet (Volume 4)

HENAN

Inside the Greatest Christian Revival in History

Paul Hattaway

PIQUANT editions

Asia Harvest

First published in 2021 by Piquant Editions in the UK
Also published in 2021 by Asia Harvest, **www.asiaharvest.org**

Piquant Editions
www.piquanteditions.com

ISBNs
978-1-909281-78-3 Print
978-1-909281-79-0 Mobi

British Library Cataloguing-in-Publication Data
A catalogue record of this book is available in the UK from the British Library.

ISBN 978-1-909281-78-3

Typeset by Fakenham Typeset Solutions, Fakenham, Norfolk, MR21 8NL

Henan

河 南

"South of the River"

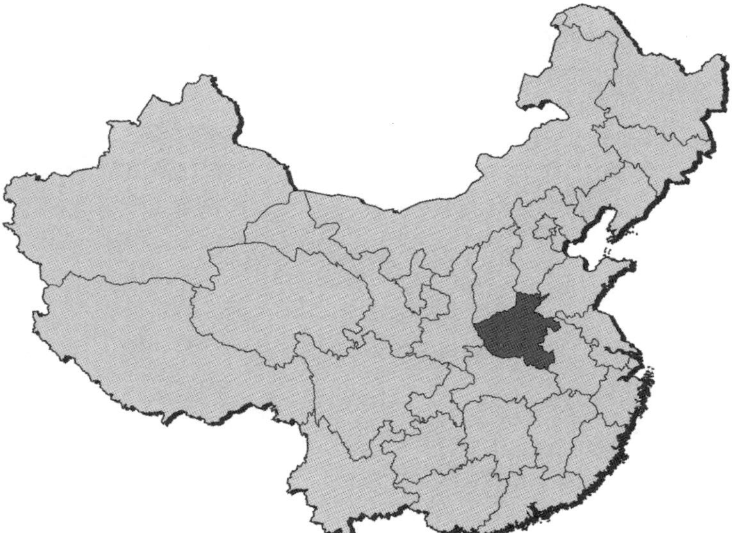

Map of China showing Henan

Henan

Pronounced:	Heh-nahn		
Old spelling:	Honan		
Population:	91,236,854 (2000) 94,029,939 (2010) 97,138,377 (2020)		
Area:	64,479 sq. miles (167,000 sq. km)		
Population density:	1,506 people per sq. mile (581 per sq. km)		
Highest elevation:	7,919 feet (2,414 meters)		
Capital city:	Zhengzhou	3,677,032	
Other cities (2010):	Luoyang	1,584,463	
	Xinxiang	918,078	
	Anyang	908,129	
	Nanyang	899,899	
	Pingdingshan	855,130	
	Kaifeng	725,573	
	Jiaozuo	702,527	
Administrative divisions:	Prefectures:	17	
	Counties:	159	
	Towns:	2,455	
			Percent
Major ethnic groups (2000):	Han Chinese	90,093,286	98.7
	Hui	953,531	1.0
	Mongol	82,170	0.1
	Manchu	61,705	0.1

Contents

Foreword

Over many years and generations, the followers of Jesus in China have set their hearts to be the witnesses of Christ to the nation. Many have paid a great price for their ministry, and the brutal persecutions they have endured for the faith have often been unimaginable.

The Bible commands all believers to "Go into all the world and preach the gospel to all creation" (Mark 16:15). Many foreign missionaries responded to this command in the past, traveling to China to proclaim the Word of God. They blessed the land with their message of new life in Christ, and also suffered greatly when the darkness clashed with God's light. Their faithful service in spite of great hardship was a beautiful example for Chinese believers to emulate as they served God.

China today still urgently needs more servants and laborers to take the gospel throughout the land. God is looking for people who will stand up and declare, "Lord, here am I. Please send me!"

The day of our Lord is near. May your hearts be encouraged by the testimonies of what the Lord Jesus Christ has done in China, to the praise of His glorious Name!

May the Lord raise up more testimonies that would glorify His name in our generation, the next generation, and for evermore!

Lord, You are the victorious King. Blessed are those who follow you to the end!

A humble servant of Christ,
*Moses Xie (1918–2011)**

*The late Moses Xie wrote this Preface for the China Chronicles prior to his death in 2011. He was a highly respected Chinese house church leader who spent 23 years of his life in prison for the Name of Jesus Christ.

Reaction from Christians in China

The book you have in your hands is part of the China Chronicles, which the author is primarily writing to bless and encourage the persecuted Church in China. Each book in the China Chronicles is being translated into Chinese, and thousands of copies are distributed free of charge among China's house church networks.

The Communist authorities in China have blocked the publication of most Christian books, especially those that deal with revival and persecution. Consequently, these books have been like living water to the thirsty Chinese believers, who eagerly desire to read of the mighty acts God has performed in their nation. Here are just a few reactions from house church leaders:

> We never had a good understanding of how the Lord has established His kingdom in our midst, but thanks to these precious books, now we know how God has achieved great and amazing works through His servants in each province. We continue to pray that more life-giving books will flow to us!
>
> (Brother Yang, Chongqing)

> We believe the revival fires of the Holy Spirit will again be lit in our generation, and the mighty power of the Holy Spirit will sweep millions of our countrymen and women into the family of God. These are really amazing books. Please send more!
>
> (Brother Jiang, Hubei Province)

It is very important for the children of God to understand the history of the Church in different parts of China. After all, history is His Story. These are precious books, offering us in-depth accounts of the history of the body of Christ. We eagerly await each book in the series, as they will give us a more comprehensive and all-round understanding of God's glorious work in China.

(Brother Zhai, Beijing)

My husband and I read your book together, and we shared many thoughts and tears as we discovered testimonies we have never heard before. Our spiritual lives have been deeply enriched and encouraged. We hope to receive new books as soon as they are available.

(Sister Xu, Shanghai)

We live in Wuhan and read your book while our city was going through its unprecedented trial. As we read how the Lord established and empowered His Church, we realized that He has been in control in the past, the present, and He will continue to be in control in the future. Thank you for sharing these priceless nuggets of gold with us!

(Brother Cai, Hubei Province)

I shared your book with my fellow brothers and sisters in our Bible study group. We all loved it. Such living and relevant Christian history is nowhere to be found in our country and we treasure it. We beg you to send more of these books.

(Brother Zhou, Zhejiang Province)

I gave your book to my son, who is a college student. He studies history, but said that none of the textbooks in his school teach anything like this. It's eye-opening and refreshing to our souls.

(Sister Ping, Jiangxi Province)

As the sovereignty of the Lord Jesus Christ was revealed to us through all the incidents in history, we grew acutely aware that He is in complete control and we have nothing to fear. As a result, we now have more confidence and faith in Him, knowing that He cares for us and the Spirit of God is at work behind the scenes, weaving together a beautiful narrative as His salvation spreads throughout our nation.

(Brother Gong, Sichuan Province)

The China Chronicles overview

Many people are aware of the extraordinary explosion of Christianity throughout China in recent decades, with the Church now numbering in excess of 100 million members. Few, however, know how this miracle has occurred. The China Chronicles series is an ambitious project to document the advance of Christianity in each province of China from the time the gospel was first introduced to the present day.

The genesis for this project came at a meeting I attended in the year 2000, where leaders of the Chinese house church movements expressed the need for their members to understand how God established His kingdom throughout China.

As a result, it is planned that these books will be translated into Chinese and distributed widely among the Church, both in China and overseas. Millions of Chinese Christians know little of their spiritual legacy, and my prayer is that multitudes would be strengthened, edified, and challenged by these books to carry the torch of the Holy Spirit to their generation.

My intention is not to present readers with a dry list of names and dates but to bring alive the marvelous stories of how God has caused His kingdom to take root and flourish in the world's most populated country.

I consider it a great honor to write these books, especially as I have been entrusted, through hundreds of hours of interviews conducted throughout China, with many testimonies that have never previously been shared in public.

Another reason for compiling the China Chronicles is simply to have a record of God's mighty acts in China.

As a new believer in the 1980s, I recall reading many reports from the Soviet Union of how Christian men and women were being brutally persecuted, yet the kingdom of God grew, with many people meeting Jesus Christ. By the time the Soviet empire collapsed in the early 1990s, no one had systematically recorded the glorious deeds of the Holy Spirit during the Communist era. Tragically, the body of Christ has largely forgotten the miracles God performed in those decades behind the Iron Curtain, and we are much the poorer for it.

Consequently, I am determined to preserve a record of God's mighty acts in China, so that future generations of believers can learn about the wonderful events that have transformed tens of millions of lives there.

At the back of each volume will appear a detailed statistical analysis estimating the number of Christians living in every city and county within each province of China. This is the first comprehensive survey of the number of believers in China—in every one of its more than 2,800 cities, districts, and counties—in nearly a century.

Such a huge undertaking would be impossible without the cooperation and assistance of numerous organizations and individuals. I apologize to the many people who helped me in various ways whose names are not mentioned here, many because of security concerns. May the Lord be with you and bless you!

I appreciate the help of organizations such as the International Mission Board (IMB), Overseas Missionary Fellowship (OMF), Revival Chinese Ministries International (RCMI), and many others, such as the Committee for the Investigation of Persecution of Religion in China (CIPRC), that graciously allowed me to access their archives, libraries, photographs, collections, and personal records. I am indebted to the many believers whose generosity exemplified Jesus' command, "Freely you have received; freely give" (Matthew 10:8).

Many Chinese believers, too numerous to list, have lovingly assisted in this endeavor. For example, I fondly recall the aged house church evangelist Elder Fu, who required two young men to assist him up the stairs to my hotel room because he was eager to be interviewed for this series. Although he had spent many years in prison for the gospel, this saint desperately wanted to testify of God's great works so that believers around the world could be inspired and encouraged to live a more consecrated life. Countless Chinese believers I met and interviewed were similarly keen to share what God has done, to glorify His Name.

Finally, it would be remiss not to thank the Lord Jesus Christ. As you read these books, my prayer is that He will emerge from the pages not merely as a historical figure, but as Someone ever present, longing to seek and to save the lost by displaying His power and transformative grace.

Today, the Church in China is one of the strongest in the world, both spiritually and numerically. Yet little more than a century ago China was considered one of the most difficult mission fields. The great Welsh missionary Griffith John once wrote:

> The good news is moving but very slowly. The people are as hard as steel. They are eaten up both soul and body by the world, and do not seem to feel that there can be reality in anything beyond sense. To them our doctrine is foolishness, our talk jargon. We discuss and beat them in argument. We reason them into silence and shame; but the whole effort falls upon them like showers upon a sandy desert.[1]

How things have changed! When it is all said and done, no person in China will be able to take credit for the amazing revival that has occurred. It will be clear that this great accomplishment is the handiwork of none other than the Lord Jesus Christ. We will stand in awe and declare:

> The Lord has done this,
> and it is marvelous in our eyes.
> This is the day the Lord has made;
> let us rejoice and be glad in it.
> (Psalm 118:23–4, NIV 1984)

Paul Hattaway

Publisher's note: In the China Chronicles we have avoided specific information, such as individuals' names or details, that could directly lead to the identification of house church workers. The exceptions to this rule are where a leader has already become so well known around the world that there is little point concealing his or her identity in these books. This same principle applies to the use of photographs.

Several different systems for writing the sounds of Chinese characters in English have been used over the years, the main ones being the Wade-Giles system (introduced in 1912) and Pinyin (literally "spelling sounds"), which has been the accepted form in China since 1979. In the China Chronicles, all names of people and places are given in their Pinyin form. This means that the places formerly spelt Chung-king, Shantung, and Tien-tsin are now respectively Chongqing, Shandong, and Tianjin; Mao Tse-tung becomes Mao Zedong, and so on. The only times we have retained the old spelling of names is when they are part of the title of a published book or article listed in the Notes or Bibliography.

Note to the reader

Note: In 2009, the author wrote *Henan: The Galilee of China* as the second book in the Fire and Blood series. Unfortunately, it came out at the height of the global financial crisis, and the series was aborted. The book you have in your hands has been revised, compacted, updated, and improved from the original version, with new testimonies, pictures, maps, charts, and graphs.

Introduction

The imposing skyline of Zhengzhou, the capital city of Henan

Geography

Henan is a landlocked province roughly midway between Beijing and Shanghai. It borders six provinces—Hebei, Shandong, Anhui, Hubei, Shaanxi, and Shanxi.

Although containing the third largest population of any province in China with almost 100 million people,[1] Henan ranks just seventeenth in area. It is slightly smaller than England and Scotland combined, or the American state of Missouri. Henan, however, has almost twice as many people as England and Scotland, and 15 times the population of Missouri.

The eastern and central regions of Henan are flat, constituting part of the vast North China Plain. The province is generally mountainous in the west and south, and is framed by the Taihang Mountains in the north-west, the Qinling Mountains in the west, and the Dabie Mountains that separate Henan from Hubei in the south.

The mighty Huang He, or Yellow River, flows through the northern part of the province. It is the second longest river in China and the seventh longest in the world. Indeed, the name "He Nan" means "South of the River." The Yellow River has been both a blessing and a curse to Henan's people since the first settlers arrived in the region. Regular flooding has claimed hundreds of thousands of lives, giving the Huang He its nickname, "the River of Sorrow." To many Chinese, the well-being of the river is intricately linked to the well-being of the nation. On the massive wall of the Sanmenxia Dam in western Henan are painted eight characters that translate: "When the Yellow River is at peace, China is at peace."

History

Henan has a long history dating back about 3,500 years and is considered the cradle of Chinese civilization. Archaeological excavations show it was one of the kingdoms ruled by the leaders of the Shang Dynasty (1700–1100 BC) at about the same time that Moses led the Israelites out of Egypt and into the promised land. The first Shang capital is thought to have been at Yanshi, west of the modern-day provincial capital, Zhengzhou.

Buddhism flourished in Henan, as attested to by the famous Longmen Grottoes, near Luoyang, which house tens of thousands of statues of Buddha and has been declared a UNESCO World Heritage site. The site is believed to date back to the fifth century AD. The Shaolin Monastery, located 55 miles (90 km) west of Zhengzhou, is the birthplace of kung fu. The monastery was founded by an Indian Buddhist named Batuo who traveled to China to spread Buddhism in AD 464.

Henan held a prominent position in China during the Song Dynasty (AD 960–1279). During this period, Kaifeng became a city of international importance, with merchants and artisans flocking to it from all over the world. Henan also became home to tens of thousands of Jews who migrated along the Silk Road. The two cities of Luoyang and Kaifeng have each served as the capital city of a long list of dynasties. In the seven centuries since its heyday, Henan has not again held a prominent place in China, but it remains an important province.

On May 11, 1938, General Chiang Kai-shek (Mandarin: Jiang Jieshi) ordered his Nationalist soldiers to blow up the dike that held back the Yellow River just outside Zhengzhou, in an attempt to halt advancing Japanese troops. Although he succeeded in this aim, Chiang's brutal action did not consider the local Chinese population, and an estimated 900,000 people perished in the ensuing flood.[2]

For eight years the river flowed uninterrupted across the eastern Henan plain. Approximately 3,500 villages and towns were wiped out, leaving some 11 million people homeless and facing starvation. The devastated area was said to be "10 to 20 miles [15–30 km] wide, and all along the length of this new channel, desperate people who had lost their homes and farmland tried to stay alive in the ways that such people are wont to do."[3]

The Second World War added to the suffering of people in Henan. One missionary described the devastation that occurred in Zhengzhou as a result of the carnage:

> The city was a white sepulchre full of people like gray ghosts. Death ruled Zhengzhou, for the famine was centered there. Before the war it had held 120,000 people; now it had less than

> 40,000. The city had been bombed, shelled, and occupied by the Japanese, so that it had the half-destroyed air of all battlefront cities. Rubble was stacked along the gutters, and the great buildings, roofless, were open to the sky. Over the rubble and ruins the snow spread a mantle that deadened every sound. We stood at the head of the main street, looked down the deserted way for all its length—and saw nothing.[4]

The suffering of Henan's people continued during the disastrous "Great Leap Forward" orchestrated by Mao Zedong in 1958. In the subsequent famines of the early 1960s, several million people starved to death in Henan.

In yet another water-based disaster in Henan, in 1975 the Banqio Dam in the southern part of the province collapsed following a typhoon, and an estimated 230,000 people drowned. This remains the greatest loss of life caused by the collapse of a dam in history.

Demographics

Henan's huge population is divided into 17 prefectures, containing 159 counties and a staggering 2,455 towns.

The overwhelming majority (nearly 99 percent) of the population are part of the Han ethnicity, with the remainder belonging to China's ethnic minorities. There are nearly one million Muslim Hui people in the province, followed by 82,000 Mongols and 61,000 Manchu. Along with the small communities of people from other ethnic minorities, the Mongols and Manchu people in Henan have largely lost their distinctiveness, having been assimilated culturally and linguistically by the Han.

A missionary in the early nineteenth century wrote of Henan:

> The people are physically strong and of an independent turn of mind. In manners they are somewhat rough and not as polite

Most people in Henan are farmers, struggling to eke out a living from the land
IMB

> as Southerners. The province might be termed a province of farmers. The people are not fond of travel, and are consequently ignorant of anything outside their own little horizon, and are extremely superstitious.[5]

A later writer said that among other Chinese, the people of Henan are often characterized as:

> honest and frugal—sometimes also a bit naive. They have, nevertheless, long been considered to have violent tempers . . . Unlike the Sinitic peoples farther south, the Henanese were not stereotyped as crafty or cunning, but like the more southern peoples, they were expected to pursue luxury if given the opportunity.[6]

The main vernacular spoken in Henan falls within the Northern Mandarin group, although there are locations where the Northwestern and Southwestern dialects of Mandarin are spoken. According to one source, "The sounds of Henanese have been characterized by other Chinese as harsh and lacking resonance. This may result from a tendency to use one-syllable words rather than the two-syllable words characteristic of most modern spoken Chinese."[7]

Economy

Henan remains a relatively poor province, despite extensive reforms by provincial authorities with a view to modernize it. Until recently, its economy was growing annually by an average of 10 percent, but this was not enough to prevent millions of rural people migrating to more prosperous parts of China in search of a better income.

Henan has long been one of China's key farming regions, ranking first in the nation for the production of wheat, cotton, sesame seeds, tobacco, and leather. Other major crops include rice and maize. Its principal industries include textiles, petroleum, building materials, chemicals, machinery, and electronics, while coal production continues to play an important role in its economy.

In the last few decades, HIV and AIDS have become a major scourge in Henan, wreaking havoc in hundreds of villages along the main transportation routes, where prostitution and drug use proliferate.

Another social ill plaguing the province is human trafficking. The Chinese government's one-child policy, which came into effect in 1979, created a huge imbalance between the sexes, with millions of female babies aborted so their parents could have a male heir. As a result, in many areas there is a lack of females available for marriage. In 2007, the *China Daily* reported that a woman named was arrested in Yongcheng for selling 118 baby girls. She had purchased the infants from impoverished families in south China, and was only discovered when a taxi in which she was transporting 13 babies broke down. She and the driver "left four babies in a field nearby and went to a garage for repairs. Residents found the babies and alerted the authorities."[8]

The Galilee of China

Among its population of almost 100 million people, Henan contains the largest number of Christians of any Chinese province, and it has become a hub for the spread of the largest Christian revival in history. The coastal city of Wenzhou in Zhejiang Province has claimed for itself the title "the Jerusalem of China" because of its numerous churches, so some house church leaders in Henan have nicknamed their province "the Galilee of China"—the place where Jesus' disciples came from.

Millions of people in Henan have come to faith in Christ since the advent of Communism, and this central province—though one of the smallest in China in size—has become an engine room for the spreading of the gospel throughout every part of China and even beyond the country's borders. Consequently, the Church in Henan has contributed many prominent leaders of China's house church movements.

The size of the Christian community in Henan is without equal in China, but its spectacular growth has come at a great price. Henan often seems to experience the most severe persecution of any Chinese province. Assaults on believers, including beatings, imprisonments, and murders, have increased in recent years.

Rules prohibiting unregistered house churches seem to be implemented more harshly in Henan than anywhere else in China. As a result of the intense spiritual environment, millions of Christians in Henan have formed into a purified, bold, and uncompromising body of believers.

In recent decades, Henan has experienced a growing economic divide between the "haves" living in the large cities and the "have-nots"—the tens of millions of peasant farmers who inhabit the countryside. It is among these impoverished, simple-hearted farmers that the gospel has found its most fertile soil.

It is hoped the stories in this book will greatly bless and challenge readers, and they will see the wisdom of God, who has chosen the simple-hearted yet tough Christians of Henan to glorify His Name throughout China. As always, He looked past outward appearances, and found multitudes of believers with hearts willing to obey and serve Him.

The Jews of Henan

A family of You Tai, or Chinese Jews, proudly display their trilingual street sign in Kaifeng
Midge Conner

The enigmatic Ai Tian

Kaifeng, the ancient capital city of Henan, holds the distinction of being the principal base for China's Jews throughout their long, 2,000-year history in the country.

The most extensive nineteenth-century researcher into the Chinese Jews believed that their ancestors first migrated to China in the earliest years of the Christian era. Other scholars think that the first wave of Jews came to China much earlier, in about 250 BC. Some came for trade—silk from China was much prized by the Roman aristocracy—and others to escape persecution.

Jews migrated in sufficient numbers to sustain synagogues along the route. In China they lived free from persecution. Indeed, they intermarried with Chinese and adopted Chinese names—the Li family was thought to have been named Levi at one time.[1]

When Jesuit missionaries reached China in the sixteenth century, a Chinese Jew named Ai Tian told them of a surviving Jewish community that was scattered throughout the empire. In June 1605, the missionaries invited Ai to visit the Jesuit mission in Beijing, where he saw a large painting of Mary, Jesus, and John the Baptist. He thought the image was of Rebekah and her two sons, Jacob and Esau, and he bowed down, saying, "I do not usually venerate pictures, but I must pay reverence to these ancestors of mine."[2]

Ai told the renowned missionary Matteo Ricci that the founder of his religion had 12 sons. Ricci initially assumed Ai was a Christian and was referring to the apostles, but he soon realized that he was a Jew and was referring to the 12 sons of Jacob, the forefathers of the tribes of Israel.

At the time, Ai stated there were just 10 or 12 Jewish families living in Kaifeng, although a fine synagogue survived and had recently been restored at great expense. Inside it, Ai said, "They kept with great reverence the Pentateuch of Moses written on parchment and mounted on five rollers . . . They had been there for 500 or 600 years."[3]

Ai went on to tell the missionaries of the existence of Jewish communities in other parts of China, though because they had no synagogues they had lost their distinctiveness. Many Chinese at the time believed the Jews were the same as Muslims, largely because of their shared refusal to eat pork.

When Ricci quizzed Ai Tian about his knowledge of the Bible, he gladly recited many stories about Abraham, Moses, and Esther, "using forms of proper names which struck Ricci as strange: *Hierosuloim* for Jerusalem, *Moscia* for Messiah. He said that many of the Kaifeng Israelites knew Hebrew."[4]

When the missionary told Ai that they had copies of the Old Testament, and that there existed a New Testament which told of the Messiah's coming into the world, the stunned Jew replied that this was impossible because the Messiah would not appear for another 10,000 years. After listening carefully to Ricci, however, Ai returned home to Henan and later penned a letter to the Italian that said: "If you will come and live with us and abstain from pork, we will make you ruler of our synagogue."[5]

The Kaifeng synagogue

The synagogue in Kaifeng was first constructed in 1163. An inscription on its wall told how an initial party of 70 Jewish families had reached Henan during the Song Dynasty (960–1279). In 1183, the emperor Long Xing granted permission for them to settle down in the city, and they soon excelled in commerce.

Interestingly, two other inscriptions in the synagogue placed the Jews' arrival much earlier. One said they came to China during the Zhou Dynasty (before 250 BC), while the other claimed they had first reached China during the Han Dynasty (206 BC to AD 220). These variant dates probably indicate that the ancestors of the Chinese Jews arrived at different stages throughout history, likely traveling down the Silk Road through Central Asia.[6] Other sources suggest they may have come by sea from India.[7]

In 1608, Matteo Ricci sent a Chinese believer from Beijing to Kaifeng to follow up reports of Christian communities there.

The spot where the Kaifeng synagogue stood for centuries. In the foreground are two stone pillars recording the history of the Jews in China

Although this man was unable to find any Christians, Ricci reported:

> The brother was very well received by the Jews there, who are not known by any other name than that derived from not eating the sinews of animals, keeping still the ancient rite with regard to the sinew which Jacob found shrunken after he wrestled with the angel. They are few, but they have a good synagogue where they keep with great respect the whole Pentateuch in Hebrew, rolled up after the manner of ancient books. We could not learn if they had any other books.[8]

In its heyday the flourishing Jewish community in Kaifeng numbered around 20,000 people, and the city became known as "the Jerusalem of China." The Jews rose to high governmental positions, earning themselves wealth and recognition.

Because of its location on the banks of the Yellow River, the Kaifeng synagogue was rebuilt on seven different occasions due to floods between 1279 and the 1650s. The synagogue had once housed 13 copies of the Law, but the constant flooding destroyed most of them. However, years of painstaking copying and the careful piecing together of fragments meant that by 1663 the dedicated members of this community again possessed 13 copies of their beloved Law.

In 1845, author James Finn wrote a letter in Hebrew to the Jews of Kaifeng, asking them a number of questions about their origins, their way of life, their style of prayer, and the holidays they observed. He received a response 25 years later, written in Chinese, indicating that they no longer knew any Hebrew. The letter was full of despair. It said, in part:

> During the past 40 or 50 years our religion has been but imperfectly transmitted, and although the canonical writings are still extant, there is no one who understands so much as a word of them . . . Morning and night with tears in our eyes and with offerings of incense, we implore God that our religion may flourish again.[9]

By 1851 the Kaifeng Jews had lost their ability to speak or read Hebrew, and in almost every way had become assimilated to Chinese culture. Their last rabbi had died in 1810, leaving them directionless and unable to read their Scriptures. For centuries they had intermarried with their Han and Hui neighbors, and damage to their synagogue from yet another flood caused them to lose heart. One source says that, "poverty-stricken and isolated for centuries from any contact with other Jews, they demolished their own synagogue and sold the bricks."[10]

By the time the famous American Presbyterian missionary W. A. P. Martin visited them in 1866, all traces of the synagogue had disappeared. Martin managed to locate a neighborhood in Kaifeng where a number of people still clung to their Jewish identity, but in name only, much as they do today.

Outreach to the Jews

A Jewish woman and her son at Kaifeng in 1911

A number of Evangelical missionaries, fascinated by the presence of Jewish people in China, visited Kaifeng and attempted to share the gospel with them, but the Jews decided the Christian message was not for them, and little interest was shown. When Dennis Mills of the China Inland Mission visited in 1890 he reported:

> I offered Kao [a Chinese Jew] copies of the Old and New Testaments, but he said he already had a boxful of our books. We tried to interest him in the promises made to Israel, and the offer of salvation in Christ, but to all this he seemed perfectly indifferent. "I know all about it," he said.[11]

The Canadian Anglican bishop William White visited Kaifeng in 1918 and became fascinated by the heritage of the Jewish community. He started archaeological digs on the site of the synagogue and uncovered two stone pillars that told the history of the Jews in China. White later wrote an extensive three-volume work, entitled *Chinese Jews*.[12]

Considering their centuries of struggle and hardship, it is amazing that even now a small community remains in Kaifeng that still proudly identifies itself as Jewish. Today, 800 You Tai, or Chinese Jews, reside in Kaifeng, and several hundred more live in other parts of China. Since the 1990 census, the Chinese government has officially noted the You Tai, although it refuses to grant them status as a distinct ethnic minority.

Most of the inhabitants of Kaifeng are aware of the existence of the Jewish neighborhood in their city, and visitors are directed to the place where the synagogue once stood, which is now occupied by a hospital. The Jewish Cemetery still remains, however.

In 1999, a Chinese house church network specifically targeted the remaining 800 Jews of Kaifeng with the message of Jesus Christ. More than 300 placed their faith in Christ, accepting God's offer of salvation through the sacrifice of His Son, and their prayer that "God's religion may flourish again" has begun to be answered.

A tenuous future

The Jews of Kaifeng, who—according to one recent source—number just 100 practicing adherents of Judaism out of a population of 1,000 people,[13] face an uncertain future due to their small numbers and recent actions by the Communist authorities to clamp down on all religion outside government control.

Beginning in February 2018, the intense atheistic stance adopted by President Xi Jinping has swept the country, resulting in the persecution and oppression of millions of religious adherents.

Because Judaism is not one of the five religions officially recognized by the state in China, the Jews of Henan have come under strict surveillance. According to a 2019 article in the *Jerusalem Post*:

> During a raid, government agents reportedly tore loose a metal Star of David from the entryway and tossed it on the floor. They ripped Hebrew scriptural quotations off the walls. They filled up a well that had served as a *mikveh* (ritual bath) with dirt and stones. And all foreign plans to build up and support the Jews of Kaifeng were summarily cancelled.[14]

A small organization called Shavei Israel, which works to repatriate "lost and hidden" Jews back to Israel if they wish, had helped 20 Kaifeng Jews migrate to Israel, but the Chinese police closed its community center in the city, and the Sino-Judaic Institute, established to promote the study of Jewish life in China, was forced to shut. In the crackdown, the remaining members of the Jewish community were banned from meeting outside their homes.

After more than 2,000 years in Henan Province, the God-hating atheists who control the Chinese Communist Party now pose a greater threat to the existence of the Jews there than at possibly any time throughout their long and fascinating history.

Early Christians in Henan

The Nestorians

Christianity in Henan has a history of over 1,300 years, but for most of that time the gospel struggled to take root in the province. The painstakingly slow and difficult progress gave little hint of the explosive growth that has occurred since the 1970s, which has resulted in the Henan Church containing more Christians than any other province in China today.[1]

The Nestorian Stone, which records the story of the first Christians in China

The first verifiable Christian witness in China occurred when Nestorian missionaries from Central Asia and the Middle East arrived in AD 635. By 638, a group of 21 Persian monks had begun spreading the knowledge of Christ, and over the next few hundred years monasteries and churches were established in various parts of the country. The Nestorian Stone, written in both Chinese and Syrian scripts, was unearthed in Shaanxi Province in the 1620s. It tells the story of how Nestorian Christians came to China.[2]

The Syriac characters on the stone contain references to "Gabriel, the priest and archdeacon of the church of Khumdan and of Sarag." These were the names of the two Tang Dynasty capitals of Chang'an (in Shaanxi) and Luoyang (Henan). Luoyang was connected to the ancient Silk Road, the strategic route linking China to Central Asia.

Besides the stone, other relics and documents refer to Nestorian churches and monasteries at various locations in Henan. One describes how a Persian monastery was constructed in the Xiushan quarter of Luoyang City. It was situated next to the southern market, which was a gathering point for all foreign merchants who lived in the city.[3]

Even today, almost 1,400 years after the Nestorians arrived, evidence of their presence in Henan occasionally emerges. In 2006, an eight-surfaced tombstone was unearthed in Luoyang that was inscribed with Scripture and Nestorian insignia.

The empress Wu Hou instigated a persecution of the Nestorians in 690 after she established Buddhism as the state religion, and the harmonious relations the Nestorians had enjoyed with China's leaders up to that point came to an abrupt end. Mobs destroyed the Nestorian church at Luoyang in 698, in the first recorded persecution of Christians in Henan Province.

Nestorianism survived for more than 600 years in other parts of China, so that when Marco Polo came through on his epic journey in the thirteenth century, he referred to many Nestorian churches in diverse locations. In Henan, however, it seems Nestorian activity was confined to the city of Luoyang.

Over the centuries, the Nestorian movement suffered a gradual spiritual and moral decline. In 1263, an official document mentioned the provision of horses by Christians and other people living in Henan, but apart from this fleeting reference the Nestorians seem to have largely disappeared from Chinese history.

The first Catholics

By the time Jesuit missionaries arrived in Henan in the late sixteenth century, they initially found little evidence that any Christians had ever set foot in the province before them, and Catholic knowledge of Nestorian Christianity seemed limited at best.

In June 1605, when the Chinese Jew Ai Tian traveled to Beijing to make the Jesuits' acquaintance, the famous missionary Matteo Ricci asked him if he had any knowledge of "Christians" in Henan. Ai did not recognize the word, but when Ricci made a sign of the cross, his visitor seemed to understand and said there were certain foreigners who had settled in Kaifeng who "adored the cross" and part of their doctrine came from the same Scriptures the Jews used.

Ai Tian said that these believers prayed over everything they ate and drank, making the sign of a cross with their fingers. He further informed Ricci that the Christians in Kaifeng—fearful of being mistaken for Muslims and caught up in hostilities between the Chinese and the Hui—had abandoned their church and met in secret.

The church building had been converted into a temple for idol worship and the Christians had vanished from public view, although Ai was sure they still survived. He reported that:

> Many kept this custom of making the sign of the cross, and were known by their look which was quite different from that of other persons. And he wrote the names of all the families in Henan who were descended from these people, and they were many.[4]

Three years later, Ricci sent a young Chinese convert named Anthony to Kaifeng to see if he could locate any of these "adorers of the cross," but he was unsuccessful. Ricci wrote:

> Sixty years ago the Chinese wished to seize the members of this religion, and they hid themselves, becoming heathen or Muslims from fear, and to this day they do not reveal themselves. And so now, when our brother asked them these questions, they were frightened, not knowing for what purpose they so unexpectedly asked them this.[5]

Further research revealed that the surviving Nestorians in Kaifeng were not known by that name, but rather were called "Terza," which seems to have been the name of the country from which their ancestors came. They were different from the Muslims and Jews in that they freely ate pork, and their religion was commonly called "the religion of the figure ten" by local people. In Chinese the number 10 is represented by a cross.

More than a decade elapsed after Ai Tian visited Matteo Ricci in Beijing before the first Catholic missionary took up residence in Henan. In the early 1620s, Nicolas Trigault of Belgium established a mission in Kaifeng. Shortly after, a Jesuit named Rui Figueredo built a church in the same city. In 1642 the church suffered the same fate as the Jewish synagogue when, in an attempt to drown 10,000 rebels, the emperor ordered the destruction of embankments along the Yellow

River. The church building was severely damaged by the flood waters and Figueredo was drowned, setting the work back many years.

The Catholic Church in Henan appears to have stagnated for the remainder of the seventeenth and eighteenth centuries, with no particular progress reported. Indeed, by 1834 there were only 500 Catholics left in the entire province.[6]

Strong anti-foreign and anti-Christian sentiment arose in Henan during the second half of the nineteenth century. The general population strongly objected to the methods employed by the Catholic missionaries, causing people to associate Christianity with the imperialistic powers that were trying to subdue China. As a result, interest in the gospel was minimal.

In the late 1860s, a mob drove a Catholic missionary out of a city in Henan with these words: "You burned our palace, you killed our Emperor, you sell poison to our people, and now you come professing to teach us virtue."[7]

The eminent mission historian Latourette wrote that the Catholic Church in Henan, lacking any spiritual vitality or access to the Word of God, became "especially decadent and many Catholics had lapsed into idolatry."[8]

When the first Evangelical missionary to Henan, Henry Taylor, traveled through the province in 1875, he visited the Catholic mission in Nanyang and gave this assessment:

> Their house is situated in a very beautiful place about four miles from the city; they are now completing a magnificent chapel, upon which they have spent a year's income . . . One of them came out, and very courteously invited us in. They showed us the greatest kindness, and told us of all the persecution to which they had been subject. At one time there were between 8,000 to 10,000 hostile people surrounding the premises, and they knew not the moment when an attack might take place. The gun never left their hands . . . They have fully 100 domestics, all of

> whom are as willing to handle the sword as to bow down before the cross: the end is supposed to justify the means.[9]

A severe famine struck Henan and the surrounding provinces in 1877 and 1878, resulting in eight million deaths. The famine was followed by a typhus epidemic. The Catholic missionaries and their converts in Henan provided shelter and medical care to thousands of desperate people, resulting in many conversions. Within a few short years, "the mission stations increased from 27 to 40 and by 1879, Catholics numbered 4,588."[10]

For approximately 250 years Catholicism had been the sole form of Christianity in Henan, but its adherents failed to make much of an impact in the province. Today, the number of Catholics in Henan remains small compared to other parts of China.

1870s and 1880s

The arrival of the Evangelicals

Although the era of Evangelical missions in China commenced with the arrival of Robert Morrison in 1807, a further 68 years elapsed before the first missionary set foot in Henan, and a further nine years passed until 1884, when the first worker was able to reside in the province. The reason for this slow progress was explained by a missionary:

> The Henanese farmer is conservative, independent, easily roused to anger, indifferent to discomfort or dirt, and in many districts, until recently, anti-foreign. For this and other reasons, it was very difficult for foreign missionaries to secure any foothold, especially in the larger cities. They were forced to settle in smaller places, to face opposition and suspicion on every hand, and patiently wait till more favorable opportunities came.[1]

George Clarke of the China Inland Mission

The first Evangelicals arrived in Henan in April 1875, when Henry Taylor of the China Inland Mission (CIM) and a Chinese evangelist named Yang visited the province. Earlier that year—in the very first issue of the CIM magazine *China's Millions* in July 1875—Taylor expressed optimism about the prospects of establishing a mission base in the province:

> I turn my eyes toward Henan's 25 million people with much desire. If God enables me—and I believe He will—to carry the gospel there successfully, I shall have cause for rejoicing through eternity . . . A whole province is a vast field to fill; but if the God of all grace fills us, power and blessing must attend our efforts.[2]

Later in the year he reported encouraging initial contact with the local people:

> We were well received in the towns and villages through which we passed. I have not seen people anywhere so readily disposed to hear the gospel; and as for buying books, we might have sold any number, but we had to limit the sale in each place. The Lord has given us encouragement from individuals who came to ask the way to Zion. I could not rest if hindered from visiting these places again.[3]

Henry Taylor and Yang had the privilege of being the first Evangelicals to lead someone to Christ in Henan. Taylor's diary records:

> An old man came in, whom we invited to be seated, and then preached the gospel to him. I have never met anyone who grasped the gospel more readily. He repeated what we had been saying very clearly . . . We knelt together, and asked God to save his soul. We then asked him if he truly believed this gospel. With much earnestness he answered, "Why should I not believe this good news?" He seemed astonished that any could disbelieve it. He is an old scholar, and reads the character readily: we gave him some books.[4]

Things did not always go smoothly, however, with Taylor recording this incident:

> Certain lewd fellows of the baser sort stirred up the people. They threw our books in the mud, stamping on them and tearing them up, cast them in our faces, and ridiculed that worthy Name by which we are called. Though this conduct was calculated to provoke us, the Lord kept us perfectly calm . . . As we left them to go to our inn, some shouted out, "Throw the foreign devils down." We rejoice to be persecuted for the Name of Jesus.[5]

Evangelical progress in Henan was slow in the early years, and the Chinese struggled to understand why there were two separate branches of the same religion, represented by Catholics and Evangelicals. An anti-Christian placard appeared which ridiculed the missionaries. It said:

> Although the adherents of the religion only worship Jesus, they are divided into the two sections of Roman Catholics and Evangelicals, and are continually railing at each other so that we have no means of determining which is right and which is wrong.[6]

In 1876, Henry Taylor was joined by George Clarke, and together they "visited a large portion of the province, selling Scriptures and preaching the gospel . . . and were blessed to see the conversion of two or three souls."[7]

On one occasion, Clarke told of a Chinese man who had received a Gospel tract. When the man "came to the cruel treatment and death of Christ, he became enraged and burnt the book, and said he would have thrashed the man who did it."[8] The missionaries sat the man down and tried to explain that Christ had offered His life as a sacrifice for the sins of the world.

During this trip across the province, Taylor found that the atmosphere in Henan had changed for the worse. Innkeepers refused to allow him to stay on their premises, and the people responded to the gospel with indifference or hostility. One morning, Taylor learned that Confucian scholars in the town of Queshan had:

> bound themselves together under a promise that they would kill the foreigner, and stationed themselves in different parts of the city with this intention. The foreigner did not preach in the streets that day, so next morning they went to the inn to seek for him, but found he was gone. Enraged by their disappointment, they tore down the landlord's sign, and threatened to set fire to the inn.[9]

Henry Taylor was obliged to leave Henan after he found his way blocked by scheming officials. Although he and Clarke had successfully preached the gospel to thousands of people in many cities, towns, and villages, the provincial authorities were not yet willing to allow missionaries to live among the people. Three times Taylor and Clarke were forced to flee the province back to their base at Wuhan in Hubei.

Tragically, the career of the first Evangelical missionary to share the gospel in Henan Province ended in acrimony, with one source stating:

> Henry Taylor, "broken" by the rough handling and "deep hate" he had encountered in Henan, tried to find a niche in Zhejiang. Resentment made him incapable of a new start. He quarrelled bitterly with his Chinese colleagues, and resigned from the CIM to take up a lucrative post in the Customs service. To dare to invade Satan's domain in the hearts of men was to invite attack, and he fell wounded emotionally and spiritually . . . The first pioneer to penetrate the first of the nine unevangelized provinces had become the first casualty.[10]

Tears of determination

It was not until 1884, nine years after Henry Taylor's first attempt, that A. W. Sambrook secured a permanent foothold in the province. He was granted permission to dwell in Zhoukou, and three years later he baptized his first converts. In 1886, a second mission station was opened by J. A. Slimmon in a market town near Nanyang in southern Henan.

On one occasion, Slimmon visited Xiangcheng, where a long drought had brought misery to the people. Members of the local community had hired all the religious practitioners they could find, asking them to pray to their idols to bring rain, but all to no avail. Now they challenged Slimmon and a Chinese evangelist to pray to their God for relief. Feeling it was a heaven-sent opportunity to present the gospel, the evangelist ran around the neighborhood gathering as many people as possible to witness the showdown, like the clash between Elijah and the prophets of Baal on Mount Carmel.

With many Buddhist and Daoist priests looking on, the two Christians prayed to the Living God. When they had finished, they started to preach the gospel to the crowd—only to find that within minutes dark clouds began to race across the sky and the people scattered to escape being drenched! Slimmon and his co-worker later returned to the town and shared the gospel with all who would listen. Many hearts had been opened by this dramatic answer to prayer.[11]

As more missionaries trickled into Henan during the 1880s, the Christian message began to impact an increasing number of people. In many instances the foreign missionaries assumed roles overseeing the work, while most of the daily preaching was left in the hands of Chinese evangelists and pastors who had accompanied the missionaries to the province.

Slowly, one person at a time, the seed of the gospel began to take root in Henan. Although the foreign missionaries were usually credited for pioneering the gospel, they would have enjoyed little success without the help of their Chinese colleagues.

Yang, the evangelist who had accompanied Henry Taylor on the first journey into Henan in 1875, continued to be a key worker in the province for many years, faithfully sharing the gospel. He later moved to Zhoukou, where "his labors were blessed to the conversion of not a few. As his strength failed, he returned to his home, where he passed away still bearing testimony to the saving power of his Lord and Master."[12]

Another key Chinese pioneer in Henan was a man named Chen. He was a salt commissioner by trade, but after his conversion he became a bold and uncompromising witness for Jesus Christ. He reportedly had "a gift of dramatic preaching and could hold a large audience spell-bound as he told them the gospel story in his own graphic way."[13] God later used Chen to establish the first groups of believers at Zhengzhou and Taikang.

In many places, people who decided to follow Jesus Christ experienced severe persecution. In some cases they returned to their old way of life, but most new believers remained true to their convictions.

One 16-year-old girl in the town of Sheqi accepted Christ with great joy. A short time later, she was obliged to marry a man she had never met, in a union arranged by her parents when she was an infant. Her bridegroom believed the Christian message was nonsense, but there was no way to cancel the wedding plans.

The girl resolved in her heart not to participate in any of the spiritual rituals customarily performed in wedding ceremonies of the era. At the point where the newlyweds were required to bow down before the gods of heaven and earth, the girl sat still and prayed to Jesus instead. This infuriated the wedding guests, and five women rushed forward and pushed her face down to the ground before the idols.

She wept bitterly, and when her husband later invited her to worship the kitchen god with him, she stood firm:

> "You must worship it yourself [she said]; I shall never join you, even if you kill me." A few days later she sent a note to the missionaries, saying, "Tell the ladies not to be troubled about me. I am still trusting Jesus, and mean to do so till I die."[14]

Breakthrough in Zhoukou

The fledgling Church in Henan experienced much persecution, as Satan and wicked people tried to prevent the gospel taking root in this proud province. Their diabolical efforts were in vain, however, and at Zhoukou on November 27,

Some of the first Christians in Zhoukou in 1888

1887, Joe Coulthard of the CIM had the honor of baptizing nine converts, who formed the first Evangelical church in Henan.[15] Hudson Taylor's daughter, Maria, married Coulthard and moved to Zhoukou the following year.

The most fervent and studious of the new believers at Zhoukou was a man named Liu. The missionaries felt they could not baptize him straight away because his business was making firecrackers, most of which were used in idolatrous ceremonies. As soon as Liu gave up this occupation, however, he was welcomed into the church, much to the joy of the other Christians.

The devil was enraged by this development, and Liu came under strong attack. One man threatened to take Liu to court on a trumped-up charge if he did not forsake his new religion. Liu went to a solitary place and wept before the Lord, asking Him to intervene. A few days later, his accuser was himself sued by another man for a large sum of money, and all thoughts of action against Liu were forgotten.

Soon after, the inhabitants of Liu's home village hired a sorcerer to curse Liu and to drive out the demon they believed had caused him to become a Christian. The sorcerer and a large mob went to Liu's home, where they found him worshipping the Lord and studying the Bible. When they entered the property:

> Liu went to the sorcerer, and laying his hands upon him, said, "In the Name of Jesus of Nazareth I command you to leave!" Immediately the sorcerer was rendered speechless and powerless, the evil spirit within being quite subdued. The crowd urged on the sorcerer, beseeching him to exorcise Liu, who then said, "In the Name of the Father, Son and Holy Spirit I command you to leave!" The man fled for his life, shouting, "He is too powerful for me! He is too great!" The crowd wanted him to come back, but he said, "Do not take me to him. His Savior is too strong for me, and his prayer is too powerful!"[16]

Later, three of Liu's relatives who had persecuted him died within a short space of time. He had visited each one and warned them of God's impending judgment and the necessity to believe in Jesus Christ before they died. None of them did so. The villagers, witnessing these strange events, decided it was better to leave Liu alone, and all opposition ceased. Within a year, all of Liu's remaining family members had started to follow Christ.

From these humble beginnings, the Name of Jesus Christ has flourished among the people of Zhoukou in east Henan Province. By 1998, the registered Three-Self churches in Zhoukou Prefecture alone numbered 160,000 members, with the source noting: "Unregistered Christians must amount to the same number if not more."[17]

Today, the gospel has flourished to such an extent that the whole of Zhoukou Prefecture (which is comprised of ten different counties and districts and has a population of nine million people) is home to approximately 1.6 million believers.[18] With 20 percent of the population professing faith in Jesus Christ, Zhoukou is one of the strongest Christian prefectures, not only in Henan but anywhere in China. The mustard seed that started with Liu and other early converts has grown into a mighty tree!

Taikang

A man named Li Zizeng, from Taikang, eagerly received the Lord Jesus Christ in the early 1880s, gaining the honor of being the first believer in his town. Li was a highly respected scholar, and his family had held leading positions in the city for generations. One day, Li was caught in a heavy downpour, so he took shelter in a doorway with another man, who proved to be a missionary. While they waited for the rain to ease, the

Li Zizeng was the first Christian at Taikang

two struck up a conversation and the missionary gave Li some Gospel booklets to take home and read.

Over time, the vital truths contained in these texts were absorbed into Li's heart. He repented of his sins and followed Christ, and immediately began to share the gospel with everyone he met. The city leaders turned against Li, and he was stripped of all the social privileges associated with his position.

According to missionary Geraldine Guinness, when Li declared his allegiance to Christ:

> Persecution, bitter and terrible, broke over his head. His father, his mother, his wife, and all the clan turned against him, and did everything they could to frighten him out of his new faith . . . On one occasion we noticed his hand bound up and in a sling. At first he would not let anybody see it. After a time the pain was severe, and he was prevailed upon to let the doctor attend to it. We were surprised to find the hand inflamed and festering from the marks of human teeth. Very reluctantly, the poor man

> confessed that his wife had attacked him in blind fury, and had bitten his hand and arm almost to the bone.
>
> This is the state in which that poor fellow lived for months. Often, when he came round to the mission house to attend the meetings, his wife would follow him . . . She would search him out, wherever he might be, and before the assembled people she would storm and swear, and order him out, working herself up into the most terrible passion. Sometimes, to avoid a scene, he would go with her, and then she would follow him home, through the streets of the city, cursing and raving openly as she went along, to the delight of the onlookers and his most bitter shame.[19]

Within a few years, five more residents of Taikang were baptized and the first Christian fellowship was established in the town. When the church had grown to 30 people, they asked Li Zizeng to become their pastor. He proved to be a faithful shepherd, and the number of Christians in Taikang grew rapidly.

One day, Li asked the Lord to give him and his wife a son, for he believed that much of her antics stemmed from the disgrace she felt at not having produced an heir. Approximately a year later, his wife gave birth to a little boy. It was the start of a change in her heart, and she later became a sincere believer in Christ. In 1890 it was said of Li:

> The very bitterness of persecution seemed to develop a remarkable strength and sweetness of character. His life was fragrant of Christ, and he was much used of God in leading others to knowledge of the truth. Numbers of men in that little Taikang church today trace their conversion, directly or indirectly, to the beautiful life and earnest witness of dear Brother Li Zizeng.[20]

After such a promising start, the Evangelical church in Taikang struggled for the next four decades, and when a nationwide survey was conducted in 1922, there were only 216 believers in the city, among a population of 415,000 people at the time.[21]

Today, while the population of Taikang has tripled since 1922, the number of Christians has exploded to nearly 200,000![22] Now, one out of every five people in Taikang is a follower of Jesus Christ. The perseverance of Li Zizeng and many other Taikang believers has produced a mighty harvest for the kingdom of God.

Kaifeng: an elusive target

In the late nineteenth century, many missionaries longed to establish a base in Kaifeng, which was the capital of Henan at the time (an honor it later lost to Zhengzhou).

Kaifeng was renowned as a proud and prestigious city, and the authorities were determined to do all they could to prevent Christianity taking root there. In the late 1800s, even Chinese

Bishop William White of Kaifeng being pushed around in a wheelbarrow—a common form of transportation in China in the late 1800s

Christians were not permitted to enter its gates and were severely punished if they attempted to do so. Despite these obstacles, however, God found a way to penetrate Kaifeng's walls and gain a witness for His Name.

In 1881, a man named Zhu noticed someone selling books by the roadside outside the city walls. He stopped and bought a book, but moments later a local scholar named Wang rushed up to him and warned him that if he tried to read it he would go blind. Wang angrily kicked over the bookseller's box, scattering his Gospel materials in the dirt, and he beat and cursed the seller.

Wang then ordered the bystanders to gather up the remaining books and burn them. None of this deterred Zhu, who went home and began to read several texts he had concealed up his coat sleeve.

Among the books Zhu had were copies of the four Gospels and two tracts. As he read God's Word, the Holy Spirit touched his heart. He was convinced that the message of Jesus was true and that the idols he had worshipped since his youth were false. Zhu felt uneasy about keeping the good news to himself, so he told his neighbors. Within a short time, everyone started calling him "Zhu the Christian."

Zhu did not meet another Christian for years, but he continued to grow in Christ by studying the Gospels and praying. He developed a deep fear of God after Wang—the scholar who had so viciously attacked the bookseller—suddenly lost his mind and became dangerously insane. The local magistrate

> had him chained to a large millstone in an outhouse. The poor maniac would not allow himself to be clothed, and he remained naked to the day of his death some 10 years later. Heaven's judgment on this man awed Zhu.[23]

In 1898, Zhu heard that missionaries had settled in the town of Jixian, several days' journey to the north. He visited them and was formally converted to Christ and baptized. In the same year, Robert Powell of the CIM spent a night in Kaifeng. Until then, foreigners were banned from even passing through the city's gates, so it was considered a significant breakthrough just to stay a night inside the walls. Another four years passed before Powell was allowed to rent a house in Kaifeng and begin to share the gospel.

Powell soon befriended Zhu, whom he described as a

> fine, warm-hearted and strong character, one who, from the way he managed his band of followers, might have been a pastor of long standing. In all there were about 13 who seemed established in the faith, while others were under instruction.[24]

Despite these encouraging signs of God's grace, the gospel continued to face tremendous obstacles in Kaifeng, and progress was painstakingly slow. In fact, by 1910 the number of Christians in Kaifeng had declined slightly. At the time, the city contained 12 foreign missionaries, 7 Chinese co-workers, and just 34 baptized believers.

The struggle for the soul of China's ancient capital city was long and difficult, but thanks to the sacrifice and perseverance of God's servants, the seed of salvation was sown and would later produce a massive harvest for the kingdom of God.

By the start of the Communist era in 1949, one report stated: "13 denominations have churches in Kaifeng, though the actual number of Christians is small."[25]

After more than three decades of Communist persecution, however, a 1985 article in *Time* magazine reported: "Government officials have recently admitted that in Kaifeng . . . approximately 10 percent of the people are Christians, compared with only one percent in 1949."[26]

The early pioneer missionaries and their converts like Zhu would scarcely have believed that, by 2002, Kaifeng City would contain 69 Three-Self churches alone,[27] in addition to hundreds of house churches. The whole of Kaifeng Prefecture, which now boasts a population of 4.7 million people, is home to more than 500,000 Evangelical Christians.[28]

Today, although the percentage of Christians in Kaifeng is still lower than in most other parts of Henan, the growth of the Church is nevertheless remarkable considering how the first preachers battled for years just to be allowed to enter the city.

1890s

The Canadians arrive

The China Inland Mission was the only Evangelical group working in Henan until 1894, when the Canadian Presbyterian Mission established a base at Changde (now Anyang) in northern Henan. The names of early pioneers such as Johnstone, Mills, Hunt, Gracie, King, and Lund are associated with many attempts to take the gospel to cities and towns north of the Yellow River.

The Canadian Presbyterian involvement in Henan had its origins in 1888, when Hudson Taylor visited Toronto and challenged the churches to send laborers into the harvest fields of China. One historian wrote of Taylor's timely visit:

Canadian members of the North Henan Mission in 1894

> His presence at the Northfield conference and his recruitment for his own China Inland Mission were both symbol and catalyst of the resurgence of fervor. From that point onwards, the enthusiasm became a movement, and its growth was dramatic and inexorable.[1]

By the end of the nineteenth century, the North Henan Mission of the Canadian Presbyterians numbered 23 missionaries at three stations: Changde, Jixian, and the small town of Chuwang.

At the same time, the CIM's work continued to expand into other parts of the province. Howard Taylor, the son of the pioneer Hudson Taylor, had grown up with a love of medicine, and he graduated as a doctor in 1888.

At the age of 26 he was already a skilled surgeon. After accompanying his father on a speaking tour of North America, however, Howard made a firm commitment to give up worldly wealth and professional acclaim to serve Jesus Christ in China. He enjoyed close companionship with his father, and the fact that his son so eagerly embraced the vision to reach China brought joy to the great statesman in the years before his call home.

Howard and Geraldine Taylor

Howard Taylor departed for China in January 1890, still a single man. Three years later he married Geraldine Guinness, who was also serving with the CIM. In 1895, the Taylors and their co-workers opened Zhengzhou (the present capital of Henan) to the Christian message. The results were very encouraging, as almost immediately people started coming to Christ. Howard's gifted leadership and medical expertise were greatly respected by the other missionaries, and greatly benefited the Chinese people.

The Taylors labored unceasingly in Henan, treating thousands of patients and taking every opportunity to share the love of Christ with all who would listen. Summarizing his ministry in Zhengzhou and Taikang, Howard Taylor wrote:

> In the providence of God we had the privilege of opening up two new stations—the city of Zhengzhou and the adjoining city, one day's journey away, of Taikang. We were the first missionaries to reside at these places, hence, speaking broadly, none of the people knew intelligently about the Lord Jesus Christ. Of course the very foundations of the work had to be laid, and they were laid, at some cost. The medical work was a means which the Lord used very greatly in enabling us to get at the hearts and the affections of the people in those two cities and the surrounding districts.[2]

The people of Zhengzhou continued to respond to the message of eternal life, especially when compared to the steely response of people in Kaifeng. In 1903, the CIM's Bessie Leggat reported on her work among the women of Henan:

> It has been one of the hardest years of work, as it has been one of the most blessed, since coming to China . . . During the second moon, we were busy almost daily from breakfast time until sunset; hundreds and hundreds of women listened most attentively to the gospel story . . .

Both Mrs. Louis Talbot and I have seldom enjoyed such liberty in telling the story of Jesus and His love, and very many of the women said they would never worship false gods again, but only seek the true.[3]

New laborers

By the late nineteenth century several new mission societies had entered Henan and established bases, but most were forced to quit China during the Boxer Rebellion of 1900. One of the most effective missions at the time was the American Norwegian Lutheran Mission, which focused on the Nanyang area in southern Henan. Within a few years its workers had opened several mission stations, hospitals, schools, and orphanages.

While the Norwegians concentrated on the south, their Scandinavian counterparts from the Swedish Mission in China

Four elderly Henan women who were baptized in 1899

targeted north-west Henan. They established a base in Xin'an, and—despite encountering great difficulties and opposition—within five years they had baptized 114 new believers and opened two boarding schools with 29 students.[4]

At this time, a vital shift occurred as many missionaries began to realize that the key to winning the country for Christ lay not in their own efforts but in the hands of the Chinese Christians. Hudson Taylor's desire was that Chinese people would ultimately assume the leadership of their own work. He wrote:

> I look upon foreign missionaries as the scaffolding around a rising building. The sooner it can be dispensed with, the better, or rather, the sooner it can be transferred to other places, to serve the same temporary use, the better.[5]

Instead of taking prominent leadership roles, many of the wiser missionaries stepped back and were content with helping and advising the Chinese church leaders. As a result, the light of the gospel began to shine more brightly in Henan, as people understood the message much more easily without the cultural and linguistic barriers that existed when foreigners proclaimed it. Writing from Xiangcheng in 1898, Mrs. Archibald Gracie reported:

> You will be glad to know that the work here is spreading on every hand; men and women come long distances, from villages that have not even been visited by us, having heard the good tidings from natives who have carried away some of the precious seed and scattered it in other hearts . . . Our Bible woman has visited a good deal in the villages, and is gladly received everywhere . . . The Spirit of God is working where the foot of foreigners has never trod, and we believe that the Lord is going to work wonders in Henan.[6]

Trouble on the horizon

The CIM had spearheaded much of the pioneer Evangelical work in Henan. It baptized its first nine believers in 1887, and by 1893 it had 117 Christians meeting in five churches.[7]

The missionaries had been interested in developing good-quality converts rather than focusing just on numbers, and the transformed lives of the Chinese believers were a powerful witness to their communities.

As the curtain came down on the nineteenth century, resentment at the presence of foreigners in China had reached boiling point. The Chinese were tired of being invaded and dominated by Western powers, and a long and severe drought across north China exacerbated the tensions. Many Chinese took the drought to be a sign of the ancestral spirits' displeasure at the presence of foreigners in the land.

In the summer of 1900 a widespread uprising erupted, which came to be known in English as the "Boxer Rebellion."

A group of Henan missionaries just before the outbreak of the Boxer Rebellion in 1900

Not only foreigners were targeted, but also the Chinese who associated with them. Thousands of native Christians—both Evangelicals and Catholics—were slaughtered, as were more than 300 foreign missionaries.[8]

The worst carnage occurred in the neighboring provinces of Shanxi and Hebei. Henan escaped comparatively unscathed, due in part to the relatively small number of Christians in the province at the time, and to God's miraculous intervention in a number of incidents where believers were able to escape their pursuers.

1900s

Remarkable deliverances

For decades a secret group known as the "White Lotus Society" had been active in north China. A subgroup of the society called the Yi He Quan (literally "righteous harmony fists") came to be known in the English-speaking world as "Boxers," because of their practice of using boxing drills for physical training. They launched the notorious Boxer Rebellion in 1900, resulting in the slaughter of thousands of Christians throughout China.

When the Henan missionaries heard of the trouble that had broken out in neighboring provinces, most made plans to flee

Missionary H. S. Conway and the students at the Sheqi Boys' School in 1900

to the coast as soon as possible, and they suffered many beatings and abuse as they passed through towns and villages on their way to safety.

At Sheqi in early July 1900, a group of CIM workers, including Whitfield Guinness (the brother of Geraldine Guinness), found that the mood of the people had suddenly become hostile. During a church service on July 8, a large mob surrounded the building, threatening to slaughter those inside. The believers prayed for God's protection and were able to return home safely. The mob reassembled the next morning, attacking the missionaries and the Chinese Christians with a hail of blows. As a full-blown riot developed, the local believers escaped, while a small group of missionaries took refuge in a loft, where they spent the whole day committing their lives to Christ and praying that God might preserve them for His glory. The house next door was set alight, and the missionaries were sure that armed men would soon ascend the stairs to kill them.

On two occasions, young boys climbed up the outside of the building and looked into the room where the missionaries were hiding, staring straight at them. Yet, for some inexplicable reason, they failed to see the foreigners or report their whereabouts to the rioters.

After darkness fell, the landlord of the house came up to the loft and told Guinness and the others to follow him. He hid them inside a trapdoor above a pile of grain. The next day, soldiers were dispatched to find and kill the missionaries, and mobs marched through the streets shouting, "Kill the foreign devils!"

For five days the missionaries huddled together, speaking in no more than a whisper, and praying that the little baby in their midst would not betray their presence by crying. The kind landlord provided for them by pushing a pot of tea and a loaf of bread through the trapdoor each morning. One day, as soldiers searched around the hiding place, the missionaries heard them ask the landlord what was inside the trapdoor, to which he replied, "This is where I store my grain." Guinness recalled what happened after the officer ordered the landlord to open the door:

> I was sitting on the door—we hardly breathed, but kept praying silently to God . . . I felt the door lift and pressed it down with all my weight. Mrs. Conway and baby were sitting on the floor a yard away, and the others were beyond. Would he come up? Again God interfered, and the officer and his soldiers departed. Three times they returned and renewed their search for us, but each time they left after a fruitless investigation . . .
>
> The hours of Tuesday slowly passed and evening found us still alive—I thought it would be our last. 'Twas dusk and in the court below I could see men piling up wood and straw and dried grass—they had surrounded the whole house with this flammable material. Listening intently we could hear a voice saying, "We will burn them out and kill them if they run."[1]

Hopes of an escape were thwarted, as it seemed the whole town was still searching for the missionaries. God, however, had them hidden safely in the palm of His hand.

Under the cover of darkness, the missionaries were moved to a new house with the help of the Chinese believers, who did not hesitate to risk their lives for their friends. Incredibly, night after night while the foreigners had been in the loft, bloodthirsty men had slept in the room beneath, yet the baby girl had not once alerted them by crying. Her father, H. S. Conway, later said: "God closed the mouths of the lions, and He also closed the mouth of our dear little baby."[2]

During the long hunt for the missionaries, the drought finally broke and heavy rain began to fall. This seemed to distract the would-be murderers, and after 12 days the river had risen sufficiently to allow boats to dock at Sheqi. Guinness believed the group's best chance of escape was by boat, and he saw the rain as God's provision. Eventually, the missionaries were able to make their way to the river undetected, where they hid inside a small vessel bound for Wuhan in Hubei Province. They were assured the journey would take five days, but it ended up taking 13, each day filled with anxiety.

On several occasions, soldiers boarded the boat and searched it, but though they discovered the fugitives, they failed to recognize them as foreigners. The women had covered their feet and hair, and they all pretended to be asleep. Guinness later wrote:

> I was rolled over and poked in the back, and the ladies were hustled over to a corner of their couch, under which a search was made, the officer merely remarking to our escort, "Your travellers are very silent." The strain of such moments was considerable—discovery, we were led to believe, meant death.[3]

Mrs. Conway, who survived the ordeal with her baby daughter

The exhausted missionaries finally reached the safety of Wuhan, which was then under British control. Their appearance was dreadful. They had been wearing the same clothes for almost a month, and their bodies were unwashed and unshaven. Miraculously, the Lord had protected His servants and they all made it out alive.

The perilous journey of three Swedish ladies

The fledgling Swedish Mission had a small number of workers in the northernmost part of Henan when the Boxer violence erupted. Three single women—Emma Anderson, Sigrid Engstrom, and Maria Pettersson—decided to head south and hide in caves until the end of the summer, but only a week into their ordeal their presence was uncovered. They fled, but were soon intercepted by a group of armed Boxers outside the city of Xiangcheng.

The rebels robbed them, even of their outer clothing, but when they threatened to cut their heads off, the three women calmly smiled and told their attackers that they were not afraid to die. The Boxers then "looked at one another, smiled, and went away without touching [them]. One of them said, 'You cannot die because you are devils.'"[4]

For weeks, the three courageous women survived, helped by local believers, including a young man who had only believed in Christ for a month before the persecution broke out. On one occasion they hid in a maize field, and the Boxers were unable to find them despite searching all day. Despite a mob of 40 to 50 evil men pursuing them, the women succeeded in finding a boat to hide in and were taken to the safety of the coast.

Alphonso Argento—the man who refused to die

Alphonso Argento was born in Italy in 1873, but despite coming from the heartland of Catholicism, he is remembered as a great Evangelical missionary to Henan. At the age of 18, Argento was led to Christ through the influence of the Waldensian Church, and he later dedicated his life to serving God in China. He applied to join the CIM, and at the interview, when warned of the risk, he boldly declared: "I am not afraid to die for Christ and the gospel . . . I was led to take this step after having known Christ's promise: 'Blessed are they which are persecuted for righteousness' sake, for theirs is the kingdom of heaven.'"[5]

Argento was fluent in English, French, and German, and upon arriving in China in 1896, he soon learned Chinese. Three years later he established the first mission station at Guangshan in south-east Henan.

During a church service on the evening of July 8, 1900, a large crowd of people armed with swords and knives rushed into the chapel. As the would-be assassins pressed forward to

Alphonso Argento with his wife and sons

kill Argento, someone knocked the lamp over and the building was plunged into complete darkness. The Italian crawled into a corner and hid under some rubble as the Boxers, presuming he had escaped, plundered everything they could find. Finally, Argento was discovered. He later described what happened:

> With a rush they got hold of me and dragged me from under the table and on to the pile of wood (with which they planned to burn the building down). Others took up the benches and struck me with them . . . They poured kerosene on my clothes and set them on fire. Friendly neighbors, however, quickly quenched the flames, tearing off the burning part of the garment . . . I was lying with my face to the ground.
>
> The rioters, seeing these neighbors wanted to save me, got hold of a pole, and began to strike me on the head and all over my body. I tried to protect my head with my hands, but had not reached the doorsteps when a very heavy blow inflicted on my head caused me to lose consciousness.[6]

Some of the ruffians dragged the Italian's body into the street, where they wanted to decapitate him, but others who sympathized with the missionary convinced them that he was already dead. When he regained consciousness two days later, the local magistrate was afraid he would die within his jurisdiction, so he ordered that Argento be carried by stretcher to a town 140 miles (225 km) to the north.

All along the route people came to stare at the half-naked missionary, who was covered in terrible bruises and caked in blood, and they urged the stretcher-bearers to put him out of his misery. Argento later said that at one place, "they thought I was dead, for I did not move or make a sound, although they pinched me, pulled my hair, and knocked me about—an ordeal which lasted an hour."[7]

On July 21, after two weeks of misery, the officials refused to accept the dying man in their town, so Argento was carried all the way back to Guangshan, where his ordeal had begun. The locals were astonished to see him still alive, but they nevertheless had the audacity to mock his God. A large crowd gathered around him, saying:

> God has brought you back safely, has he? Your God cannot save you. Jesus is dead; He is not in this world. He cannot give real help. Our god of war is much stronger; he protects us, and he has sent the Boxers to pull down your house and kill you.[8]

Argento later recalled his ordeal at the hands of these wicked people:

> [They] spat in my face, and threw mud and melon peel at me, and did what they liked. Some pinched me, others pulled my hair, and others expressed themselves in the vilest way. All the time I did not answer a word. Some of the Christians came to see me, but had to run for their lives.[9]

The cowardly magistrate, still afraid the missionary would die in his jurisdiction, ordered Argento's journey to recommence, though now in a sedan chair. This time, they went west to Xinyang. A group of 30 armed Boxers pursued them, determined to kill the Italian once and for all, but by obeying the inner promptings of the Holy Spirit, he managed to evade them and was eventually delivered to safety on July 31, after he had spent 23 days on death's doorstep in excruciating pain.

The people of Guangshan thought they had finally seen the last of the stubborn missionary, but after a year recuperating in Europe he returned, to the astonishment of everyone in the town. Alphonso Argento was a man who had learned to overcome fear and intimidation. In 1901 he wrote:

> It was the greatest joy I have ever experienced in my life to see the Christians again, and hear what the Lord had been doing during my absence; how they had been keeping close to Jesus

and to one another; and how, though subject to fiery tests, they shone more brightly and were a living witness for Jesus, as well as a rebuke to their accusers.

It seemed to us all like a dream that I was back again in Guangshan. Many of the people could not believe that I was the same person they had killed![10]

For the next seven years, the Italian continued to boldly serve the Lord in Guangshan, and the church grew steadily. In 1905 he married Aasta Bjorgum, a nurse with the Norwegian Mission, and together they raised two fine boys. Argento's head injuries continued to cause him much pain, but he carried on regardless. Finally, in 1908, his deteriorating health obliged him to leave China, after a fruitful ministry that had resulted in 385 baptisms. When he arrived back in Europe, doctors found that his condition was dire:

He was suffering from severe pains in his head, and in spite of the best surgical skill, he gradually became blind. He also lost his memory, and the use of his limbs. His interest in the work in China never flagged, however, and in a letter at the end of May 1917 he wrote: "I will use my strength in prayer and in intercession for China."[11]

Finally, on July 3, 1917, Alphonso Argento was released from the pain of this life and went to be with Jesus forever. He was 44 years old. The CIM paid him this tribute:

He was a man of great zeal and energy and of entire devotion to the Lord, and the work at Guangshan owed much to his intercessions during the years in which he was laid aside. The church there has prospered greatly in recent years, and there are now nearly 800 communicants. There are 29 outstations in the surrounding district . . . The central church has seating for 1,400, and at the time of the annual meetings it is crowded out.[12]

God cannot be mocked. In Guangshan County, where evil people once declared that "Jesus is dead; He is not in this world. He cannot give real help," today there are some 80,000 Evangelical Christians[13]—nearly one fifth of the population—following the example of the beloved pioneer missionary Alphonso Argento.

Henan's Christians stand firm

The CIM alone had 28 workers in Henan during the Boxer Rebellion, but all survived. Extraordinarily, no known Chinese believers were killed by the rebels in the province either, although hundreds were beaten and robbed of all their possessions, including their animals and tools, which plunged them into dire poverty.

Considering the widespread carnage in neighboring provinces, what happened in Henan can only be explained in terms of the sovereign intervention of Almighty God, who must have determined that His children there could best advance His kingdom by remaining alive.

As the dust settled on 1900, it became apparent that the large majority of Chinese believers had not only survived the ordeal with their faith intact, but had also grown spiritually as a result of the experience.

Far from destroying the Church, the Boxer persecution provided impetus for strong growth in the province. In 1900 "there were only four mission agencies and 12 stations, but 20 years later there were 16 agencies, 67 stations, and 394 missionaries in Henan."[14]

Jonathan Goforth

The Canadian evangelist Jonathan Goforth must rank among the greatest foreign missionaries of any era. After years of struggle, he became an instrument used mightily by God in the early twentieth century. Although his work expanded to take in many parts of China and beyond, he spent the bulk of his ministry, including the early years, in northern Henan Province.

Goforth was born in 1859 on a farm near Thorndale in Ontario, the seventh of 11 children. After giving his life to Jesus Christ at the age of 18, he soon began winning others to the faith.

Jonathan's interest in missions was piqued when he heard an appeal by George Mackay, a veteran evangelist to Taiwan,

Jonathan and Rosalind Goforth

who had spent two years crisscrossing Canada in an attempt to recruit new missionaries to continue his life's work. Sadly, he had been unable to find a single person to take up the challenge. Goforth recalled: "I was overwhelmed with shame. There I was, bought with the precious blood of Jesus Christ, daring to dispose of my life as I pleased. From that hour I became a foreign missionary."[1]

In the spring of 1885, Jonathan met a young lady named Rosalind Bell-Smith. While he was from poor farming stock, she was the daughter of wealthy, upper-class parents, but she had been praying for a husband who was fully dedicated to God and His work. One evening, before a meeting they were both attending, Goforth was called out of the room. Rosalind recalled:

> As he rose, he placed his Bible on the chair. Then something happened which I could never explain, nor try to excuse. Suddenly, I felt compelled to step across four or five people, take up the Bible and return to my seat. Rapidly I turned the leaves and found the Book worn almost to shreds in parts and marked from cover to cover. Closing the Book, I quickly returned it to the chair, and returning to my seat, I tried to look very innocent. It had all happened within a few moments, but as I sat there, I said to myself, "That's the man I would like to marry!"[2]

Rosalind was able to see a rough diamond in Jonathan, and she quickly fell in love with him. Later that year they were engaged after he asked her, "Will you join your life with mine for China? And will you give me your promise that always you will allow me to put my Lord and His work first, even before you?" She immediately replied, "Yes, I will *always*."[3]

Rosalind soon

got her first taste of the sacrifice she would encounter the rest of her life as the wife of Jonathan Goforth. Her dreams of an engagement ring were dashed when he told her that the money

> he would have spent for a ring must instead go for Christian literature.[4]

The couple were deeply affected by Hudson Taylor's message when the great statesman visited Toronto in 1888. When Goforth expressed an interest in working in Henan Province, Taylor told him, "Brother, if you would enter Henan, you must go forward on your knees."

After studying Chinese for nine months, the Goforths arrived in the city of Anyang (then called Changde) in northern Henan, which was to be their home for decades to come. Their early years in Henan were difficult. Although the small North Henan Presbyterian Mission had only about 20 workers, they spent much of their time in committee meetings, arguing over contentious issues while thousands of lost souls perished in the streets outside. The atmosphere in the mission frustrated Goforth, who "often got his dander up and pounded the table."[5]

At the time, the Chinese in Anyang were strongly opposed to the missionaries and their message. Rosalind recalled: "There we were, a mere handful of missionaries in the midst of a bitterly hostile people, many of whom were only waiting and watching for an excuse to attack and murder us."[6]

One day Jonathan and a colleague attended a fair, where they planned to preach the gospel to the thousands of people gathered there. Although they wore Chinese clothing,

> their identity was soon recognized, and in a few moments the crowd rushed upon them, hooting, yelling, and throwing sticks, stones and clods of earth. Just when death seemed imminent, a sudden gust of wind blew a tent over and scattered the articles offered for sale. As the Chinese scrambled for these, the missionaries escaped.[7]

Rosalind struggled to gain acceptance among both her fellow missionaries and the local Christian women of Anyang. She thought the problem lay with those people, until one day she overheard two Chinese women talking outside her window. One said, "She speaks our language well and is a zealous preacher." The other admitted, "And she does love us. But it's her impatience, her quick temper! If she only would live more like she preaches!"[8]

At first Rosalind felt angry, but when she realized the women had spoken the truth, she fell to her knees in prayer, asking the Lord to humble and break her, and to cut the rough edges off her character.

Rosalind had earned a reputation for being short-tempered, and many cooks and other workers had lost their jobs after failing to live up to her standards. Some had been angrily dismissed. Sometime later, one of the Chinese evangelists came to the Goforths' home and asked to speak privately with Jonathan. Jonathan told Rosalind:

> He came as a deputation from the other evangelists and workers to ask what the secret was in the change in you. Before, none of the servants wanted to serve you, but now they all want to be your servants.[9]

Rumors and suspicions about the missionaries were so rife that the only way to defuse the situation was to be completely open and friendly to the Chinese. The Goforths started what they called "open-house evangelism," which involved them leading groups of up to 50 curious people at a time through their house.

After showing off their furniture, glass windows, organ, and sewing machine to their amazed guests, "Rosalind would first preach to the women, and Jonathan would preach to the men."[10] This strategy was so successful that "as many as 1,835 men and 500 women passed through the house on a single day and all heard the gospel message."[11]

Many of the other missionaries treasured their privacy and disapproved of the Goforths' open strategy. Untroubled by their criticisms, Jonathan wrote:

> Some may think that receiving visitors is not real mission work, but I think it is. I put myself out to make friends with the people and I reap the results when I go to their villages to preach. Often the people of a village will gather around me and say, "We were at your place and you showed us through your house, treating us like friends." Then they almost always bring me a chair to sit on, a table to lay my Bible on, and some tea.[12]

At death's door

The powerful revival that God brought to China through the Goforths in the early twentieth century nearly didn't happen, for Jonathan was almost killed during the Boxer Rebellion. As the couple attempted to flee in a donkey cart, a large mob attacked them with swords, knives, stones, and clubs. The backs of the donkeys were broken to prevent escape, and then Jonathan was

> struck down with the blunt edge of a sword, nearly breaking his neck. As he fell and held his arm up to protect himself, it was slashed to the bone in several places. When he struggled to his feet, the evangelist was struck unconscious with a club. As he regained some consciousness, in God's providence a rider galloped through the crowd to where their carts were and was thrown from his horse. The thrashing horse now formed a barrier between the attacking men and the missionary. As Jonathan dazedly got to his feet, a man stood over him as if to strike him with a club, but instead whispered, "Get away from the carts." When they moved away, their attackers ignored them and started fighting among themselves over the goods in the carts.[13]

The beleaguered missionaries received help from sympathetic villagers, who hid them in a hut and gave them food and water. The next afternoon they were sent on their way, after learning that their rescuers were Hui Muslims who had been fearful of incurring the wrath of Allah if they had taken part in slaughtering the Goforths.

Jonathan had been hacked about his back, neck, and head with a sword, but he miraculously survived. For weeks, he and the other missionaries continued their flight, though they were again attacked and robbed along the way.

Finally, the fugitives reached Fangcheng in southern Henan, where a boat dispatched by the American consulate collected them and brought them to safety on the coast. They arrived in Shanghai with nothing but the blood-soaked clothes they had on.[14]

The search for God's power

The Goforths returned to Canada to recover from their ordeal, but the following year they recommenced the ministry that would earn Jonathan Goforth the nickname of "China's greatest evangelist." The Chinese also referred to him fondly as "the flaming preacher."

The fact that Jonathan had been at death's door contributed to the fearless and tireless soul-winning that characterized the remainder of his life. When he returned to Henan in 1901, Jonathan was a changed man. He had been grieved by the dead Christianity he encountered in Canada and was dissatisfied, too, with the lukewarmness he found among the churches in China. Many believers had embraced a new, liberal Christianity which made them carnal and indifferent toward the things of God.

Goforth studied the Scriptures for an answer and also read many books on revival. He was deeply affected by the writings of Charles Finney, and he felt the Lord impress on his heart that the Holy Spirit would be poured out on any servant who confessed his or her sins, repented, and was obedient to His leading. In 1904, thrilling news of the Welsh revival reached China, and Goforth was convinced that God wanted to pour out his Spirit in a similar way throughout China.

In 1906, Goforth was preaching in a remote town when he fell under heavy conviction. When the Lord commanded him to go and reconcile with a Christian brother, Jonathan attempted to argue with God by pointing out that their dispute was the fault of the other man. He tried to continue preaching, but his message was awkward and without power, so he stopped speaking, bowed his head, and promised the Lord he would go and see the man immediately after the meeting.

The spiritual atmosphere immediately lightened, and there were many tearful confessions of sin throughout the congregation. In the months that followed, similar repentance occurred at every meeting Goforth addressed. The Holy Spirit moved mightily and many wrongs were made right.

Rosalind observed the changes in her husband, and she also desired to be deeply transformed by the Holy Spirit. Before that occurred, however, she went through an intense struggle, and the Spirit of God put His finger on the root of hatred and bitterness that had lodged in her heart. For years the conflict in the missionary community had caused her not to speak to one of the male missionaries. Rosalind recalled:

> I bent my head and cried to God to fill me with His Spirit as He had filled my husband. Unmistakably clear came the inner voice: "Write a letter to [this man] and ask forgiveness for the way you have treated him!" My whole soul cried out, "Never, never can I forgive him!"
>
> Again I prayed as before, and the inner voice spoke clearly as before. Again I cried out in my heart, "Never; never. I will never

> forgive him!" . . . Then followed the saddest part of my life. For several months I preached and prayed to keep up appearances but all the while my heart was becoming harder, colder, and more hopeless.[15]

Finally, after a long struggle, Rosalind yielded to the Holy Spirit and wrote the letter, and her burden was lifted. A new liberty came into her life, and her ministry in conjunction with Jonathan experienced new power and fruitfulness.

For the next decade, Jonathan Goforth led revival meetings across China, although he concentrated on Manchuria (now north-east China). He would often preach for eight hours a day to crowds of up to 25,000 people. Multitudes of sinners experienced the saving grace of Jesus Christ, and countless Christians were awakened to a vital relationship with God.

Meetings were often characterized by the public confession of sin, and such was the speed of the revival that swept through Manchuria that Rosalind remarked: "Jonathan Goforth went to Manchuria an unknown missionary . . . He returned a few weeks later with the limelight of the Christian world upon him."[16]

This expanded ministry excited Jonathan, and he made plans for his family to travel around with him as he spread God's revival fire. Rosalind was less than enthusiastic, however, fearing the impact that such an itinerant lifestyle would have on their family. She told her husband: "The plan sounds wonderful, except for the children. Think of all the infectious diseases and of our four little graves [their children who had already died in China]. I can't do it. I cannot expose the children like that."[17]

Jonathan saw the situation in a very different light. He believed that God was about to do a great work in China, and he expected his family to play a full part in it. He told Rosalind: "I fear for the children if you refuse to obey God's call and stay here at Anyang. The safest place for you and the children is on the path of duty."[18]

Husband and wife were divided in this matter, but just hours after Jonathan had warned Rosalind that the safest option was to obey God's call, their son Wallace fell ill with dysentery. After two weeks he began to recover, and Jonathan set out on an evangelistic tour alone, while his family remained in Anyang. The very next day, baby Constance fell ill. Jonathan hurried back to find the little girl close to death, and she passed into eternity.

Rosalind was overcome with sorrow and prayed, "O God, it is too late for Constance, but I will trust you hereafter for everything, including my children."[19] From that point forward, she and the surviving children traveled constantly with her husband, traversing thousands of miles across north China. Despite the hardships, they never lost any more of their children to sickness.

Revival in Anyang

Although the Goforths now had a nationwide revival ministry, they never forgot their roots in Henan and they frequently returned to the province. In the town of Guangshan—where missionary Alphonso Argento had suffered terribly for the gospel—the number of Christians increased from 2,000 to 8,000 in four years, largely due to the impact of Jonathan's preaching.[20]

Once, when they returned to their base at Anyang, the local church leaders immediately asked Goforth to lead a week's revival meetings among them. Some of the other Presbyterian missionaries were less than enthusiastic, however, believing the revival was nothing more than human hype and emotionalism.

A group of Henan Christians in the early 1900s

When Jonathan addressed the congregation at Anyang the next Sunday morning, he felt as though he was talking to a brick wall. Halfway through his message, he suddenly stopped and announced: "The Spirit of God is being hindered. It is no use for me to go on speaking. Will several brethren pray?" Prayers were offered, but they were of a very ordinary nature and clearly without spiritual power. "Stop!" Goforth cried. "Plainly there is someone in this audience who is hindering God."[21]

The meeting was dismissed, and everyone returned home.

Over the following months, it became clear to the Goforths that the problem in Anyang lay with the defiant attitude of the other missionaries. The boys' school had become so unruly that there were thoughts of closing it down, and the entire Presbyterian work seemed to be unraveling.

In faith, Jonathan scheduled eight days of renewal meetings in the spring of 1908. The church building could seat 600 people, and a large pavilion was erected in an adjoining yard to accommodate the anticipated overflow of seekers.

On the morning of the second day, a number of people broke down and contritely confessed their sins. That evening, two female missionaries, trembling under the conviction of the Holy Spirit, begged one another's forgiveness and were reconciled. When the principal of the girls' school confessed to specific sins that she felt were obstructing God's work, many of the students broke down, confessing their own sins with tears streaming down their cheeks.

Hu Fenghua, one of the leading evangelists in Anyang, was asked to lead the prayer meeting on the evening of the fourth day. He bowed his head and said:

> I must confess my own sins before I attempt to lead this meeting. When the reports of the Manchurian revival began to reach us, I said to the other evangelists, "This is not the Holy Spirit's work. It is just Goforth's way of manipulating an audience by a sort of mesmeric power" . . . On the second morning when I saw teacher Fan, from my own village, down in the dust, weeping like a little child and confessing his sins, I was more than disgusted. I assured myself that this could not possibly be the Spirit of God . . . As the day progressed, I became more and more scornful at the way things were going. What weak creatures they must be, I thought, to give way as they were doing!
>
> On the third day, as the movement increased in intensity and the people seemed to be swept along in spite of themselves, I became a little uneasy . . . What if it should turn out that I am actually opposing God? Last night I hardly slept a wink, and this morning I was like a man demented . . . My heart was broken and I sobbed like a little child. I knew then that I had been pitting myself against God the Holy Spirit.[22]

This heartfelt confession from one of the prominent leaders of the Anyang church brought a spiritual release to the proceedings. Goforth remarked: "The whole audience gave way and melted like wax."[23]

The fire spreads

In 1909, Goforth conducted another series of tent meetings in Anyang. This time he found an "open heaven," and the results were even greater than the earlier meetings. The evangelist reported:

> The Anyang blessing was the most wonderful I have ever seen. We had decided on eight days of meetings, but we continued 10 days of three meetings a day. Each succeeding day was more wonderful in power than the preceding. On seven different occasions I went prepared to give an address and could not, so mighty and awful was the pressure on the people. They crowded to the front in dozens to pour out agonized confessions. Day by day this continued . . .

The missionaries at Anyang in 1910. Jonathan is seated on the left, with Rosalind fourth from left. Four of the Goforth children are among the children seated at the front

> Such praying! I never heard the like. Sometimes every few minutes it would, like great waves, sweep over the assembly, hundreds joining and many in tears. They grasped the Unseen and were able to get what they asked for. Many prayed for were seen kneeling on the platform confessing all with agonized weeping. Oh, how good is our Heavenly Father![24]

As the power of God continued to move in Anyang, many who attended the meetings rushed back to their villages and encouraged relatives and friends to come and experience God for themselves. On the seventh day the place was packed out, and so many people were gripped with the fear of God that their sole desire was to confess their sins and be cleansed by the blood of Jesus Christ. As a result, Goforth was unable to deliver any message for the remainder of the meetings.

Visitors who traveled from outlying areas were often deeply affected by God's Spirit even before they reached the meeting place. Many people were found kneeling in the street or in their rooms, confessing their sins and desiring to enter into right relationship with God. Goforth recalled those life-changing days:

> A number of people, who had held out up till then, felt that things were becoming too hot for them and tried to run away. But they found out what a difficult thing it is to escape from a seeking God. Some only got half-way home, when the pressure became so unbearable that they had to turn around and come back. Others got all the way home, but, finding no relief, they returned to Anyang.[25]

A wealthy man, to whom the thought of publicly confessing his sins was abhorrent, went back to the church and begged to be allowed to nail his sins to the cross. When he found a long line of people waiting to do the same, he was distraught:

> "I can't wait [he cried]. I'll burst if I'm not given a chance to confess my sins right away" . . . Then followed the confession—coming like a torrent, bursting through the dam which had tried to hold it in check.[26]

Heaven came down to Anyang during those blessed days, and thousands of people met Jesus Christ for the first time. Many Christians repented of their sins and found new freedom in their lives. People who had stolen items from their neighbors went and gave them back, and broken marriages were restored. Many opium addicts were wonderfully delivered and never returned to the drug again. Perhaps the greatest result was the new unity and love between Christian leaders. Goforth recalled:

> Pastor and elders and deacons all besought God to forgive them for the coldness and laxity of their Christian service. Many prayed earnestly for a deeper experience of the spirit of brotherly love. Others in shame confessed how they hadn't read their Bibles, how they hadn't prayed, and how they made no attempt to save those around them.[27]

Although Anyang had been mightily blessed by the revivals of 1908 and 1909, the Church in the city continued to ebb and flow in the following years. By 1922 there were only 390 baptized Evangelical believers in Anyang, meeting in ten churches.[28] The population of the city at the time was estimated at 290,000, meaning that only one in every 743 residents of Anyang were followers of Jesus at the time.

Today, however, the revival that impacted Anyang over a century ago has helped sow the seeds of a bountiful harvest. There are currently more than half a million Evangelical believers—in both registered churches and house churches—throughout the entire Anyang Prefecture,[29] meaning that one in ten people in Anyang are followers of Christ.

Lives well spent for Jesus

For almost 50 years, Rosalind Goforth proved a wonderful partner to her husband. The couple had seen multiple thousands of people transformed by the power of the gospel, but following the call of God had cost the Goforths dearly, and five of their 11 children had been buried in China.

In the early 1930s, Jonathan's eyesight began to deteriorate, and after a while he became totally blind. In 1934, the Goforths retired to Canada, although Jonathan's idea of retirement was quite different from that of most other people. A historian noted:

> At the age of 74 he returned to Canada, where he spent the last 18 months of his life traveling and speaking at nearly 500 meetings. He carried on to the very end, speaking four times on the Sunday before he peacefully died in his sleep. He left behind a striking testimony of what one man could do for God among the teeming millions of the Orient.[30]

Rosalind and Jonathan in 1925

"China's greatest evangelist" finally went to his eternal reward at the age of 76, and the influential *Moody Monthly* eulogized Goforth with these words: "The hand of God was upon him in a mighty way, and his ministry was almost like that of Charles Finney and Evan Roberts combined."[31]

Prominent preacher Charles Turnbull said: "Jonathan Goforth was an electric, radiant personality, flooding his immediate environment with sunlight that was deep in his heart and shone on his face. God used him in mighty revivals."[32]

Rosalind, who was five years younger than Jonathan, died in 1942 at the age of 78. Three years after her death, a book she had been working on, *Chinese Diamonds for the King of Kings*, was published.[33] It contained a series of testimonies of Chinese believers whose lives had been transformed by Christ. The Goforths continued to fascinate and inspire Christians for decades after their deaths. A bestselling biography, *By My Spirit*, was published in 1942, and *Miracle Lives of China* has been reprinted many times.[34] Both titles are still in print today.

In the early 1980s, 50 years after the Goforths had left China, their daughter Mary Goforth Moynan traveled to Henan to visit the places where she grew up. With "deep gratitude and joy she reported that revival was once again spreading in China, and some of the people God was using were spiritual heirs of the fires that her father had started many decades before."[35]

1910s

Trophies of grace

The powerful, life-changing ministry of Jonathan Goforth and others continued to impact Henan during the 1910s, and Evangelical churches throughout the province saw steady growth. Entire families experienced God's salvation and forgiveness, and countless testimonies emerged of how lives were transformed by the power and grace of Jesus Christ.

One trophy of God's grace was Mrs. Chu of Taikang. She died in 1910 at the age of 53, leaving behind a strong

Mrs. Chu

impression on all who knew her. The Chu family had moved to Taikang in 1896, living next door to Henry and Mary Ford, missionaries serving with the CIM. Chu's brother-in-law soon believed the gospel, but she herself was bitterly opposed to God. Her startled missionary neighbors later recalled: "She hated the sound of our singing and worship, which she could plainly hear. Often during service or prayers she stood in her courtyard screaming curses at us—even cursing us several generations back—parents, grandparents, and great-grandparents!"[1]

Blinded by her pride and stubbornness, Mrs. Chu carried much bitterness in her heart, and her violent temper spilled over whenever she thought someone had wronged her. The Fords prayed daily for her salvation, asking the Holy Spirit to soften her heart and convict her of sin, righteousness, and judgment. Mrs. Chu gradually adopted a friendlier attitude toward the Christians, and when her son tragically died it broke her and she became receptive to the good news.

Although Mrs. Chu was a woman of little worth in the eyes of the world, she was precious to God, and what little she knew about Christ she believed and acted upon. Within a few months she made a firm commitment to follow the Savior, and she slowly changed from being a bitter woman to one with a warm and gentle heart.

In time, Mrs. Chu proved to be a great blessing to the missionaries. She often traveled with Mary Ford into the countryside, visiting the scattered Christians and offering encouragement from the Scriptures. When she died in 1910 after a short illness, Mrs. Chu was sorely missed by the Christians of Taikang and was fondly remembered as one of the trophies of God's grace in that town.

The jailer of Zhengzhou

A number of startling conversions took place in Zhengzhou, which was considered a hotbed of witchcraft and idolatry in the early twentieth century. Superstition flourished, and numerous amulets and charms were worn by people in a bid to ward off evil spirits and curses. God brought His truth and power to people, however, and in a short space of time three new men joined the local church from an interesting array of backgrounds: a tax collector, a head cook, and the city's jailer.

The jailer started attending church meetings in the years following the Boxer Rebellion, but after becoming acquainted with the story of Jesus he drifted away. One day he was returning home when a group of robbers attacked him. The jailer had no money on him, just three melons. He offered the melons to the outlaws, and they let him go without using their clubs on him.

A Chinese evangelist demonstrates the use of the Medicine Tree. People believed that by passing through the trunk they would be cured of sickness

The jailer continued his journey, amazed that he had been spared a beating, and declared: "This is surely the Lord's hand." Hearing his own confession brought conviction, and he realized he had been unfaithful and had hardened his heart to Jesus Christ. Right there, in the middle of the road, he knelt down and dedicated his life to God.

The jailer was soon baptized and became an effective member of the Zhengzhou church. Not willing to keep his faith to himself, the blessing was "extended to the prisoners, for he witnessed to them and gave them gospel portions, with the result that a number became interested and worshipped God in the prison."[2]

Jesus proves stronger than demons

The people of Xinye in southern Henan had resisted the gospel until an interesting incident set the town talking and piqued the curiosity of many people toward Christianity for the first time.

One day, a Lutheran missionary decided to visit Xinye to do some repairs. After reaching the town in the evening, he looked for a place to sleep. He was offered a downstairs room at the inn, but finding it dirty and damp he decided to sleep in the upstairs room, even though it contained an idolatrous altar. He moved the altar to one corner and enjoyed a good night's rest, not realizing that the locals never went near that room, for many people had encountered a demon that lived there. In the words of one resident: "[It] sometimes looks like a big snake, sometimes like a tiger, sometimes like a lion. It is fearful!"[3]

When news spread around the community that a foreigner was staying in the haunted room, many rushed to the inn to see what would happen. They pleaded with him not to sleep there, but the missionary was untroubled and calmly declared: "Don't be afraid! There are certainly many evil spirits in China, but my God is stronger than all of them, and He will protect all who believe and trust in Him."[4]

The next morning a crowd gathered outside the gate of the inn, waiting to see whether the missionary had survived the night. When he appeared healthy and happy, a report "spread like wildfire throughout Xinye, and helped to announce the coming of the gospel. Many came to see the foreigner and to hear the new teaching."[5]

Nonetheless, progress in Xinye proved difficult, and by 1922 there were only 203 baptized believers in the county.[6] Today, however, the story is totally different. After decades of powerful revival, Xinye boasts one of the highest percentages of Christians in any part of Henan. At the present time there are approximately 147,000 Christians in Xinye County—about 25 percent of the population.[7]

Yang the boxing champion

Guangshan, the town where missionary Alphonso Argento had planted such good seed, was visited by Jonathan Goforth in December 1915. It was home to probably the strongest church in Henan at the time, and during eight days of meetings 154 people were baptized, with thousands hearing the gospel for the first time.

One of those who came to Christ was a man named Yang, a former boxing champion. He had been the greatest prizefighter in the region, and nobody had ever knocked him out. Many gamblers lost their fortunes betting against him and consequently held a grudge.

When news got around that the great fighter Yang had become a Christian, his enemies saw it as an opportunity to take revenge. One day, while he was in the marketplace, a mob surrounded him and almost beat him to death. He was found by friends and carried home. The missionaries wanted the perpetrators arrested, but Yang begged them not to get involved and refused to bring charges against his attackers.

A few months later, Yang had recovered from his injuries and was again seen walking around the town. His enemies were furious and decided they would finish him off for good. Yang was so terribly beaten the second time that for months his family despaired for his life. He slowly recovered, and again insisted that no charges be brought against the thugs. Goforth recalled:

> As soon as he had recovered, he went around the country preaching the gospel. He died a few years after I met him. But it was not before he had led many of his old enemies to Christ. He left a church of 600 members in his own village, and 10 other churches scattered throughout the surrounding country.[8]

The wolf boy

In a village west of Anyang lived a 14-year-old boy named Zheng Wuze. One winter's day, he left his home to visit an aunt. On the way, a hungry wolf rushed out of the woods, jumped up on him, and clawed and chewed his face. For months, the people of the village did all they could to relieve the boy's suffering, but their efforts were in vain and he seemed to be in worse pain as time went by. When it became apparent that he would soon die, they carried Zheng down from the mountains and took him to the mission hospital in Anyang.

His injuries were so horribly severe that the "wolf boy" (as he came to be known) spent almost a year in the hospital. The doctors tried to give him a "new face," but after numerous skin grafts it was clear that he would remain horribly disfigured for the rest of his life. A mask was fashioned for him to wear.

The "wolf boy" in dire condition after being mauled by a wolf

Through all the months he lay in hospital, Zheng impressed everyone with his positive attitude and his gratitude to the doctors and nurses. They shared the gospel with him, and found that he possessed a soft heart which soon fell in love with the Lord Jesus. His mother also became a Christian.

One evening at a prayer meeting, the "wolf boy" spoke out in public prayer for the first time, saying, "O Lord! I thank you for letting the wolf eat my face, for if he had not I might never have heard of this wonderful Savior."[9]

After recovering from the worst of his injuries, the missionaries gave Zheng a job as a water carrier. He lived and worked with the other believers, and daily grew in grace and knowledge. All who met him were struck by his patient and gentle spirit, and some followed the Lord because of his witness. Four years after his conversion, Zheng went to bathe in a nearby river. He was swept away and drowned, but his spirit soared to be with the Living God who had counted him among His treasured possessions.

How the gospel reached Gong Village

In 1910 many families turned to Christ at Gong Village, located near Yancheng in central Henan. The gospel first made an impact there when a man named Yang and his friend Feng attended a county fair and met a Christian bookseller. Yang purchased a copy of Matthew's Gospel and took it home with him—but, finding the genealogy of Jesus in the first chapter hard to understand, he put the book on a shelf, where it lay unread for the next three years.

Banditry increased in the area, causing the people of Gong Village to be filled with terror at the plundering and murder around them. One night Yang was so afraid that he was unable to sleep. He remembered the strange book he had purchased years earlier and took it off the shelf. As he read through the

The Zhangs of Xihua, one of many Christian families in Henan

Gospel, his heart became strangely attracted to Jesus Christ. He seemed a good and trustworthy leader, the kind of hero the villagers wanted to protect them from the wicked bandits.

When Yang reached the account of Peter's denial of Jesus and the rooster's crow, his own rooster let out a loud crow. This startled him, and he was convinced that the God of the Bible was speaking directly to him, warning him to flee the coming wrath. Yang and his friend Feng traveled at once to the nearest town that had a church and inquired about the way of salvation. They were just in time to hear a Chinese preacher proclaim the gospel, and both men received Christ with great joy. They submitted themselves to Bible instruction over the following months.

When Yang and Feng returned home, they smashed the idols that their ancestors had trusted in for centuries. Their hearts were so deeply touched by the Holy Spirit that they determined to stand for Christ, regardless of any opposition they encountered. Yang became the leader of a small church in Gong Village, until he was taken ill in 1917. A missionary reported:

> Yang died full of the peace which had come to him through faith in our Lord Jesus . . . Even on his deathbed he asked the nurses to read to him certain passages from the Bible that he had learnt to love. His friend Feng was appointed the church leader. He had been an opium-smoker, but God delivered him from this awful habit . . . The Christians at Gong village have now built a small chapel entirely at their own expense, and there are a number of enquirers in that village.[10]

Medical missions

Dozens of medical missionaries worked throughout Henan during the early twentieth century. These skilled and tireless

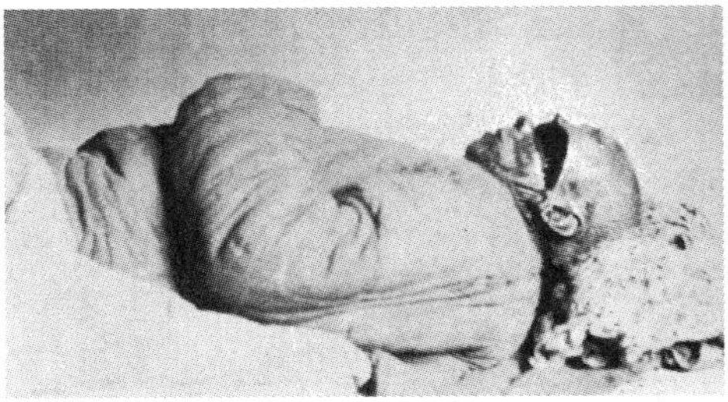
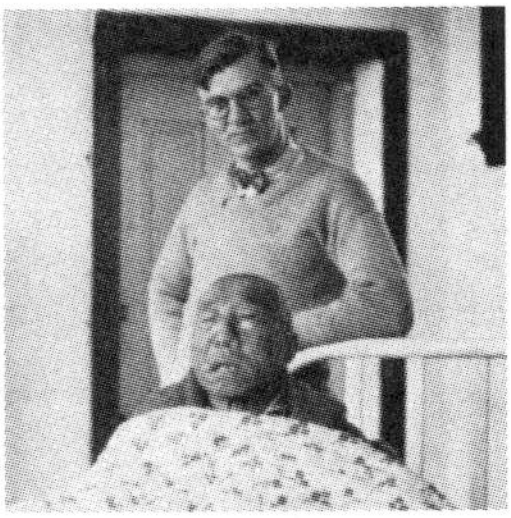

This man was brought to the hospital with his skull almost severed in two, but was stitched up and released just a week later

workers willingly gave up the prospect of wealth and acclaim in their home countries to serve Christ in bandit-infested and disease-ridden China.

Many of the cases brought to the Christian hospitals were severe. One 60-year-old man, admitted to the Lutheran Hospital at Xuzhou, was attacked by robbers and had been left for dead with his skull almost split in half by a deep sword cut. The doctors, who had witnessed all kinds of human suffering, were aghast at the man's condition. They stitched his skull up and gave him large doses of morphine to ease his pain. Incredibly, he was released from the hospital little more than a week later, fully recovered.

Perhaps the two kinds of people most uplifted by the help Christians provided were the lepers and the blind. Both groups were despised by society and were obliged to beg in order to survive. Hundreds of thousands of men and women in Henan were blind, often because there were no doctors for hundreds of miles to carry out simple cataract removals and other common procedures.

The missionaries provided Braille Bibles and set up schools where the blind could learn how to read. Some blind Christians became great preachers of the gospel in Henan, and crowds

Two blind Henan evangelists: Yang Dedao and Zhong Mo

often gathered to listen to them, amazed to see them "reading with their fingers."

Two of the better-known blind evangelists in Henan were Yang Dedao of Zhengzhou, who led many people to faith in Christ, and Zhong Mo, a man who often told people, "If I had not lost these eyes, I might never have gained my spiritual eyesight."

Henry Brown's faith

The General Conference Mennonite Mission was one of the most successful Christian organizations in northern Henan in the decades preceding Communist rule in 1949. Its work was centered on the eastern suburbs of Puyang City, which at the time was named Kaizhou.

Mennonite work in Puyang commenced in 1911 with the arrival of Henry and Maria Brown, but progress was slow. In 1913 the Browns baptized the first eight believers, but a number of them drifted away into sin and unbelief.

In 1917, the residents of Puyang ridiculed Henry Brown when he constructed a church building with enough seats to accommodate 700 people. At the time few local Chinese showed any interest in the gospel, but the missionary must have had a glimpse of the future, and he pressed on with the work, undeterred by the criticism and laughter. In 1922, five years after the church building was completed, there were still only 42 baptized Christians in the entire city,[11] who met in the huge empty building every Sunday.

After the Communists came to power, the Mennonite church was confiscated and used for secular purposes. Brown had left China in 1941 during the Japanese occupation, and the building gradually fell into disrepair.

Decades later, the spiritual environment in China began to change, and the church property was finally returned to the Christian community in 1993. There were holes in the roof, and many repairs needed to be done before it could again serve as a house of worship, but the believers set about the task with boundless enthusiasm.

A foreign Christian brought a gift of $12,000 from a Mennonite mission in America to help with the restoration, but the local believers politely refused the money, saying they had enough of their own to finish the job. Puyang was one of the poorest counties in the province, but they completed the repairs and the church was officially reopened in October 1994. More than a thousand people crammed into the sanctuary for the ceremony, with many more standing outside in the courtyard. The church has continued to overflow with worshippers ever since.

Although he had long before gone to be with the Lord, Henry Brown's faith and foresight were finally vindicated. He had envisioned a day when God would pour out His Spirit in Henan and churches would be filled with hungry souls. In 1995 the director of the Inter-Mennonite China Educational Exchange wrote an open letter to the late Henry Brown in which he posthumously commended the missionary for the great faith he had displayed many decades earlier. Part of the letter reads:

> I wonder what the people thought when you began building this church in what was then their small town. Perhaps there were comparisons to the foolishness of Noah and his ark. After all, who would come and fill your building, thus identifying themselves with this religion of the West?
>
> But on this Sunday morning, 78 years after the building was completed, I just thought I would tell you that you really should have built it a bit bigger. Even though I was a half-hour early, I had to struggle and be pushed forward to the front of

Hundreds of believers spilling out of a church meeting

> the church. How many people did you intend for this place to hold, anyway? . . . I took a few minutes to do a rough estimate of the size of the crowd. Yes, there were really about 700 sitting and some 300 standing in the aisles for the four-hour church service.
>
> Just a word about the courtyard: You could have made that larger as well. They had to shut the front gate because there was no more room there either. I think the overflow is gathering by the school you helped build across the road.[12]

Today, the seed of the gospel that had taken so long to germinate in the first half of the twentieth century has bloomed into a mighty tree that gives shade to many weary and thirsty souls. Puyang has become a large prefecture with 3.7 million people. Of these, more than 500,000 are Evangelical Christians, meeting in both registered Three-Self churches and unregistered house fellowships.[13]

Only someone with the faith of Henry Brown could have foreseen such a harvest as this.

1920s

Feng Yuxiang, the Christian general

Despite the work of the Goforths and many other faithful missionaries, the gospel had progressed agonizingly slowly in Henan. By 1922—47 years after the first Evangelical missionaries came to the province—Henan contained just 46 foreign missionaries, 57 Chinese workers, and 520 church workers. The number of believers in Henan at the time numbered 20,636, of whom two thirds were men.[1]

The 1920s was a dire decade in Henan and throughout the country. The economy collapsed and inflation reduced wealthy families to beggars. Hundreds of gangs of bandits, ranging

General Feng Yuxiang in 1922

from a few individuals to large armies of 10,000 men, brought terror to the entire society.

In the midst of this mayhem emerged a Chinese Christian named Feng Yuxiang, who was a senior general in the Chinese army. His remarkable story divided Christians at the time. Some believed his faith was a front, assumed for convenience, and that he was really a renegade warlord; others, including the veteran missionary Jonathan Goforth, befriended him and held him in high regard.

Feng had an imposing physical appearance, standing 6 feet 2 inches (1.88 meters) tall and weighing more than 200 pounds (91 kg), enabling him to tower over other Chinese of his generation. His manner was described by Jonathan Goforth as

> every inch a General, yet without a trace of the bombast so often seen in higher class Chinese. His manner is a curious and striking mixture of humility, dignity, and quiet power. He has a handsome, good face. He at once impresses one as true and sincere, a man to be trusted.[2]

Feng was just 16 when he joined the army in 1899. He was one of a detachment of soldiers sent to quell the Boxer uprising in Hebei Province, and found himself inside the mission compound where many missionaries and Chinese Christians had been cruelly massacred a short time earlier. A single female missionary came out and pleaded with the soldiers to spare the lives of the survivors. With great power and passion, she recounted what she and the others had been doing to help the Chinese people, and her words touched the young soldier.

Later, Feng was stationed in Beijing when John Mott—the American preacher who founded the Student Christian Movement—conducted a series of meetings. Feng signed up for one of the classes, and the gospel gradually sank into his heart. He became a true follower of Jesus Christ in 1914.

Because of his integrity and God-given wisdom, Feng rose through the ranks from brigade commander to be appointed as governor of Henan Province in just 13 months. He later became a general. While the rank-and-file troops in most army divisions were known for their unruly behavior and for pillaging and raping wherever they went, Feng's division was markedly different. One resident of Henan noted:

> Other soldiers when they came seized our houses and public buildings and made off with anything they took a fancy to, and our wives and daughters were at their mercy, so that the people called them the soldiers of hell. Now General Feng leads his men through the city and nothing is disturbed or molested. Even the General lives in a tent, as his men do, and everything they need, they buy, and no one is abused. The people are so delighted they call them the soldiers of heaven.[3]

Feng was greatly respected by the 10,000 troops under his command, who knew their commander had their welfare at heart. No smoking or gambling was permitted. Illiterate men were taught to read, and their wives and children were well cared for. Missionary Marshall Broomhall commented on the radically different approach Feng and his army took toward their enemies:

> He spared the lives of many southern spies who were caught and brought to him in fear and trembling. Instead of issuing orders for the firing squad, he took the men by the hand and led them throughout the city, showing to them the strength of his regiments, his horses and guns, his grenade corps and other arms, and then, handing them a sum of money, sent them back to tell his enemies what they had seen.[4]

On several occasions when he was stationed in Henan, Feng invited Jonathan Goforth to address his troops and teach them the Bible. At one of these events the evangelist reported:

General Feng Yuxiang preaching to thousands of his troops at Kaifeng in 1922

"500 men have already been baptized, and hundreds more are enquiring."[5]

According to one visitor, every Sunday:

> Fourteen separate church services were conducted for Feng's troops. Twelve preaching places were erected, apparently out in the open so that large numbers could assemble—and it was estimated that, on an average Sunday, 6,000 of his soldiers attended these services and listened to sermons.[6]

Robert Mathews, a member of the CIM, was another missionary inspired by his encounters with Feng and his soldiers. In 1921 he reported:

> It was an inspiration to speak to such eager faces. Young men, strong, in perfect health, and with astonishing earnestness, daily

A mass baptism of hundreds of General Feng's soldiers at Puyang in 1927

> took notes of the lessons. I spoke on Ephesians and questioned them daily on the preceding subjects . . . 1,500 voices answered as one. It was glorious! I asked, "What were you before you knew the Lord Jesus Christ?" and like a thunder-clap came the reply: "Dead in sin." "What else?" "Following like silly sheep the course of the world; serving the prince of the power of the air; giving rein to passion; without hope, without God."[7]

After being stationed in Kaifeng for six months, Feng was transferred to another province by the new governor, Wu Beifu, who was wary of the Christian general. Much of the good work that had been accomplished in the capital city was quickly undone.

The later years of Feng's life are somewhat clouded in mystery and controversy, and it appears he fell away from the faith. Many missionaries described Feng as an apostate, while Rosalind Goforth lamented: "Through all the years, when Feng undoubtedly had backslidden . . . Dr. Goforth never gave up hope for him, praying daily for his return."[8]

Feng was finally defeated and his army disbanded in 1930. He eventually died in September 1948, aboard a Russian ship which caught on fire.

Daniel Nelson

Daniel Nelson was born in the Norwegian town of Søndhorland in 1853. Four years after marrying Anna in 1878, he migrated

Daniel Nelson

with her to America, where they bought and operated a successful farm in Eagle Grove, Iowa. Their lives were hard-working and happy, and they raised their four children in the fear of the Lord.

Many missionaries went through an elaborate and lengthy process before they were able to discern the call of God. Nelson, on the other hand, said that while he was laying shingles on the roof of his house in 1889,

> The call of God came upon him to become a missionary to China. He got up, threw down his hammer, climbed down the ladder, and told his wife his experience of the unmistakable call of God to become a missionary to China. Anna, the winsome wife of the shingler, answered, "I'll go where you want me to go."[9]

Nelson's call to China may have been simple, but the task of getting there was anything but. His son later recalled the reaction his father received when he told people of his intentions:

> The pastor told him he was foolish and advised him to return to his farm. He was reminded of his responsibility to his family. He was reminded that there were enough heathens in America not to mention far-away China. He was reminded that he lacked educational training. He was reminded that he was not an ordained man. He was reminded that there was no Church which had called him.
>
> He was reminded that there was no organization which would undertake to support him. He was reminded of a hundred and one difficulties. His friends thought he was unbalanced. His relatives thought he was a fool. Neighbors thought he was crazy. At best he was branded an impractical and radical idealist. Nobody encouraged him. The future looked black indeed.[10]

Nelson applied to a missionary organization, only to be turned down. Countless reasons for him not to go were recited, but he was sure of his call from God and refused to lose heart. Deciding to obey God at all costs, the couple sold their farm and all their worldly possessions and booked passage for the family on a ship to China. When church and mission leaders saw that the Nelsons were determined to go with or without their blessing, they allowed Daniel to attend the Augsburg Seminary from 1889 to 1890, after which he and his wife were appointed to work with the Lutheran United Mission. Then, after tearful farewells, the couple and their four children set sail for China, arriving in November 1890.

Life was difficult for the new missionaries. They succeeded in renting a small, one-room mud house near Wuhan in Hubei Province, where a fifth child was born. The summers were terribly hot, and their humble home was filled with mosquitoes.

In winter, subzero winds howled through the cracks in the roof and walls.

Deep sorrow soon came to the Nelsons. Not long after their arrival, their co-worker Sigvald Netland died of cholera and his wife, Oline, also passed away. The Nelsons then lost their 14-year-old daughter, Nora. A few months later their infant daughter also died. This was the darkest moment, when all the forces of hell seemed to be attacking them. Daniel's wife Anna then fell sick with cholera,

> and all the children had dysentery. Hundreds of Chinese succumbed to the cholera epidemic and their dead bodies lay unclaimed in the baking sun . . . For six whole summers the Nelsons and their children endured the intense heat of the Oriental climate. It was only a miracle that they did not lose more of their loved ones.[11]

After six years of traveling and preaching with few times of rest, Daniel suffered a physical and emotional breakdown. The Lutheran Mission sent the exhausted man back to America for eight months in the hope that he would recuperate, but funds were not available to send the whole family, so Anna remained in Wuhan with the children.

In due course, Nelson returned to China in better health and threw himself into the work with renewed vigor. He fixed his sights on southern Henan Province, but "his enthusiasm and zeal again overtaxed his strength and he suffered another breakdown."[12] This time, funds were found for the entire family to return to America. They arrived in 1899, and so escaped the Boxer persecution of the following year.

The Nelsons again returned to China in 1902 and continued to serve in Henan for many years. From 1911 to 1917, Nelson served as the superintendent of the American Lutheran Mission, a startling achievement considering how he had been ridiculed and rejected when he first applied for missionary service. Eventually, he was killed in his home at Xinyang on February 8, 1926. A large mob of bandits had laid siege to the city for a month. Government troops had defended it stoutly, but:

> One evening during a fierce encounter a bullet came through a barricaded window of the Nelson dwelling. It struck the pioneer above the temple and he passed away three hours later without regaining consciousness. For 36 long years he had given unreservedly of his strength and talent to the Chinese people—now he was killed by those he had come to serve.[13]

Because of the fighting, Daniel Nelson's funeral could not be held for a month after his death. His son Bert, who had seen his own bride die of illness soon after their wedding, rushed from his station at Luoshan to comfort his grieving mother.

When the funeral finally took place, the overwhelming response from the local people showed how much respect they had for Daniel Nelson. Hundreds of Chinese followed the coffin as the procession slowly wound its way to the cemetery. Anna was calm and brave, and when asked how she felt, she answered: "I can only thank God for giving us so many happy years of friendship together."[14]

Through his faith in God, and despite the discouragement of other people, Daniel Nelson had been an outstanding missionary to China. His son Bert, who was just two years old when the family first arrived in the country, was himself later martyred in Henan in 1932.

Whitfield Guinness

Whitfield Guinness, an Englishman, was born in 1869. His father, Grattan Guinness, was a preacher who had once spoken

Whitfield Guinness

at the tabernacle established by the great eighteenth-century evangelist George Whitefield, and when his son was born he named the boy after him.

From 1883 to 1886, while he was still a teenager, Whitfield and his sister Geraldine lived with relatives on the Australian island of Tasmania. While there, the siblings heard Hudson Taylor speak, and decided to become missionaries. Whitfield sailed back to England and studied to be a missionary doctor.

Guinness finally arrived in Henan in 1897, where his sister Geraldine Taylor was already stationed. She was later to have the honor of writing her brother's biography. In it she described the huge task that faced him as he commenced work as one of just two missionary doctors in an area of thousands of square miles:

> Including Kaifeng, there were in Henan, south of the Yellow River, no fewer than 80 capitals of counties—each one representing an average population of over 350,000—in which no witness for Christ was to be found. There was, moreover, only one medical missionary in the same region—larger than the whole of England . . .
>
> Imagine 30 million people in this southern part of the province, suffering from all the ills that flesh is heir to, practically without the succour of trained physician, surgeon, dentist, or nurse, without provision of any kind for the sick, blind, crippled, or mentally afflicted—what a mass of unrelieved human misery![15]

As detailed in a previous chapter, Guinness, along with three other missionaries and a baby, had miraculously escaped martyrdom at the hands of the rebels. One day, he scribbled this note on a dirty piece of paper:

> Dear Home Ones: This may be the last time I can write to you. I sit in the dust and dirt on the floor of a barn. For three days we have been rioted, and have fled to three different spots to escape the awful wrath of the people. They little know what they do. We have had to lie down in order to be hid . . . We lay still and pray. We are tired, yet rejoicing . . . We shall meet yonder in heaven.[16]

Weeks later, the fugitive missionaries managed to escape by boat. God had spared their lives. From that point on, Guinness never saw things in the same way again. The world held no attraction to him, and the rest of his days were spent wholeheartedly for eternal purposes. He served the Chinese faithfully and energetically, always putting other people's needs before his own.

In 1902 Guinness moved to the prized city of Kaifeng, where he was appointed chief doctor at the CIM Hospital. During a trip to Europe in 1905, he married Jane Af Sandeberg of Sweden.

They enjoyed a brief honeymoon in Japan before returning to the work in Kaifeng. The harshness of Chinese society was difficult for his new bride to cope with, however. She came from a well-heeled family, and later expressed some of her burdens in a quote that became famous around the world:

> A great "without" has been written about heathenism. Men and women are toiling without a Bible, without a Sunday, without a prayer, without songs of praise. They have rulers without justice and without righteousness; homes without peace; marriage without sanctity; young men and girls without ideals and enthusiasms; little children without purity, without innocence; mothers without wisdom or self-control; poverty without relief or sympathy; sickness without skilful help or tender care; sorrow without any to bind up the wounded hearts; sin and lying and crime without a remedy; and worst of all, death without hope.[17]

After many years of faithful service, 1927 was to be Whitfield's last in this world. Lawlessness reigned, with gangs of bandits terrorizing, raping, and killing the people of Henan. Guinness caught typhus while he was treating wounded Chinese soldiers, and was already critically ill when anti-foreign mobs decided to attack the hospital.

His friends could not bear to see the servant of God helplessly left behind to die, so they smuggled him—still lying in his bed—out of the building to the railway station. They squeezed his bed into a crowded wagon heading for Beijing, where they hoped he would be protected from harm. However, two bumpy days and nights in that unventilated box proved too much for the weakened missionary doctor, and he died on April 12, 1927, soon after the train reached the capital.

Although he didn't meet a violent end, the life and death of Whitfield Guinness were nevertheless those of a martyr for

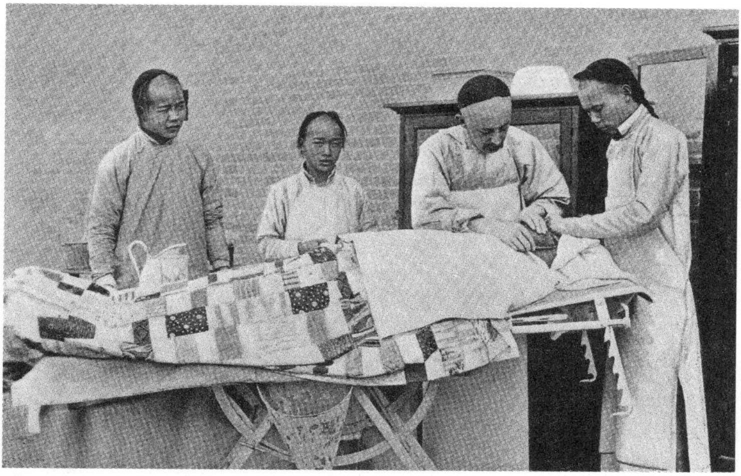

Whitfield Guinness and three student doctors operating at Kaifeng

Christ. His sacrificial service to the King of kings expedited his demise and ushered him into the glorious presence of his Master. Tributes came flooding in after the news of his death spread around the world. One friend remembered him with these words:

> My chief impression of Dr. Guinness was that Christ had been formed in him to an unusual degree. His whole life radiated Jesus . . . and his heart was glowing with love for the people of China. I well remember how naturally he spoke of spiritual things and how trustful his prayers were. There was nothing strained or artificial about his Christianity. He lived an overflowing life, for he knew how to receive of the fullness of Christ, not to keep it to himself, but to share it with others, making many rich.[18]

A Chinese Christian from Zhoukou, who had been trained as a doctor by Guinness, said:

Dr. Guinness, with a burning heart, sought to save men. Except at such times as he was treating patients, he was constantly bringing them the gospel. His object was not only to save their bodies but their souls. Whenever there was a baptismal service, seven or eight out of ten received into the church would be sure to be ex-patients, converted in the hospital.[19]

Marie Monsen

The Norwegian Lutheran China Mission, whose headquarters were in Norway, sent ten new missionaries to Henan in 1901–2 to reinforce its work. One of the new recruits was a single woman named Marie Monsen, who reached China on September 1, 1901, just a year after the Boxer violence had exploded across the country. Nobody would have believed that this small, humble figure would have such an impact over the next 30 years that many Christians in Henan still refer to her as "the mother of the house churches."

Marie Monsen

Born in 1878, Monsen was trained as a schoolteacher and had just completed a year studying nursing when she felt a strong call from God to become a missionary. She was ready to travel to China in the summer of 1900, but the outbreak of the Boxer Rebellion delayed her plans for a year.

Almost as soon as she arrived on Chinese soil, Monsen faced serious challenges that threatened to force her to go home. Just a month after arriving, she fell down an iron staircase and lay unconscious for several days with severe concussion. She was afflicted with severe headaches for six years, which ended only after she received special prayer and anointing for healing.

The mission doctor who was responsible for overseeing Monsen's recovery from the fall strictly forbade her from both language study and teaching for two years. This was a huge blow to the fledgling missionary. Every worker she knew had been devoted to language study in order to communicate with the people, and the other deep desire in her life, to teach, had also been denied. She felt extremely frustrated—but God had other plans for this young disciple.

Monsen was still struggling with the tumultuous start to her missionary career when she contracted malaria a few months after her arrival. The fever took her close to death, and the agony she experienced in body, soul, and mind broke her. At the time, she could see only Satan in these attacks, but years later she realized that God had allowed these afflictions so that she would value this life less than eternity, and would become a broken and humble vessel in God's hands. Eventually, she reached a point where she was able to truly surrender her future to God's will. She was healed that day, and her temperature returned to normal.

Over time, Monsen realized that her desires for teaching and studying were not God's plans for her. The bouts of malaria and the severe headaches from her fall continued for years, leaving her chronically weak and listless. She recalled how,

> each time I was about to take up school work, malaria sent me to bed and it had to be postponed. This happened again and again. In the end, I realized that the Lord Himself had closed that door to me. It came as a heavy blow, and not until long afterwards did I see the wisdom behind it.[1]

Due to her inactivity, Monsen was afraid that her mission might send her home, so whenever she was strong enough, she threw herself into the work to try to make up for lost time. On one occasion, she honestly stated:

> I became fully convinced that if a Boxer Rebellion should happen again, there would be nothing of the stuff of martyrs in me. In the end the thought of a possible repetition of those sufferings became a nightmare to me, and I began to pray sincerely and earnestly, "O Lord, take the call away from me and send me home."[2]

One night, Marie had a vivid dream in which she was being chased by murderers. Just as they were about to catch her, she said,

> I was lifted up and carried in a sitting posture so that I could see over their heads . . . I was filled with abundant peace and joy. Then I awoke and quite distinctly heard the words: "As thy days, so shall thy strength be."[3] And I sighed that it was only a dream. But the dream had a mighty influence, for from that moment I was set free from fear of death at the hands of brutal heathen men.[4]

A godly discontent

Toward the end of her first term of seven years in China, Marie started to feel deeply discouraged about the methods and poor results of the mission to which she belonged, and the lack of power in her own ministry. She asked many missionaries why their experiences were totally different from those of the early believers in the book of Acts, and was distressed when a senior missionary stated that she and her fellow workers

> could not expect to see real [Chinese] Christians like those in the West before the third generation . . . In her heart there was, from the first time she heard this view expressed, one continual, inveterate protest against it: "The Bible doesn't say so."[5]

Monsen found a clue as to why the missionaries were so ineffectual when the faith of an elderly, uneducated Chinese woman challenged her to the core. The old sister had moved into a room right next to hers, and the paper-thin walls meant that Marie could hear all of her prayers and petitions to God. The woman prayed loudly and frequently, and was never afraid to ask her Heavenly Father for things the Norwegian didn't dare to request because of her conservative Lutheran upbringing. She later recalled:

> I could hear everything she prayed about, and could watch how her prayers were answered. There seemed to be a great difference between the result of her prayers and mine. More than once when I heard her pray, I thought, "That will never happen," but just "that" did happen. It took some time for me to discover the explanation. She had a living, childlike faith, and to her God, difficulties were not difficulties. I had more doubt than faith, so to me difficulties were so tremendous that it would have to take time for God to answer. That is to say, I discovered that I was an unbelieving believer![6]

In 1907, news of the tremendous revival that was sweeping the Korean Peninsula reached Marie, and something clicked inside her heart. Here was New Testament Christianity being demonstrated, with similar results! She longed to travel to Korea and experience the revival for herself, and she asked God to provide the necessary funds for the journey. She recalled:

> As I prayed for money and looked for an answer, a definite word was sent instead: "What you want through that journey you may be given here, where you are, in answer to prayer." The words were a tremendous challenge. I gave my solemn promise: "Then I will pray until I receive."[7]

The moment Monsen accepted this promise from God, a fierce spiritual battle ensued, which she later described:

> Having pledged myself, I set out to cross the floor of my room to my place of prayer, in order to pray this prayer of revival for the first time. I had taken no more than two or three steps before I was halted. What then happened can only be described as follows: it was as though a boa constrictor had wound its coils around my body and was squeezing the life out of me. I was terrified. Finally, while gasping for breath, I managed to utter the one word: "Jesus! Jesus! Jesus!" Each time I groaned out the precious Name, it grew easier to breathe, and in the end the "serpent" left me. I stood there dazed . . . That experience helped me to endure through the almost 20 years which were to pass before the first small beginnings of revival were visible. Truly, God works unhurriedly![8]

Her methods

The Holy Spirit began to stir the diminutive Norwegian, and both Christians and non-believers were astonished at the power and authority with which she ministered His Word to them. The power was spiritual in nature, for her voice was always soft and calm, and she never shouted or bellowed out her message. All traces of the fear of other people left her, and all Marie desired was to know Christ and to stand up for truth and for the purity of the Church.

Monsen was deeply troubled by the compromised lifestyles of many missionaries and Chinese church leaders, and she challenged them strongly. The question "Have you ever really been born again?" burned throughout Henan and in many parts of China as God expanded her ministry and made it nationwide. When their faith was held up to the searching light of God's Word, many professing Christians realized that they had never been truly born again. Christianity might have been pasted over their lives as a veneer, but they had never been thoroughly converted to Christ, nor had they forsaken their sins.

When she visited the town of Zhenping, one of the Lutheran missionaries described Monsen's methods in great detail:

> Her plan was first to destroy the false security of the church members. She spoke of the various kinds of patches the unsaved used to hide behind when they tried to persuade themselves they were saved. She then spoke of sin, one sin at a time. It had cost her several days of prayerful struggle before she became willing, as she expressed it, to "descend into the miry cesspool of sin" in connection with the sixth commandment, against adultery. It turned out that one of Satan's well-nigh impregnable strongholds was at last broken into when this particular sin was brought out into the open.[9]

As news spread throughout the country that a single woman was challenging missionaries and church leaders about their salvation, a chorus of criticism broke out. Ironically, one of the main charges brought against her was that she was a Pentecostal and her ministry was based on emotionalism. The facts, however, were that she belonged to a conservative Lutheran mission, and all or most of her ministry was among Lutherans, Baptists, Methodists, and CIM workers, none of whom were Pentecostal.

Far from trying to stir up people's emotions, Marie was a very quiet woman, as was indicated in every report. One contemporary historian even seemed a little confused as to how she was so effective for Christ. "She was by all accounts soft-spoken," he wrote, "and it is not altogether clear why she prompted such [a] strong response."[10]

Monsen never attempted to argue with her detractors, but simply continued to share the gospel as doors opened to her, resting in the knowledge that God was with her. Brother Yun, a modern-day house church leader from Henan, has said:

> Marie Monsen was different from most other missionaries. She didn't seem to be too concerned with making a good impression with the Chinese church leaders. She often told them, "You are all hypocrites! You confess Jesus Christ with your lips while your hearts are not fully committed to Him! Repent before it is too late to escape God's judgment!" She brought fire from the altar of God.
>
> Monsen told the Christians it wasn't enough to study the lives of born-again believers, but that they themselves must be radically born again in order to enter the kingdom of heaven. With such teaching, she took the emphasis off head knowledge and showed each individual that they were personally responsible before God for their own inner spiritual life. Hearts were convicted of sin and revival fires swept throughout the villages of central China wherever she went.[11]

Confession and restitution

In many places, Monsen's messages were followed by deep confessions of sin and practical acts of repentance. People who had stolen items from their neighbors were convicted by the Holy Spirit and returned them. One man filled a wheelbarrow with things he needed to take back to their rightful owners.

Long-standing grudges between people were renounced and forgiven. Men confessed to beating their wives, and women confessed their own sins—including infanticide, which was prevalent in Chinese society then, even as it is today through gender-selective abortion. At one meeting, Monsen was taken aback when the women broke down in tears. One by one, they admitted:

> "I have killed three."
> "And I five . . ."
> "I took the lives of eight of my children."
> "And I of thirteen, but they were all girls."[12]

Marie was horrified by the dark deeds the women had committed, yet thrilled that they had confessed them before the throne of God. She wrote:

> It was the first time . . . that I heard women, who knew we regarded the killing of infants as sin, confess that they themselves had committed this particular sin. They all knew, of course, of many others who had done it. This was the first time I had seen the Holy Spirit deal with a whole group—a miracle indeed.[13]

Six Henan evangelists in 1933. God raised up many preachers during the revival

After the Holy Spirit had dealt with church members in a particular place, there invariably followed a time of evangelism, as cleansed men and women went to surrounding towns and villages, proclaiming the life-changing gospel of Jesus Christ. Whereas previously many believers had only been able to speak of God's transforming power, now they were able to demonstrate it in their own lives. Thousands of people, seeing the difference, put their trust in the Lord.

On numerous occasions, people came to faith in Christ after having a dream or vision of God's impending judgment. Some dreams revealed to people the true condition of their lives, while one woman testified that "a shining figure had appeared to her and told her that this was her last chance to receive salvation."[14]

Monsen's deep longing that the Chinese would experience a biblical Christianity was being answered. In one meeting, the convicting presence of the Holy Spirit was so real that a soldier who had strayed into the building knelt in repentance and received new life in Jesus Christ. The joy of being forgiven overwhelmed him, and peace flooded his beaming face. He stood up and declared:

> It will be a short life of joy for me here on earth, but I shall be saved from myself and my sins forever. Will you pray together for me until you hear a shot from the military camp? I stole some ammunition and sold it, and there is a death penalty for that. I must go back now and confess to the Captain . . . We shall meet again in heaven.[15]

The soldier had not been pushed into the kingdom of God by theological arguments or human persuasion. Indeed, he had never heard a word of the gospel until he walked into the church that day, but the presence of the Almighty God was so tangible in that meeting that he was now willing to die in exchange for the new life he had just experienced. The young man ran off with a radiant smile on his face. Monsen recalled:

> We stood there praying in a ring, holding one another's hands. We thought it was a very long time we had to wait, praying and listening for that shot. Suddenly he was there again in our midst, smiling. He had confessed everything and given a careful, detailed account of what he had stolen. The Captain sat silent a moment, then sighed heavily and said, "As you have now become a new man and will not steal any more, I don't see why you should die. You may go."[16]

The response of people to the conviction of the Holy Spirit was not always positive. Occasionally people fled in terror when the terrible power of God descended upon them, including some church leaders and elders. People often said to Monsen, "Your words are like knives" or "Your words strike me like thunderbolts." One elderly Christian lamented, "All my wrong-doings have been spread out before me like wares piled up on a counter."[17]

A wall of fire

One night, even as the town she was in was being ransacked by outlaws, Monsen received a powerful vision that greatly strengthened her faith. After feeling two heavy blows on her right shoulder, she clearly heard the words: "The Lord is a wall of fire round about his people."

Immediately, fear was replaced by the peace of God. She recalled:

> It was as if the roof had been lifted off the house, and sitting up in bed I was surrounded by a very high wall of fire. It gave out no heat. A swarm of arrows came flying from beyond the wall, but not one of them reached me. The vision lasted perhaps only a second or two.[18]

Most missionaries in China at the time, and especially women, were too afraid to travel because of the threat of violent crime. Monsen was often advised to stay at home, but she would always pray and if God guided her to go, she would set out regardless of the dangers. On one occasion, as her raft drifted down a bandit-infested river, a robber came to the bank, pointed his gun at the passengers, and ordered the boatmen to stop. Marie turned to face the man and began to pray for God's intervention. Suddenly, "he began to run more swiftly than we had ever seen a Chinese run before."[19] The boatmen were later told that the man had fled because he saw a great angel protecting the raft.

On another day, three armed men jumped out from behind a rock as Monsen was passing by in a donkey cart. They seized the donkeys and pointed a gun at her, but she prayed, "Lord, thou art a wall of fire between them and me." She stared at the men for a few moments, and later said:

> I was kept perfectly calm and without fear, even peaceful. The wall of fire was there between us. Not a word was spoken. Then the bandit who had been aiming at me turned to the other two and said, "Let go the animals, these people may continue their journey."[20]

Marie's profound confidence in the Lord's promises spread to many Chinese women, for she taught them that no harm will befall a child of God apart from His will. This revelation banished their fears. Often when their town was threatened with attack, the Christians came together to call on the Lord in prayer, only for the bandits to unexpectedly change direction and leave them unmolested. On numerous occasions, lustful men tried to lay hands on Monsen with evil intent, but she prayed and trusted God, and each time the danger passed.

Once, a mob invaded the town where Marie had been sharing the Word of God. Dozens of people from the neighborhood climbed over the walls of the mission compound, clutching little bags of valuables, as they thought there was less chance of being attacked and robbed at the mission than in their homes. Bullets whistled about the heads of the people gathered there, and gunfire and loud explosions were heard for several hours as the bandits plundered and killed in the town. Throughout the ordeal, the Christians calmly prayed for God's protection.

The next day, neighbors from across the street visited Monsen and the other believers and told them that from time to time, when the firing was less intense, they had poked their heads out of their front doors to see what was going on. One non-Christian family asked whether they could come into the compound next time there was such an attack, "since you have protection." Monsen asked them what they meant, and they explained:

> Three soldiers stood on guard up on the high roof of the Gospel Hall, one at each end and one in the middle. A fourth was seated on the porch over the main gate. These soldiers had kept watch in every direction . . . They were taller than any soldiers we have ever seen.[21]

"My Father runs the trains"

At the height of her ministry in China, Monsen was in great demand. From her base in Henan she traveled widely to more than a dozen provinces, sharing the message God had placed on her heart. Everywhere, both individuals and entire churches were transformed, and many sinners repented and began pressing forward into the kingdom of heaven.

At one town, she planned to leave by train on a Saturday afternoon after the meetings concluded. She had an appointment at a city some distance away and needed all the connecting trains to arrive on time. As she was praying that morning, however,

Marie Monsen in 1929 with the widow of Chinese pastor Xi Shengmo

the Lord clearly told her that she should not leave the town until Monday.

When she told this to the senior missionary, he replied that it couldn't be God telling her to stay, for there were no trains on Mondays and she would surely miss her appointment. She returned to her room and again asked God for guidance. Again the words came: "Leave on Monday."

Her colleague became increasingly agitated, but the peace of God filled Marie's heart and she was assured that all would be well. She told the senior missionary, "My Father runs the trains," but he angrily expressed his displeasure.

On the Sunday evening, the local Chinese pastor asked Monsen if he could talk with her. He admitted that he had never experienced the inner peace of God in his life and asked how he could be saved. She led him to true faith in Jesus Christ, and he received the Lord with great joy. Monsen realized this was the reason why God had delayed her departure.

At breakfast on the Monday morning, she asked the missionary whether he would be kind enough to drive her to the station. He protested and said there was no point, because trains didn't run through the town on Mondays. After some discussion, however, he acceded to her request—perhaps to show her how foolish it was. They made their way through the narrow streets, and just as they pulled up outside the station, there was a train on the platform, preparing to depart! Marie later testified:

> In the few seconds before the whistle sounded for departure, I heard that the provincial Governor had telegraphed for the new carriage he had standing there, and it had to be sent immediately at express speed to the capital—the very city I had to reach that Monday in order to catch a north-bound train. We flashed past every station. Never before nor since has it been my lot to travel in such a magnificent carriage.[22]

An enduring legacy

In the early 1930s, Monsen received news that her elderly mother in Norway needed care. She was torn between continuing the fruitful ministry God had given her in China and returning home, but over time the Holy Spirit showed her that her service in the Orient had reached its conclusion. She returned to Europe in 1932, leaving behind thousands of new believers in Henan and other parts of China, and hundreds of zealous churches that had once been full of lukewarm Christians.[23]

Although she never set foot in China again, the impact of Marie Monsen's ministry was felt for decades. Many people tried to explain how she had been so effective, but all attempts to do so in mere human terms have fallen short. Her power came not from any human technique, but from the supernatural power of the Holy Spirit.

The Church in Henan was to experience great anguish and testing when the Japanese invaded in 1937. Later, the rise of Communism inflicted decades of oppression on the body of Christ, so that many onlookers believed the Church had been totally obliterated.

Many Christians were able to withstand the storms because of the message and example of the little woman from Norway. In 1950, as fierce persecution raged in Henan, one church leader declared:

> We could never have been able to face the attack that came if the Lord had not sent us the revival in the 1930s. Now, we are able to stand in the evil day. The foundation that was laid then stands sure.[24]

In the early years of Marie Monsen's ministry, after she fell down the stairs and contracted malaria, she often felt tempted to return to the comforts of her home country. She remained in Henan, however, and persisted in the call God had placed on her life. At her lowest point, when the mission work in Nanyang seemed entirely fruitless and no one showed any interest in the gospel, God consoled her with this promise from His Word: "The least of you will become a thousand, the smallest a mighty nation. I am the LORD; in its time I will do this swiftly."[25]

There were only a few dozen Christians in Nanyang when God sent Marie Monsen there at the start of the twentieth century, and there was no mass turning to Christ in that locality during her years in China. By 1922, there were only 318 baptized believers in Nanyang,[26] but in the decades since, the Church in this predominantly rural area has grown exponentially, transforming Nanyang into one of the strongest Christian regions in China.

Today, the entire Nanyang Prefecture contains over ten million people, and the number of Evangelical Christians living there is estimated at 3.2 million, or nearly one third of the population.[27] Nanyang includes the counties of Fangcheng, Tanghe, and the Nanyang City area—each of which has lent its name to major house church movements that have reached a combined total of tens of millions of people throughout China in the past several decades.

Many key house church leaders have emerged from this blessed part of southern Henan. God has truly made the body of Christ in Nanyang into a powerhouse for revival in China. For this reason, many Christians in Henan today, more than a century after Monsen began her ministry in China, continue to refer to her fondly as "the mother of the house churches."

Honoring Marie Monsen

Marie Monsen continued to live in the Norwegian city of Bergen until 1962, when she went to her eternal reward at the age of 84. Decades later in 1999, a native of Nanyang, Brother Yun, happened to be visiting Bergen and was asked by a group of local pastors whether he would like to visit Monsen's grave. Yun was very excited at the prospect, and later wrote:

> Now I had the great privilege of visiting her grave in her homeland. I wondered if any other Chinese Christian had ever enjoyed the privilege I was about to enjoy. When she came to our part of China there were few Christians and the church was weak. Today there are millions of believers. On their behalf I planned to offer thanks to God for her life.[28]

The memorial headstone in honor of Marie Monsen at Bergen, Norway

On arriving at the cemetery, however, Yun was shocked to discover that Monsen's grave had been left untended for many years and was now just a patch of grass without a headstone. In Chinese culture, such dishonor is considered an insult to the deceased, and Yun was deeply grieved. With a heavy heart he sternly told the Norwegian Christians who were with him:

> You must honor this woman of God! I will give you two years to construct a new grave and headstone in memory of Marie Monsen. If you fail to do this, I will personally arrange for some Christian brothers to walk all the way from China to Norway to build one! Many brothers in China are skilled stonecutters because of their years in prison labor camps for the sake of the gospel. If you don't care enough, they will be more than willing to do it![29]

Thanks to Brother Yun's prompting, on September 1, 2001—exactly 100 years to the day since Marie Monsen first set foot in China—more than 300 Norwegian Christians gathered in the Bergen cemetery for a special prayer and dedication service. A beautiful new headstone was unveiled in her memory.

1930s

Refugee children learning Christian songs from the Salvation Army's Harry Woodland in the 1930s

"Days of heaven upon earth"

The 1930s was a desperately difficult decade for Christians in Henan, with crime and violence destroying entire communities; yet the churches in the province had struggled in the late 1920s when hardship and lawlessness brought fear and despondency to many believers. In 1928 alone, about half of the missionary force left their stations due to failing health and low morale. The Episcopal church leader Cheng Chingyi wrote in 1929:

> Not a few of our Christian people feel utterly depressed and exhausted; a kind of flatness seems to reign in the hearts of many—a lack of spirit and energy to make any forward move.

> The bitter experiences of the past and the uncertainty of the future have made many shy of attempting great things for God and expecting great things from God.[1]

By the early 1930s, millions of people in Henan had been reduced to poverty, forced to roam the streets, scavenging for food in order to survive. In the midst of these difficulties, however, the body of Christ continued to grow in grace, and waves of spiritual refreshing swept over the followers of Jesus. More than 20 years later, when the veteran Lutheran missionary Victor Swenson looked back on his many years serving Christ in Henan, he fondly recalled the impact of the 1930s revival:

> The hearts of Christians were burning within them. The joy of a close, new walk with the Lord spread from one community to another, from one province to others, and even across the ocean . . . These were days of heaven upon earth, days when Christians' minds were occupied largely with eternal values, when there was a willingness to listen for hours to the Word of God and to make restitution, and when there was a willingness to testify and spread the Word.[2]

Anna Christensen

The powerful impact made by Marie Monsen's ministry in Henan did not fade after her return to Norway in 1932. Indeed, the fire of the Holy Spirit that had burned so brightly in her meetings was carried forward by several other key Christians.

The many critics who had attacked Monsen's ministry because they were opposed to women preachers may have felt relieved when they heard that she had departed China, but their relief was short-lived, for it seemed the Norwegian's spiritual mantle was passed to another female Scandinavian revivalist: Anna Christensen from Denmark. Her ministry was very similar to Monsen's. She preached the same kind of messages, and great results were achieved through the power of the Holy Spirit. Like Monsen, Christensen had spent many years in China being prepared by God before her ministry blossomed.

In 1924, after a decade of service in Henan, Christensen visited Denmark for a lengthy break. She returned in 1926 to assist an evangelist who was conducting special meetings in a village. After three weeks of services, 19 families had repented of their sins and placed their trust in Jesus Christ.

In the 1930s, Christensen's ministry quickly expanded and had a nationwide influence. Everywhere she went, Christians were refined and empowered, and scores of unbelievers found salvation in Jesus. In the summer of 1933 a revival broke out among the staff and patients at the Kaifeng Hospital, where Whitfield Guinness had faithfully served for many years. According to the historian J. Edwin Orr:

> The staff were deeply moved, conscience money being presented, along with the restitution of many things stolen or pilfered. In Zhoukou and Zhengzhou, in the same province, Anna Christensen's message was given with searching power. Men and women were gripped by her messages, and many were the results recorded. Powerful in the autumn of 1933, the revival was still continuing in Kaifeng, Zhoukou, and other Henan cities, the work of grace having been thoroughly effective . . . The Holy Spirit mightily convicted men and women of sin, resulting in confessions in spite of the risk of "loss of face."[3]

When Christensen visited the central Henan town of Yancheng in 1933, a deacon who lived at an outstation walked 60 miles (97 km) to hear the Word of God. A tremendous visitation of the Holy Spirit occurred, prompting missionary Henry Guinness to report: "Praise God, we had a wonderful time of blessing . . . No appeals were made, and there was no special emotion, but the spirit of conviction was present and hidden sin was brought to light and put away."[4]

Liu Daosheng

In Marie Monsen's later years of ministry, she had often been accompanied by two Chinese Lutheran evangelists: Liu Daosheng and Wu Zhenming.

These two men—and others—did such a good job proclaiming the gospel that it helped to soften the blow when Monsen left China. Their ministry was so effective that revival reportedly broke out among the churches of six different mission societies in Henan. When Liu visited Miyang in 1933 he preached just one message: "You must be born again." The meetings reportedly produced "intense conviction. The

Liu Daosheng

missionaries had never seen such contrition, Chinese beating their fists against the wall, or on the floor, before pouring out their hearts in confession."[5]

An insight into Liu Daosheng's contrite heart can be seen in a prayer request he wrote in 1934 while in the midst of white-hot revival:

> During these years the grace of God has been great toward me. As to the future I have to rely on the grace and love of God and to press on. I hope that my friends will pray for me, that I might be saved from backsliding and causing disgrace to His Name. At the same time, I pray that the Lord may protect me and keep me, so that my completed life story may redound to the glory of the Lord.[6]

John Sung in Henan

In 1933 the influential Bethel Evangelistic Band—whose members led tens of thousands of people to Christ throughout China—traveled to Henan, with the famous Chinese evangelist John Sung (Chinese name: Song Shangjie) often remaining behind to minister in dry churches. When the band members visited Anyang—the city where Jonathan Goforth had blazed a trail of revival earlier in the century—they found that most of the Christians there were backslidden, having embraced the liberal Presbyterian theology that Goforth had spent years resisting. The missionaries in Anyang mocked the "out-of-date stuff" that John Sung preached, such as repentance from sin and consecration to Christ. Despite the cold reception, Sung reportedly

> wielded the two-edged sword of the Spirit, preaching the great and essential truths of salvation. The congregation was so moved that they all began to cry to God, among them the pastor of the church, who acknowledged that he was not born

John Sung

again. After being fully converted, he determined that he would henceforth preach only the fundamental doctrines of the faith.[7]

When Sung revisited the city later that year, he found things had greatly improved. This time, "instead of a couple of hundred hearers, 1,000 people attended the meetings. The whole situation had changed since the conversion of the pastor."[8]

John Sung was a man with the fire of God in his heart and an uncompromising commitment to truth. During one of his trips through Henan, he and another evangelist, Chu Huaian, reached the town of Zhoukou late at night. They went to the mission compound and asked the gatekeeper if two evangelists could stay the night. The man went and asked the resident missionary, who said the two preachers were not permitted to stay inside the buildings but they could sleep on a haystack in an outer shed. That night, Sung could not sleep on account of the smelly feet of one of the missionary's servants, who also slept in the shed.

The next morning, before the two preachers continued their journey, Sung wrote a letter in English rebuking their host, who did not realize that the man nicknamed "China's greatest preacher" was one of the two evangelists he had sent to the haystack. Chu recalled that the highly educated Sung, who held a PhD from an American university,

> accused the missionary of lack of loving hospitality for other preachers of the gospel, and advised him to examine himself carefully. Our rickshaw had travelled about six miles [10 km] when the foreign missionary and his wife caught up with us on their bicycles. They felt very sorry that it was Dr. Sung they had mistreated. They apologized profusely, begging Sung to return for breakfast with them. He refused, saying, "We are not going back. You are showing your hospitality to a Ph.D. rather than an evangelist. You must thoroughly repent of your behavior!"[9]

On another occasion, Sung was invited to hold revival meetings in Xuchang. After arriving, he was taken to a special Christmas banquet attended by all the social elite and VIPs of the town. Sung was introduced to the mayor of Xuchang and seated to his right, alongside the police commissioner and the publisher of the local newspaper. The evangelist felt uncomfortable being placed with these "important" people and ordered one of his co-workers to swap places with him. He declared:

> I am a servant of the Lord. I came to lead evangelistic meetings. I should be seated with brothers and sisters from the church. You go and mingle with these officials . . . We are one family as brothers and sisters; we should have the joy of eating together as a family. Why do we invite these big shots? It would be fine to invite them to come for the message. But to solicit their flattery and to have them for show, that is wrong.[10]

Remarkable answers to prayer

The revival in Henan was accompanied by many miraculous answers to prayer. The sick were healed, the demon-possessed were delivered, and thousands of sinners received a clean conscience through the blood of Jesus Christ.

An elderly Christian widow lived in a poor house that had fallen into a state of disrepair. The straw roof leaked in several places, and one of the large wooden beams had slipped out of its socket and was in danger of falling. News came that a large storm was bearing down on the town, so the widow searched for straw to patch up the holes in her roof and also tried to hire a workman to put the beam back in its place, but there was no straw available and no one was willing to help her.

The woman's son wanted her to leave the unsafe house and stay with a friend, but she believed that God cared for her, and she asked Him to protect her from danger. When the storm struck that night, a fierce wind shook the house—and, to her joy and wonder, shook the beam into its place again! It poured rain, but none came through the roof. In the morning they found that the wind had blown a lot of straw from a neighbouring roof over to theirs and filled up the holes![11]

On another occasion, a terrible famine reduced millions of people to poverty. The collapse of the economy in Henan meant that many missionaries, too, were struggling to survive. One family went without any protein for months because of food shortages. One day, they noticed many pigeons roosting on the tower of their mission house. They thought what a delicious meal the birds would make, and considered how they might catch them. They built a catapult, but it proved hopelessly inadequate. Other ideas were tried, without success.

The father realized they would never be able to catch the elusive pigeons, so he knelt in prayer and simply asked his

Heavenly Father to let them have some. A short time later, a fierce snowstorm engulfed the town. Early the next morning, the missionary heard someone calling, "Do you want any pigeons?" He recalled: "I looked out, and there scattered about were the frozen birds, fallen to the ground. We hurried out and picked up nine pigeons straightaway. What a delicious dinner we had that day!"[12]

Lasting fruit

The greatest miracle during the 1930s Henan revival was the number of hardened sinners whose lives were transformed through faith in the Son of God. Whereas just a few years earlier it had been considered a great breakthrough for even one individual to come to Christ, now it was not unusual for a hundred people to be saved in a single meeting.

The challenge of establishing so many new believers in the faith was articulated by many leaders of the time. William Nowack of the Ebenezer Mission described the scene when the revival swept through Miyang:

New Christians at a baptism class in Xuzhou in the 1930s

> At our main station the new inquirers have been coming in so fast that it is almost impossible to keep track of them all, and many homes have been taking down their false gods during the past few months . . . The Lord visited us with the most powerful revival that we have had thus far . . . Never before had we seen such mighty conviction of sin rest upon a Chinese audience, though we had seen much of God's wonderful working in the past. Some were pounding the benches with their hands and calling out, "I am face to face with God. I am face to face with God," while others could be heard to say, "I am going straight to hell, there is no hope for me."
>
> Several struck their heads with their fists out of sheer hatred of themselves, while one or two seemed to feel that even hell itself was too good for such great sinners as they were. Many were unable to eat or sleep for several days and nights, until they had made full confession of their sins [and] received the assurance of His forgiveness.[13]

The events of the 1930s shook many of the Lutheran missionaries, most of whom came from ultra-conservative churches in their home countries. Nonetheless, the majority found themselves swept along by the streams of living water that flowed in Henan. Victor Swenson, who served in China for 45 years, summarized the effect of the 1930s Henan revival:

> Those who had lived through those days of brokenness before God could never be the same again. Life had a new quality of devotion to Him. We had seen God's Spirit working at floodtide, and we had a new concept of His greatness. The Christians were bathed in a new spirit of love that bound them together as never before.
>
> Thousands were given grace to confess their sins, and through faith in the cleansing power of Christ were filled with power, love, and zeal for their fellow men . . . Through the revival they had come to know Him as a living Savior. They now knew His saving power and mercy. This created a new and

living fellowship between them and their Lord . . . The revival flames spread from person to person, home to home, city to city. The church became a Bible-reading church, and a church with a baptism of love.[14]

1940s and 1950s

These seven sisters from the Ding family were all dedicated Christians during the 1940s

Anointed for burial

The effects of the extraordinary awakening that impacted Henan in the 1930s continued to last into the following decade. The 1940s was in many ways a period of consolidation for the churches. The gains from the revival had stretched the missionaries and the Chinese leaders to the limit, and the overwhelming need was for theological training so that the thousands of new believers—many of whom were illiterate—would have a strong foundation in the truth of God's Word.

The fruit of the 1930s visitation of the Holy Spirit was evident throughout Henan. In Fangcheng County, missionary David Adeney visited a mountainous district in 1941 where he discovered "at least 1,000 Christians . . . Many of them really love the Lord and have a very strong faith in the power of Christ to heal the sick."[1]

Throughout the 1940s, the churches in Henan began to place a greater emphasis on reaching those parts of society considered shameful. Daniel Nelson Jr., whose father and brother were martyred for Christ, continued to serve in Henan and reported:

> Buddhist vegetarians, opium sots, adulterers, thieves, and hypocrites have been converted, and the testimony of their renewed lives is powerful. There has been a fresh impetus to witness for the Lord, even children taking part in the spreading of the gospel.[2]

Many of the missionaries in Henan at this time were godly, no-nonsense types. When Oscar and Mina Hellestad prepared to leave China in 1940, after almost 40 years' service, the local believers at Guangshan wanted to honor their faithful service by erecting a monument in their memory. At the crowded farewell service, just as someone was about to announce the plans for the monument, Oscar Hellestad stood up and declared:

> I want to make it very clear that no monument of any kind should be erected to my wife and me—now or ever. I appreciate your kind thought, but if you want to honor us in the best possible way, carry on the work that we have been doing here. That will be the best monument.
>
> If you have already collected money for this, there are so many ways in which it could be better used . . . Remember that my wife and I are but servants of God. It is to Him that any honor you want to express should go. By your love you have

> already erected a lasting monument in our hearts. Let any other expressions of your love be in the form of service to God and to man.[3]

Compared with the meager results from the first 50 years of Evangelical mission work in Henan, the 1930s and 1940s witnessed explosive growth. By the time the People's Republic of China was established in 1949, there were an estimated 100,000 to 120,000 Evangelical Christians throughout the province.[4]

The Catholic Church, meanwhile, had also experienced startling growth during the first half of the twentieth century. There had been 18,487 Catholics meeting in 161 churches throughout the province in 1907,[5] but by 1922 the number had nearly tripled to 51,592 communicants in 477 churches. There were four times as many Catholics as Evangelicals in Henan at the time.[6]

Then, between 1922 and the advent of Communist rule in 1949, the number of Catholics in Henan again more than tripled to 170,000.[7]

The 1950s—the Church goes underground

When Chairman Mao Zedong announced the foundation of the People's Republic of China on October 1, 1949, roughly half of Henan had already been under Communist control for years. Missionaries were divided in their opinions of what would happen to the Church under Communist rule. Some feared the worst, citing the grim fate of Christians in the Soviet Union. Others, however, looked forward to the dawn of a new era of freedom and progress for Chinese Christianity.

Just four months later, in February 1950, news emerged from Henan of a crackdown on Christian activity, and by the end of 1951 there were very few foreign missionaries left in the province. Many churches had been forced to close, and

Chinese pastors were being detained and questioned. Some congregations had the foresight to prepare for the approaching storm, and had made plans to survive without the aid of church buildings, clergy, or organized meetings. Others were caught unprepared when the persecution commenced, and believers were left to find spiritual sustenance by themselves.

Throughout the 1950s, each successive year brought more severe persecution to the Church. Hundreds of Chinese pastors were rounded up and sent to prison labor camps, and by 1954 it was clear that Mao desired nothing less than the complete eradication of Christianity from his new China.

Brother Yun told of the horrors of those years for the Christians in Henan:

> In my home area of Nanyang, believers were crucified on the walls of their churches for not denying Christ. Others were chained to vehicles and horses and dragged to their death. One pastor was bound and attached to a long rope. The authorities, enraged that the man of God would not deny his faith, used a makeshift crane to lift him high into the air. Before hundreds of witnesses, who had come to falsely accuse him of being a "counter revolutionary," the pastor was asked one last time by his persecutors if he would recant. He shouted back, "No! I will never deny the Lord who saved me!" The rope was released and the pastor crashed to the ground below.
>
> Upon inspection, the tormentors discovered he was not fully dead, so they raised him up into the air for a second time, dropping the rope to finish him off for good. In this life the pastor was dead, but he lives on in heaven with the reward of one who was faithful to the end.[8]

During the 1930s revival, Henan's Christians didn't realize that the blessing being poured out was designed to fortify them for life under a godless Communist regime. With the benefit of hindsight, a missionary wrote in the late 1950s:

> As we consider the grip of godless Communism on China today, we realize how God was preparing a people for His Name. We are often short-sighted, but God takes the long view. He was making preparation then, by the work of His Holy Spirit, for a sturdy, earnest Church that could stand persecution.[9]

The tragic death of Dong Shaowu

After all missionaries had been expelled from Henan, a curtain of silence fell, and for decades little information emerged from Christians behind the Bamboo Curtain. Later, when news did leak out, it was often harrowing accounts of martyrdom and suffering.

Born into a poor but godly Christian family in Xiangcheng County, Dong Shaowu made a commitment to serve Jesus Christ at an early age. When he was old enough, he attended

Dong Shaowu in 1956

seminary, where a wealth of Bible knowledge was deposited into his heart and mind.

In 1949, after the Communists had swept to power, Dong was placed on a list of the ten most wanted people in China. In 1950 he went into hiding, and by the following year all the other nine men on the list had been found dead.

Dong had no income at this time and was barely able to survive. His poverty caused him to move to a remote rural area. This saved his life, as the authorities couldn't find him. At Easter 1954, he received some money from his son and was able to travel to Beijing, where he visited the Christian Tabernacle, led by the great patriarch of the Chinese Church, Wang Mingdao. Dong stayed in Wang's home and was asked to speak at the Easter services. He and Wang became close friends, and Dong later described his time in Beijing as the happiest of his life.

By May 1958, Dong was back in Henan and the winds of persecution were howling all around him. His friendship with the hated Wang was seen as proof that he was a counter-revolutionary, and he was accused of betraying China to the Western imperialists. A "struggle session" was organized to break his spirit. It lasted 21 days, and ended only because everyone had to break to gather in the wheat harvest.

Dong returned home with his mind in turmoil from the constant strain of being interrogated. When he was called back for more questioning in mid July, one report said:

> Struggles became fierce and cruel. Dong was scolded, beaten up, spit at, forced to kneel . . . All kinds of vicious abuses were hurled at him . . . A month of endless struggle left Dong without rest. His health deteriorated rapidly. He was infected with acute hepatitis and jaundice. His whole body turned yellow . . . He was no longer able to sustain the torment, either physically or mentally.[10]

September 7, 1958, was a day off for all prisoners except Dong. After a long morning of physical and mental torture by Public Security Bureau (PSB) officers (including one man who at the time, and for more than 30 years after, was an active committee member of a Three-Self church in Henan), Dong reached a stage where he could take no more. Sometime after five o'clock in the afternoon, he asked his interrogators if he could go to the toilet. After a long while waiting for his return, one of the guards went to fetch him and found Dong's body slumped over in the urinal. Tortured past the point of resistance, he had drowned himself.

That evening, as news spread around the town that Dong Shaowu was dead, a local deacon boldly came to claim the body, which he washed and prepared for burial. Six other people volunteered to help bury it, at great personal risk—among them a 14-year-old believer. They wrapped Dong's corpse in an old mat and buried him in a hole in the ground outside the south gate of the city.

Dong Shaowu's death caused some believers to boldly proclaim their faith. At a meeting the following evening, the deacon who had come for his pastor's body stood up and publicly declared his commitment to Christ. He was immediately arrested and sent away to a prison labor camp, and was never heard from again.

Catholics throughout Henan also suffered terribly during the 1950s. An Italian missionary, Amelio Crotti, was tortured in the Kaifeng Prison until his expulsion from China in 1954. He shared this powerful and touching story:

> From my cell I heard a mother speak soothing words to her child of five, whose name was Xiaomei. She had been arrested with the child because she had protested against the arrest of her bishop. All the prisoners were indignant at seeing the suffering of the child. Even the prison director said to the mother,

"Don't you have pity on your daughter? It is sufficient for you to declare that you give up being a Christian and will not go to church any more. Then you and your child will be free."

In despair, the woman agreed and was released. After two weeks she was forced to shout from a stage before 10,000 people: "I am no longer a Christian."

On their return home, Xiaomei, who had stood near her when she denied her faith, said, "Mother, today Jesus is not happy with you."

The mother explained: "You wept in prison. I had to say this out of my love for you."

Xiaomei replied, "I promise that if we go to jail again for Jesus I will not weep."

The mother ran to the prison director and told him, "You convinced me to say wrong things for my daughter's sake, but she has more courage than I."

Both went back to prison. But Xiaomei no longer wept.[11]

1960s and 1970s

An elderly house church pastor teaching the Bible

The silent years

In 1958, Chairman Mao launched the Great Leap Forward, and millions of people starved to death in Henan. The extreme hardship and Mao's xenophobia led to severe persecution for Christians. By the 1960s, practically every church building in the country was closed, and thousands of believers had been killed or imprisoned for their faith in Christ. China shut itself off from the rest of the world, and a long period of silence began.

Throughout the 1960s and 1970s, the Church in Henan was at its lowest point and all activities were driven underground. Despite the harsh environment, God preserved a remnant of faithful believers, who continued to meet in secret during those dark years. No pastors remained to shepherd the flock, but in many places the flame of the gospel was kept alive by small groups of illiterate women. To all outward appearances, the Church in Henan had died. God, who is able to raise the dead, was at work, however, and He would have the final word.

In the 1960s, Henan was chosen as one of three experimental zones (along with Zhejiang and Inner Mongolia) in an anti-religion drive by extreme elements within the Communist Party. The ultimate aim was to obliterate Christianity once and for all, and to consign it to the history books. Horrific persecution ensued, with many officials reveling in acts of diabolical cruelty.

Although it would seem to be practically impossible to gather statistics for Christians in Henan during these silent decades, government sources in later years estimate there were 78,000 Evangelical believers in Henan in 1965, just before the start of the Cultural Revolution.[1] If this figure is accurate, it would represent a huge drop in the number of Christians since 1949, when there were 120,000 Evangelicals in the province.[2]

In all likelihood, the 1965 estimate was too low. Testimonies from believers who endured those dark years suggest that in fact the body of Christ actually continued to flourish and grow in Henan even during its darkest struggles.

A pastor from Shaanxi Province, Zhu Chengxin, told how a visit to Henan in 1975 invigorated his faith. He spent 28 days traveling across the province, conducting many services each day. The following account of Zhu's travels gives us a clear sense of how the Holy Spirit was moving in Henan at the time:

> Every evening [Zhu] hurried out after eating in order to reach the place of worship in time for the midnight service. Seeing the hunger and thirst of the Christians moved him to tears.
>
> When he felt it was finally time to leave, local Christians were reluctant to let him part. One Christian brother stood up and said: "You cannot leave; I have prayed to the Lord

> not to let you go." He then abruptly rode off on his bicycle. Zhu was puzzled by the man's statement and action; not until two days later did he understand what they meant. Knowing exactly what route Zhu would take in leaving the village, the brother had rushed to inform the woman in charge of the home gathering along the road that the servant of God was coming her way. She immediately sent several sisters to wait at the crossroad.
>
> When Zhu passed that way, he was easily identified because of his Shaanxi accent. He pleaded with the women to let him proceed. Instead, they fell on their knees and cried out for God's mercy. They had been longing for someone to preach to them, and had waited two days on the road for his arrival. Seeing no way out, Zhu and his companion agreed to return to the village with them . . . Over 100 people came to hear Zhu preach that evening.[3]

Feng Jianguo, a leader of the Tanghe house church movement, remembers the Cultural Revolution as a time of great tension and darkness, but also a time when God poured out His Spirit through powerful signs and wonders. In 2001, the author asked Feng to share what it was like to be a Christian in Henan during the 1960s and 1970s. He replied:

> During meetings we had to turn off all lights and cover the cracks in the doors and windows so nobody could spy on us. The believers would come to the meeting one by one, so that neighbors wouldn't notice. We were very close to one another in those days. If caught, we would be made to wear large dunce hats and be paraded in public. People would attempt to humiliate us by shouting and spitting on us.
>
> Many church leaders were persecuted during the Cultural Revolution, especially pastors with foreign connections. Some of them fell away under pressure and denounced Christ. In a short time, almost the entire church leadership was wiped out and the sheep were left without shepherds. They had no

direction or Bibles, so each person did what seemed right in their own eyes.

At Zhoukou, there was a demon-possessed man who had raped and murdered his own mother. He had become more like a demon than a human being, and the whole community was afraid of him. His own family rejected him and brought him to us to see what we could do. We prayed for him for 46 days, and he was delivered. Through this and other experiences the news spread that Christians were trustworthy and God was alive. This was the start of the house church movement in Zhoukou.

I was imprisoned for five years, and was treated very cruelly the first year, with frequent beatings and tortures. Our food was terrible and often we had to sleep on human waste because the toilets in our cells would overflow. Being "counter-revolutionaries" made us the worst kind of criminals.

Each month we were taken to different towns to be mocked and "struggled against" by the public, often before huge crowds in stadiums. I remember, however, that sometimes when the crowds were riling against us, they would fall silent when it was announced that we were Christians. It was obvious that many people didn't believe we were enemies of the state. Some believed that China had benefited greatly from Christianity in the past.[4]

Peter Xu Yongze, who later established the millions-strong Born-Again house church network, recalled the conditions for Christians in Henan at the time:

During the Cultural Revolution no one could be trusted. The government had spies everywhere, and normal citizens were encouraged and rewarded to spy on people in their communities, and to report any suspicious or "unpatriotic" activities. All public gatherings were outlawed, so the Church truly went "underground." Many believers did not meet for years, while others met in tiny groups of just two or three people, where they would whisper prayers to the Lord and encourage one another.

Even those tiny meetings were dangerous. If caught, the participants would be arrested and sent away to a labor camp.

The light of the gospel was truly like a flickering candle during those dark days. Satan wanted to completely extinguish the flame, but God had a great plan. It was a time of burial. The Church went underground, awaiting the resurrection power of the Lord.

People at the time were so desperate and spiritually dry that the slightest spark from the Lord would set them ablaze! In those remarkable days, the Lord instantly healed every sick person who was prayed for, and the fame of Jesus spread rapidly. On one occasion, when the authorities investigated reports of conversions by three elderly women in Zhenping, they found out that many undeniable miracles had been performed by these sisters. The fear of God fell on the officers, who decided it was more prudent to leave them alone![5]

Going the extra mile

Throughout the years of brutal suppression, the Christians in Henan often asked the Lord to give them an attitude that would enable them to embrace suffering as a gift from God. With that outlook, they were willing to go the extra mile, and there was little that evil human beings or the world could do to destroy them.

During the Cultural Revolution, Brother Shui of Fangcheng was one of a group of people sentenced to parade in public wearing a large "dunce" hat made of heavy bamboo. Crowds of people came out to mock and abuse him and the other "criminals."

When it was Brother Shui's turn to be exhibited, the police were unable to find a spare hat for him, so he had to walk without one. This deeply upset him, because he wanted to bear the reproach of the Lord. Each prisoner's "crimes" were written

An accused criminal forced to wear a dunce hat in 1967

on his or her hat, and for Christians the notice often read: "This person believes in Jesus," so many Christians wore the hat as a badge of honor. It was also a witness to unbelievers, who could see the peace and joy on the Christians' faces. Deeply anguished because no hat was available for him, Brother Shui cried out, "O Lord, why did you forget me?"

On the second day, a dunce hat was found for Brother Shui and he was overjoyed. His face shone and tears welled up in his eyes as he walked through the streets. Now he was considered worthy to suffer for the Name of the Lord! After the parade, he asked the police officers if he could keep the hat and take it home with him when he was released from prison, as a reminder of his "crimes." Although they found his request strange, they consented.

When Brother Shui returned to his farm, his neighbors were amazed to see him herding his cows and sheep while proudly wearing his dunce hat. They thought he had lost his mind and had no shame, but he was a man who loved Jesus with all his heart. For him, the hat was a treasured souvenir of the day the Lord allowed him to suffer for the Name of Jesus.

The authorities were furious when they saw him embracing what was meant to be his humiliation, but they realized there was nothing they could do to make him change his ways or renounce the Lord. Brother Shui served God wholeheartedly until his death in 2000.

In 1966, in the small town of Yunyang in Nanzhao County, another Christian was made to wear a dunce hat and was paraded through the streets as a criminal. Everyone knew that the man had been completely blind for many years, and the people came out to beat and smear dirt and excrement on him.

Guards were placed on either side of him to lead him forward, but suddenly this brother began to shout loudly: "Please don't guide me anymore! I can see! I can see!" God had miraculously opened his eyes right in the midst of his persecution.[6]

A famine of the Word of God

In 1967, with the Cultural Revolution in full swing, the fire of God continued to burn brightly throughout many parts of Henan. In Lishan Village of Fangcheng County, a small boy was afflicted with smallpox and his life hung in the balance. A doctor was summoned, but after taking one look at the boy he shook his head and left. The house church historian Danyun records what happened next:

> A young believer got up, laid his hands on the child, and the boy immediately got up and began to play!
>
> There were only a handful of Christians in this village at first. But eventually all the villagers believed in Jesus. After that, nobody was interested in taking part in commune plays or other entertainment. On the hillsides, the shepherd boys sang

During the "silent years," Henan's Christians could only gather secretly in small numbers for prayer and fellowship

> and danced before the Lord. In the fields, the laborers praised God aloud as they worked. The village women who usually gathered by the stream to do their laundry ceased arguing and sang from the depths of their hearts. The whole village was full of the harmony of praise . . .
>
> The number of believers increased by leaps and bounds, as neighboring villages turned to Jesus. Before long, there were more than 300 Christians, and they quickly outgrew the meeting place.[7]

As the years of hardship dragged on, people had become so deprived of truth and reality that there was a tremendous hunger for God's Word among both Christians and unbelievers. Peter Xu shared one example of how desperate people in Henan were to hear the gospel in those days:

People could not get enough Bible teaching. Their souls were so dry that they were willing to sit under the fountain of God's living water for as long as they could. All other activities were meaningless compared to the chance of learning the Bible and being in the Lord's presence.

I visited a mountainous area in Nanzhao County where a Christian there was also a respected government official, so large meetings could be held in his neighborhood without any security concerns. He had come to Christ after God healed him from a serious illness. When this brother heard that I was in the area, he asked me to teach the believers.

There were so many people crowded into the house that there was no room for me to stand at the front. Instead, I propped myself up in the doorway and taught God's Word. By the late afternoon I was exhausted, so I asked the leader to come and take my place, but he refused. I continued, expecting that when the sun went down the meeting would be dismissed. I was wrong! The leader said: "We have notified many brothers and sisters and they are coming from afar. You cannot leave; they haven't even arrived yet!"

Some of the believers walked more than 40 miles [65 km] to the meeting place. They were so hungry for God's Word and they lapped up everything. I shared [the gospel message] for five days straight, stopping only late at night. I spoke so long that my mouth became dry and my lips almost stuck together.

One afternoon, heavy rain began to fall. I was sure the meeting would be halted, because many believers were sitting on the ground in the courtyard of the house. The leader, however, said: "Let's cut the branches from the trees!" Using the leafy branches, they constructed makeshift shelters for people to sit under in the rain. They didn't care that water was trickling down their necks and soaking their bodies. All they cared about was hearing more of God's Word.

That day I continued preaching until midnight. The Holy Spirit came in great power and many people repented of their sins with intense agony. I knelt down next to some of them and listened to what they were praying. They were in pain because they realized their sins had pierced the Lamb of God. They continued, and by the time the sun came up the next morning, many were still kneeling in the dirt, deep in travail. Finally, God's light dawned in the believers' hearts. Agony and pain was replaced by joy and peace, and we all stood up together and praised the Lord for His grace and mercy.[8]

God's wrath leads many to repentance

Those who have persecuted Christians in Henan have done countless detestable acts over the years, but they have not always had things their own way. Some government officials who ordered persecution against God's children were suddenly struck with cancer, while family members of others have died in accidents. Both the officials and the community knew that God had judged those people for their actions against the Church.

One officer had been particularly brutal, showing neither mercy nor remorse for his evil deeds against God's servants. The one person this man loved dearly was his young daughter, who was the apple of his eye. One day, he returned home to find that she had suddenly lost her mind. For weeks she was unable to respond to her parents or anyone else. Leading doctors and psychiatrists were brought in to treat her, but to no avail.

The girl could utter only one sentence this whole time. Constantly, day and night, she declared: "You must stop persecuting the Christians. You must stop persecuting the Christians." Finally, realizing God's wrath had fallen on him, the official decided he would not persecute God's children anymore. On the very day he relented, his daughter was restored to sanity.

During the Cultural Revolution, one cruel man loved to persecute God's children. He constantly blasphemed the Lord and was always making plans to arrest more believers. One day, this man stuck out his tongue and was unable to pull it back into his mouth! He visited many doctors, but nobody knew how to help him, until finally one of them told him he should ask a Christian to pray for him.

In desperation, the man visited the home of one of the Christian leaders he had persecuted. At first the family was afraid, but when they saw his tongue sticking out and that he was unable to say anything intelligible, their fear turned to pity.

They understood that he wanted them to pray for him, but they knew if he was healed he would go straight back to persecuting them. They told him:

> There's no way we will pray for your healing until you give your heart to Jesus Christ and believe in Him. And after you receive Christ, you must agree that you will come to our meetings regularly, and learn to love and serve God with all your heart.

The officer was told to kneel down and repent, and as he did so, God healed his tongue. The man stopped oppressing the Church and remained a true believer for the rest of his life. This incident was the catalyst for a great revival in that village, and many families came to know Jesus.

From persecutor to preacher

Believers in every part of Henan have stories to tell about the importance of the Bible in their lives. A woman named Ying had grown up in a Christian home, but when persecution broke out, she opposed her own mother and told her to abandon her "superstitious belief" in Jesus. When her mother refused, Ying prepared a list of 800 names of Christians in the area and

A precious handwritten Chinese Bible

handed it to the Red Guards, who promptly arrested many of them.[9] Even her own father was sent to prison. Still not content, Ying burned all the Bibles and hymnals her mother had been safeguarding on behalf of other believers in the community.

The loving Heavenly Father, who sees the pain in people's hearts, did not abandon Ying. He reached out and saved her, causing her to repent in deep sorrow for her wicked deeds. A seed of faith was planted in her soul, but she was unable to nourish it because of the lack of Bibles during the Cultural Revolution. How she wished there had been just one Bible that she had not destroyed!

Ying cried out to the Lord for a year, asking for a Bible so she could learn His Word. She was willing to give everything she had for a copy, but her family was very poor. When she visited some Christians and offered them bags of grain in exchange for a Bible, they told her that no amount of grain would ever make them part with the beloved Scriptures.

One day, Ying heard there was a Bible in a nearby village. Clutching her baby, she staggered through the rice field to the village and begged to see it. The Christians there thought it was a ploy to get them into trouble, and they sent her away.

Finally, after a year of seeking, her desperate prayers were answered. An old woman who had hidden copies of the four Gospels took the risk of lending them to Ying. Like a starving beggar she devoured the Word of God, memorizing as much as she could before returning the Gospels to their owner. She managed to borrow other parts of the Bible, and she copied down every word by hand. After a while, she had copied half the Bible, while another Christian was busily copying the other half. Together, they had a complete Bible, painstakingly written by hand.

Sister Ying, like the apostle Paul, was transformed from being a persecutor of Christians to a defender of the faith. God used her throughout the Luoyang area to lead hundreds of people to Jesus Christ.

The obedience of Sister Chang

One day, God spoke clearly to a house church believer named Sister Chang, instructing her to do something that made no earthly sense. He told her to preach the gospel on the steps of the Public Security Bureau headquarters. The more she prayed about it, the more certain she was of the inner voice of the Holy Spirit. Finally, Chang realized she had no option but to obey God. She packed a small bag, fully expecting to be arrested and taken to prison.

Standing on the top step outside the PSB office, she bravely proclaimed the gospel to astonished onlookers. Within a few minutes, several officers dragged her inside and placed her under arrest. She was sentenced without a trial and sent to the local women's prison, where she found herself among thousands of lost souls.

Sister Chang boldly proclaimed the message of Jesus' love and forgiveness to her fellow inmates and to the guards. The fire of the gospel spread quickly, and within three months 800 women had believed in Jesus. The whole atmosphere of the prison was transformed, and now sounds of praise and worship were heard echoing down the corridors and around the courtyard.

The prison director was greatly impressed by the change of atmosphere and traced it to the preaching of Sister Chang. He brought her into his office and told her:

> You have made my job easy. There is no more fighting between the women, and they have become gentle and obedient. We need more people like you working here. Today we have decided to set you free. We want to give you a fulltime job here in the prison, and every month we will pay you 3,000 Yuan [about $375]. We will also provide you a car with your own driver, and will find a comfortable place for you to live.[10]

Sister Chang considered his offer. Although the salary was extremely high for any job in China at the time, she replied:

> Twenty years ago I became a disciple of Jesus Christ, and He has been wonderful to me. I don't believe that your offer of a car, driver, and salary falls in line with what Jesus wants to do with my life, and I belong to Him. All I want to do is preach the good news.[11]

Despite her rejection of his proposal, the director released Chang from the prison that very day, and she continued her ministry for the Lord.

1971—a turning point

Many church leaders in Henan view 1971 as a significant year for Christianity. Looking back, Peter Xu believes that:

> It was a real turning point in the history of the Chinese Church. It was in 1971 that many people became disillusioned with the empty Marxist system and they contemplated the purpose of life.
>
> Christians were called by the Holy Spirit to fully repent of their sins and to present their bodies as living sacrifices. As we shared the gospel amazing things happened, the likes of which we had rarely witnessed in China before this time. Sick people were healed, demons were cast out, and the precious blood of Jesus Christ changed many lives. Before the Cultural Revolution, many Christians in Henan came from a conservative Lutheran background. Prayers were read from a book, and hymns were sung with expressionless faces and joyless hearts. In 1971, however, God transformed his people and crowned them with overflowing joy.

The Church in Henan continued to grow in the 1970s despite severe persecution

> By the power of the Holy Spirit, small prayer groups of three or four believers were the links in a chain of blessing throughout Henan. As these small groups made contact with each other, God brought forth a huge revival. The Cultural Revolution was still in full swing in 1971, but the Lord Jesus launched His own revolution!
>
> Who could have ever believed that in the midst of our darkest struggle God would bring revival and resurrect the Chinese Church? It was completely the sovereign work of God, as all resurrections are. As thousands of house churches emerged across China, not a single person could claim any of it to be his or her work. There were no church growth manuals, and no human strategies or programs, just an outpouring of God's love and power on people who had been totally demoralized.[12]

In the Tongbai Mountains in southern Henan, an elderly sister named Su Xing had been illiterate her whole life. She had never attended school, but she was a warm-hearted sister who liked to share the gospel with people.

Because she could not read the Bible, however, church leaders were reluctant to send Su Xing out as an evangelist. The believers prayed earnestly for her, and a miracle took place. Without anyone teaching her to read, Su Xing was suddenly able to read fluently from the Bible! When asked how this occurred, she simply replied: "I just point my finger at a word, and the Holy Spirit tells me what it means."

Interestingly, Su Xing could only read words in the Bible. She was unable to read any other text, whether in newspapers, on street signs, or any other place except in the Word of God! She zealously preached the good news far and wide, and testified to the great miracle God had done for her. Later, Su Xing was imprisoned because of her bold witness and she suffered much for the Name of the Lord.

Amazed and confounded

Some house church leaders, when asked about the different miracles that occur in China, respond by saying: "All the miracles recorded in the Gospels happen at least once in China every year." One such miracle that both amazes and confounds onlookers is the supernatural multiplication of food. In southern Henan, this miracle occurred at various times during the 1970s.

A Bible teacher named Qinlu hosted large groups of believers who came to his house to hear him teach the Word of God. His family wanted to feed their precious guests, but they were poor and had already exhausted their resources. Then one day

> Qinlu's sister took a basket of wheat to make flour. Who would think that, when this one basket of wheat was milled, it would become two baskets of flour? Qinlu's house had only one small

Lunchtime at a house church training center
RCMI

> wok, and usually when they made porridge, at the very most, it could only provide food for six people. There were often 20 or more guests to feed, yet they always had leftovers. For many years there were meetings in Qinlu's home. Sometimes there were 40 or 50 people, sometimes over 100. Qinlu used his wok each time to make food and everyone ate until they were full. Hallelujah![13]

During the harvest season, another Christian family heard sounds like small explosions coming from their granary. They raced into the granary and found that the sides of the wheat container had split open and a huge amount of wheat was spilling all over the floor. The barrel had not been able to contain the Lord's blessing!

By the late 1970s, the leaders of China began to realize that their systematic efforts to obliterate Christianity had failed, and pockets of zealous believers had sprung up all over the country! In 1979 the police rounded up more than a hundred house church members at Fangcheng in southern Henan. The raid was carried out after dark, so the guards decided to lock the believers in a cell overnight before processing the detainees the next day. The house church leader Zheng Shuqian recalled what happened:

> Throughout the night we prayed and worshipped together. It was a time of glorious fellowship. With tears in our eyes we sang about the Lord's suffering in the Garden of Gethsemane. It was as though we were there with Jesus. We all wept and wailed from the depths of our hearts.
>
> At three o'clock in the morning, a 14-year-old girl who had been arrested with us shared that she was deeply concerned because her school had warned the students that if they ever attended a Christian meeting they would be expelled and would forfeit any chance for future education. She pleaded with me, "Uncle, please help me go home!"

I gently said to her, "How can I help you? The iron door is securely locked and the windows all have iron bars across them. There's no way out."

The girl's earnest pleas deeply touched my heart, however, so I decided to do whatever I could to get her and the other children out, even if it meant a worse punishment for me the next day. I took a chair and tried to smash the windows, and then kicked against the door with all my might, but nothing budged.

Then one of the brothers asked, "Uncle, why don't you pray and ask God to open the door? Command the door to open in Jesus' Name!"

I put down the chair and ran to the door, crying out in prayer for God to act on behalf of the children, but nothing happened.

Feeling emotionally spent, I prayed again, and suddenly one of the brothers who had his back against the door said he felt something move behind him. He stood aside and we all watched the heavy door open by itself!

When the police awoke and saw the prison door open, they knew it would be more difficult explaining the escape to their superiors, so they acted as though nobody had been arrested in the first place. The incident passed without any of us being arrested.[14]

The Born-Again Movement

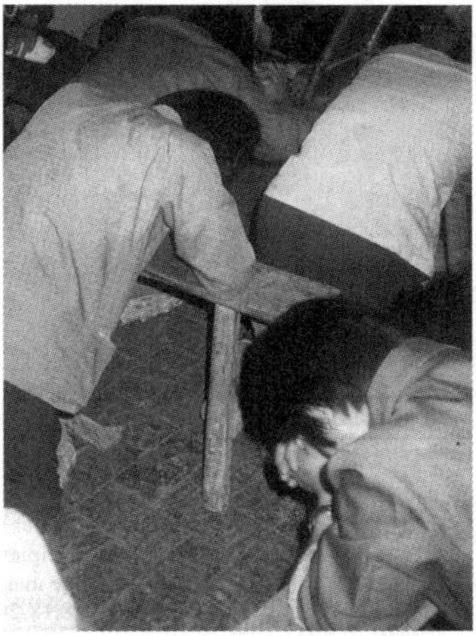

House church believers interceding for their nation

One of the largest, most influential, and controversial house church movements to emerge from Henan Province is the Chong Sheng Pai, or Born-Again Movement.

This group is known by a variety of names. The Chinese government has labeled it an "evil cult," and calls its members the "Crying Sect," or simply "Criers" or "Weepers," but the group calls itself Sheng Ming Zhi Dao Hui ("Word of Life Church").[1] Other names attributed to it have been "Living Truth," "Word of Truth," and Quanfanwei Jiaohui, which has been translated into English as "Full Scope" or "Total Scope" Church. Most Christians inside and outside China, however, call the group Chong Sheng Pai ("Born-Again Movement").

Of all the large house church networks in China, none seems to have attracted as much controversy as the Born-Again Movement. For years, it has been a major target of the Communist authorities. Waves of brutal persecution have been unleashed against its members, and all manner of slanderous accusations have been leveled at its leaders.

One reason for the special hatred the government seems to have for this group is that it is highly organized and systematically structured. The Born-Again Movement has dozens of efficient training centers throughout the country, which equip hundreds of evangelists and church leaders through a variety of Bible courses. The Born-Again Movement is not afraid to make specific and ambitious plans to win people to Christ, and it generally achieves its goals. Its mission statement encapsulates its ambitious vision:

> *With spiritual life as the foundation,*
> *Building up the Church is the central task.*
> *Breakthrough comes by the training of workers.*
> *With our present localities as our bases, we will expand outward in all directions,*
> *Radiating to cover the entire country.*

Inside a typical Born-Again meeting

Many Christians who have never visited China may find it difficult to imagine a typical house church meeting. Although meetings vary in style from place to place and from fellowship to fellowship, they are almost always marked by a tremendous intensity of commitment and zeal. In 2000, an American visitor to a Born-Again Movement leaders' meeting in Henan shared his impressions:

> This was a time of retreat and refreshing for them, and a hardship tour for me. We started before 6:00 each morning and

> finished between 10:30 and 11:00 each night. I taught a little over ten hours each day.
>
> We took time out to eat three meals a day which we ate in the training room. The men also slept in the room. The rest of the time was spent in prayer and worship. They usually stand to sing. Whenever they sit, it is on short stools about six inches high.
>
> The morning prayer time, which averages about two hours in length, is always done kneeling on the concrete floor. I must confess that I had to stand and stretch every 10 or 15 minutes. They often weep during prayer, and rolls of toilet paper are available to use, although some people don't bother and just blow their nose directly on the floor, so it can become quite a mess after a while.
>
> When standing to pray, everyone may be asked to raise their hands. Again, their endurance put me to shame. Some of these prayers lasted up to 30 minutes, during which they would never lower their arms. I had to rest my arms every few minutes.
>
> They pray with great fervor and focus. I would say that their prayer times are a primary method used to communicate ethos and passion, as well as to teach. Prayers, songs, and testimonies are contributed by any member as he or she feels led by the Spirit. They usually read the Scriptures in unison.[2]

Fueled by this kind of passion for God, it is little wonder that the members of the Born-Again Movement have been able to win millions of people to Christ from across China, and it also explains why the Communist authorities feel so threatened by them.

The early 1980s—a brutal beginning

Throughout the 1970s, a small cluster of home fellowships in southern Henan Province had a loose connection with one another. Later, they connected, shared resources, and expanded with remarkable speed under the sovereign hand of God, emerging as the Born-Again Movement. The fire of the gospel spread rapidly from family to family, village to village, and the Christians were busy trying to keep track of all the wonderful things God was doing.

In 1982 the churches decided to send a team of 17 young evangelists to the neighboring province of Sichuan. Previously, their work had been confined to their home area, and this was the start of what was to become a nationwide ministry.

After arriving in Sichuan, the evangelists spread out to different areas. God did a wonderful work and many people gave their lives to Christ. The authorities responded with severe persecution, and most of the evangelists were caught and badly beaten.

When the battered and bruised evangelists returned to Henan, Xu and four colleagues went to the Zhenping train station to welcome them home. There, officers pounced on them and dragged them to the local Public Security headquarters, where they were cruelly beaten for weeks, and Xu and the other leaders were sent to prison. Undeterred, the churches regrouped and dispatched more workers to Sichuan to replace those who had spilled their blood. Over time, their courage and persistence reaped a great harvest of souls for the kingdom of God.

In 1983, a widespread crackdown on criminals resulted in the arrest and ill-treatment of hundreds of house church leaders. Many fled to other provinces, where they remained constantly on the move while the authorities hunted them. As they scattered throughout the country, God gave many of these leaders a nationwide vision for the salvation of China. Within two years, the Born-Again Movement had expanded from being a group of churches based predominantly in southern Henan to one that was sending teams of on-fire workers to distant parts of China.

Life meetings

After a while, most of the evangelistic teams would return to Henan, tired and desperate for fellowship and keen to learn more of God's Word before heading back to the field. To meet this need, Peter Xu and his leadership team established what they called "Life meetings," after recognizing the need to develop a theological foundation for the thousands of new believers in their churches and to provide more extensive training for those called to the ministry. David Aikman noted:

> Xu thought that, in the excitement about all of the healing miracles taking place, China's house church networks were not doing enough to disciple and develop solid Christian lives among the new converts. He focused on building up a network of Christians that, in his view, were really attentive to a repentant, moral lifestyle.[3]

One of the strongest supporters of the Born-Again Movement throughout the 1980s and 1990s was the late Jonathan Chao, the head of China Ministries International. Chao, who was widely respected around the world as a balanced commentator on Chinese Christianity, defended the movement against charges of heresy. In 1997 he wrote:

> The Life meetings of Peter Xu's church are a marvelous way of giving inquirers and new believers a thorough grounding in the entire plan of salvation from Genesis to Revelation, with opportunities to respond in prayer and confession to the conviction of the Holy Spirit . . .
>
> I have not found this type of evangelistic meeting anywhere else in China. It is like the apostolic preaching of the cross, and is presented by those who have dedicated themselves to its preaching. Their changed lives bear witness to the working of the Holy Spirit. No wonder people want their relatives to attend them, even though they have to wait their turn. No wonder

the gospel is spreading like wildfire throughout many parts of China.

After my field trip I have come to appreciate the ministry of this group. It seems that their critics have not been there to see for themselves, and have therefore based their criticism on rumors. In view of this, I would encourage people to be absolutely sure of the facts before labeling such groups as heretical. I personally look forward to the time when I can again attend one of these Life meetings and be revived by the Holy Spirit.[4]

Peter Xu Yongze

Known as a quiet and contemplative man, highly educated and well versed in the Chinese classics, Peter Xu Yongze rarely talks about his life and experiences. For this book, the author is thankful for several extensive interviews he conducted with Xu, both before he left China and after he moved overseas.

Although he cannot recall a specific time when he became a true follower of Christ, Xu remembers sneaking into his

Peter Xu in 1975

grandparents' room at the age of five so he could kneel at their bedside and pray for them. Such was his burden for prayer that he was often unable to sleep until he had interceded for people the Lord placed on his heart.

Xu, from a well-to-do family in Zhenping County, came to be recognized as the principal leader of the Born-Again Movement almost by default. He had made a firm commitment to publicly preach the gospel in 1968, in the midst of the Cultural Revolution. That bold stance and his knowledge of the Bible won the respect of other Christians, and they gravitated toward his leadership.

Fleeing for the gospel

In 1968, Xu began to preach the gospel openly, which was almost unheard of during the Cultural Revolution. As a result he was forced to flee from the authorities, who were eager to crush his ministry before it took root. On one occasion in 1971, he hid with his parents and sisters inside a cave in a remote part of Yunmeng County. The police discovered their whereabouts, but Xu managed to escape by slipping past 20 armed officers who had surrounded the cave. His parents and sisters were captured and faced a public trial near their home in Zhenping. Xu recalled:

> Many people came to watch the spectacle. Some came to lie and shout accusations at my father. Others came to watch silently like spectators at a play. During the staged performance, certain "witnesses" were produced as evidence of my family's crimes. Despite the pressure of the situation, my father and sisters had an unusual calm on their faces, and a peace that only comes from knowing the indwelling Jesus.
>
> The trial took an unexpected turn when the Holy Spirit came upon my sister Yongling with great power, and she started

shouting at the top of her voice, "Hallelujah! Hallelujah!" The officials were both shocked and furious. They commanded her to shut up, but she continued to shout God's praises as loudly as she could. My father finally turned to her and calmly said, "Precious daughter, we don't need to be alarmed. If we live, we live with Jesus, and if we die, we will be with Jesus."

At the end of the trial my father and sisters fully expected to be executed, but for some reason the sentence was delayed, and they were sent home to wait until a verdict had been reached.[5]

Miraculously, Peter Xu was not arrested again for the whole of the 1970s. The Lord supernaturally protected him from harm, and he was able to travel widely and build up the body of Christ.

The Billy Graham incident

Throughout the 1980s, Xu's fellow church leaders were under such tremendous pressure from the authorities that they asked

Peter Xu in the 1980s

him to go into hiding for an extended period. For four years he ran the church movement from a secret location, with key leaders slipping into the hideout at night for fellowship and prayer. Xu finally emerged into the public eye again when he attempted to visit Billy Graham in Beijing during the American evangelist's first visit to the country in April 1988.

Graham was scheduled to speak at several registered Three-Self churches and official functions, and Xu wanted to consult him on behalf of the millions of house church Christians who faced relentless persecution for their faith. Before he got to meet him, however, Xu was captured and put behind bars. According to the *South China Morning Post*, he was the leader of 3,000 house churches at the time.[6]

Although he was unaware of it until years later, news of Xu's arrest spread like wildfire around the world. Television networks, newspapers, and magazines all gave it prominence. It even became a major political issue, with the governments of the United States and the UK expressing their grave concerns to Beijing and demanding his release.

Xu's arrest overshadowed Billy Graham's trip to China. The authorities refused even to acknowledge the arrest for a week while the evangelist continued his tour of the country, but every press conference was dominated by questions about the incident, and Graham was subjected to strong criticism for his apparent failure to intervene. Alex Buchan, a long-term advocate for the persecuted Church around the world, wryly noted:

> While the world's most famous evangelist was moving from one luxury hotel suite to another, China's most famous evangelist was moving from one prison cell to another. Human hands could not have choreographed a more perfect, more dramatic, more revealing contrast.
>
> At the press conference in Hong Kong following his trip, Dr. Graham read a positive message about the changes in China,

> the relaxation in religious laws and the warm welcome that he received from his hosts. But to the visible annoyance of some of Graham's entourage, when he invited the press to respond, virtually all the questions were about Xu Yongze.
>
> I felt that justice was done. Dr. Graham had properly highlighted some positive changes in the religious situation. These changes were not cosmetic. China was relaxing, but that was by no means the whole story. And the event of Xu's arrest contradicted the unalloyed picture of progress that Graham presented, highlighting the darker colors that also belong on the canvas. As the negative and positive stories clashed, people got a more accurate grasp of the truth.[7]

In the providence of God, Xu's arrest became a catalyst for millions of people around the world to learn about the house churches of China. The international media examined the reasons why house churches were refusing to register with the government, and the fact that Christians in China were persecuted for their faith became widely known. Jonathan Chao issued a statement to the media, which concluded:

> Xu Yongze went to Beijing intending to share the phenomenon of Church growth, revival, and persecution with fellow-evangelist Billy Graham, but he was arrested before he had a chance . . . With regards to the nature and impact of his work, Xu might rightly be regarded as the Billy Graham of China, so it is somewhat ironic that he should be arrested while attempting to see Billy Graham. May Christians concerned for the evangelization of China and people concerned for religious freedom remember Xu Yongze in their prayers.[8]

Although his arrest was much commented upon throughout the world, Xu himself had rarely spoken about it until 2003, when he shared the following details:

> Many rumors did their rounds among the prisoners as they discussed when I would be killed. All kinds of predictions were

> made as to how I would die. Some said I would be put in an electric chair, others that I would face a firing squad. The whole prison seemed to know that my case had not only gained local awareness, but was being followed even by the national government in Beijing.[9]

Instead of execution, however, Xu was transferred to the Nanyang Prison. On one occasion, a furious prison warden drew his electric baton and threatened Xu by waving it in front of his face. The man picked up a spoon and touched it with the end of the baton, causing sparks to fly from the metal. Xu remained completely calm, which infuriated the warden, who decided to electrocute Xu. He shouted, "Not afraid, are you? Let's see how you feel after I give you some treatment!" Xu recalls:

> I was sitting on a chair, and he reached out and placed the electric baton on the back and side of my neck. As I prayed, calling on the Name of the Lord, I felt the baton roll across my neck but didn't feel any shock!
>
> My would-be torturer was enraged. He again tested the baton and it worked. But when he placed it on me again, there was no electric charge! This time his anger gave way to fear. He sensed a greater power was at work, and a look of horror came across his face. I sat still and thanked God, while smiling at the man. Finally he nervously told me: "Okay, you can go back to your cell now."[10]

The founder of the Born-Again Movement spent three years in prison without ever being formally charged. He was released in 1991, but his health had deteriorated, and he now suffered from tuberculosis and gastric problems. It was only years later that Peter Xu learned that many Christians around the world had been praying fervently for him. He reflected:

> I was told the worldwide publicity my case attracted probably spared my life, as the government was afraid to do anything to me that would result in their gaining a bad image in the eyes

of the international community. Many other house church pastors have not enjoyed this privilege and have been treated like animals while being brutally tortured.[11]

Many years later, a co-worker of Billy Graham met with Xu, who recalls:

> At the time of my arrest in 1988, Billy Graham had personally tried to do all he could to gain my release, but the government had lied to him and said: "We have no such person by that name. Nobody in China is persecuted for their religious beliefs." The representative of Billy Graham officially apologized and told me Mr. Graham had been personally concerned for my well-being all these years.
>
> I was taken aback by this kind gesture and told him, "Please, dear brother, you have nothing to apologize for! I have not held any hard feelings toward anyone over this incident. My arrest was part of God's plan for my life, and I am thankful that he allowed me to go through the experience."
>
> Let me state on record that I have had nothing but respect and appreciation for Billy Graham and his ministry.[12]

The years went by, with Xu frequently being arrested and forced to endure suffering. Meanwhile, the Born-Again house church movement continued to expand throughout China until it had a presence in every province. In 1997, a special meeting was organized in Zhengzhou, where a group of senior house church leaders gathered to discuss unity.

The authorities were tipped off about the meeting and all the participants were arrested, including Brother Yun who broke his legs when he tried to escape by jumping from a window. During their first night in prison, the Christians were beaten viciously. Xu testified:

> I was punched and kicked by officers trained in the martial arts, until my whole body was bruised and battered. My face

> was punched at least a hundred times during the night as I was forced to kneel on the ground. It was a brutal bashing. I never tried to cover up or protect myself. As each blow rained down on my body, I tried to meditate on the Scriptures.
>
> Finally, the guards who had been kicking and punching me grew tired. They didn't allow me to sleep, but kept questioning me until morning. The next day one of the guards came and said, "I was exhausted after beating you last night. After I went to bed I found I had a fever."
>
> I looked at this poor man, loved by God, and replied, "Friend, can I pray for you to get well?" I pitied these young men and felt that I owed them a great debt. If we had shared the gospel to all people—like Jesus commanded—their hearts would not have been so full of violence. We failed to reach their families, and this was the consequence. Whenever I looked into their eyes I saw individuals deeply loved by God. Jesus died for them. He knew every hair on their heads and every breath they took, and He longed for them to be saved.[13]

In the days following the arrest, Xu was told that he would be executed by firing squad. Multitudes of Christians around the world were praying for him and the other prisoners, especially after the Hong Kong newspaper *Pingguo Ribao* reported that Xu had been sentenced to death.[14] The news shocked Christians everywhere.

Thankfully, Xu's sentence was changed to ten years in prison after worldwide Christian protests and intervention from the US State Department. At the trial, Xu refused to defend himself or answer the charges, claiming the proceedings were little more than a stage play to legitimize a prearranged verdict.

Peter Xu, meanwhile, experienced a rollercoaster ride of emotions in the prison. One high point came when he witnessed Brother Yun escape from the maximum-security facility. By a miracle of God, Yun simply walked past a succession of armed guards and out through the front gate. The lowest point came when Xu was cruelly tortured in an unusual way:

> The guards took me to a retractable iron gate that stretched across the prison corridor. It was similar to the folding gates you can sometimes see on old elevators. The guards were not happy with the answers I had given them during interrogation sessions, so they handcuffed my hands behind my back onto the gate, in such a way that I was facing the guards in front of me. After making sure I was securely handcuffed, they opened the retractable gate so that the force lifted me off the ground.
>
> This was one of the most agonizing experiences of my life. My hands swelled up from the pain, and sweat poured from every part of my body. My internal organs were torturously stretched, and my heart felt like it would explode inside my chest. The pain was absolutely unbearable. I wished my toes could touch the floor, so I could put some of my weight on them, but my straining was to no avail.
>
> The guards left me in that suspended position for four hours. I was certain that my time had come to die. I longed for death.
>
> Finally, after what seemed like an eternity, the chief interrogating officer unlocked my handcuffs and I fell on the floor in a heap. All feeling in my upper body was completely gone. My arms, back, and shoulders were numb. The officer gruffly pointed toward the interrogation room and gave a one-word command: "Walk!" I staggered along the corridor the best I could, using the walls to prop myself up. After I slumped on the floor he continued his interrogation. "Xu, this is your last chance. Confess all your crimes! How do you feel about the treatment we have given you today?"
>
> I looked at him with compassion in my eyes. I didn't hate him at all. He had been a young boy in Henan once, just like me, only he had never once heard the gospel. I looked into his eyes and said just one brief sentence: "Thank you."
>
> The officer stormed out of the room without saying another word.[15]

On September 25, 1997, Peter Xu was sentenced to four more years in prison, which was reduced on appeal to three years. This was good news to many Christians around the world, who just a short time earlier had grieved after reading reports of his impending execution.

Labeled an "evil cult"

The Chinese government became increasingly afraid of the Born-Again Movement because of its highly organized methods and the success its evangelists seemed to enjoy wherever they went. Severe persecution had done little to stop the progress of the movement, so in the late 1990s a new tactic was employed in an attempt to stall it. The rearrest of Xu in 1997 provoked an international outcry against China. Diplomats, human rights advocates, and the media all took Beijing to task over its treatment of the evangelist.

In response—with Xu behind bars and therefore unable to answer—the authorities spread a succession of allegations about him and his church movement. Beginning with articles published in *Tianfeng*, the official magazine of the Three-Self Church, Xu was branded a heretic and the Born-Again Movement a cult. At the same time, the government launched a sustained clampdown on the churches, invoking a new law against "evil cults" to try to crush them once and for all.

Initially, the principal criticism against the movement concerned its supposed overemphasis on crying. It was claimed that people were taught they must cry for days to prove they had truly repented; otherwise they could not be saved. Rumors circulated among other Christian groups in China about secret rituals lasting for days in dark rooms, at which people were whipped into an emotional frenzy so that they would cry and shout to the Lord. Some who were unable to cry had even (it was said) been physically beaten by leaders in a bid to "help" them gain their salvation.

For his part, Xu found the accusations ludicrous, saying:

> One of the strangest accusations that has been leveled against us, and me personally, is that we are the "Crying Cult." This stemmed from a lie first circulated in China by the Three-Self Church magazine that we teach that if anyone wants to be saved, he or she must first cry for three days and three nights. Let me clearly state that this is absolutely ridiculous. I have never taught any such thing, nor have I preached anything that could possibly be construed that way.
>
> If this were true, then I would not be saved myself! I sometimes weep before the Lord, especially during times of intercession, but these are not frequent and may last for a few minutes, not three days and nights. Perhaps once or twice I may have made some people cry because my preaching went on too long.
>
> Now, I should say that it is true that people in our meetings often weep before the Lord when the Holy Spirit touches them and convicts them of sin. But never have we said this is a requirement for salvation or that people need to do it to obtain some level of spirituality. We have always held that it is only by the grace of God, through faith, that a person can be saved. Nothing else. Certainly not by crying.[16]

These stories and rumors all contributed to the general impression that the Born-Again Movement was either a straight-out cult or, at best, a marginal sect worthy of deep suspicion. Some other house church networks, perhaps angered by incidents of the Born-Again Movement "stealing" their sheep, were quick to believe the accusations. Yet several Western Evangelical leaders, with intimate knowledge of the church network and its leaders, strongly defended the Born-Again Movement against the attacks.

By launching continual waves of propaganda, the government attempted to change the perception that Xu was a prisoner of conscience—a hero of the faith—and to reduce him to the rank of a dirty criminal and dangerous heretic. It is no coincidence that the attacks on his character came at the start of his prison sentence, meaning Xu was unable to defend himself against the accusations.

A number of other outrageous claims were made against the leaders of the Born-Again Movement, with one Communist Party member claiming:

> Xu Yongze has been getting more and more unorthodox in recent years, as well as abusing his power within his own movement . . . Some of his followers are total charlatans who have been hiding lights up their sleeves and then shining them in dark, crowded rooms as "the light of the Spirit."[17]

In 2001, the author traveled to a small town in Henan and met with all the senior leaders of the Born-Again Movement and specifically mentioned this charge about hiding lights up their sleeves. None of them had ever heard it before—it was apparently only reported overseas—and they all burst out laughing when the charges were repeated to them. They assured me that nothing of the sort had ever happened and that they would never tolerate such behavior in their midst.

To the land of the free

After Xu was released from prison in 2000, he found that things in his church movement had changed dramatically during his absence. He explained:

> It would be fair to say that my leadership role in our church had diminished during my three years in prison from 1997 to 2000. I prayerfully considered my future. Ministry had become

Peter Xu in 2003
Paul Hattaway

difficult in China for a number of reasons. One of them was I had been arrested so many times that maintaining the security of our meeting places proved difficult. If government agents followed me, they would soon discover many of the places where we hosted Bible schools and training centers.

The United States had long taken an interest in me, for which I was appreciative. While I was in prison in the late 1990s, a delegation from President Clinton's administration came to China and asked to visit me in prison, but Beijing did not permit them to do so.

Certain Christian organizations in America had been a blessing to me for many years, and now that I was out of prison, some of those brothers came to Beijing to meet with my wife and me. An opportunity was placed before us, and we were assured that if we could get to the United States we would be welcomed by the government and be permitted to stay there. We prayed earnestly about this offer, seeking the

Lord's guidance. We knew that regardless of how we personally felt about it, if God was not behind it, then we would be out of His will. We would rather stay in China the rest of our lives and suffer mistreatment than leave China and find we had missed God's plan for our lives.[18]

Peter Xu was 60 years old and had never left China. The more he prayed, the more he realized there were great opportunities for ministry that weren't available if he remained in China. After many years in prison and decades spent on the run from the authorities, he felt it was time for a change of direction. After arriving in New York on May 31, 2001, he reflected:

I had left my blood and sweat on China's soil and had been granted the rare privilege of witnessing God's mighty power sweep across my nation. Life in China was all I knew. It had been my heart and soul.

The friends who had arranged our departure from China warned us not to tell anyone; otherwise all the plans would be jeopardized. Unfortunately, this resulted in many believers in our churches being upset when they heard we had suddenly left. It was a shock to many, and I was sad that I had been unable to say proper goodbyes to my own church family.

My first impression of America was a sense of great freedom. It took some time for us to get used to the fact that we weren't being followed when we walked down the street, and for the first time in more than 30 years I didn't have to go to sleep at night with the threat of being arrested and hauled off to prison.[19]

Deborah Xu Yongling

One of the most joyful and bold Christian leaders to emerge from Henan Province is Deborah Xu Yongling, the younger sister of Peter Xu. Born in 1946, she grew up close to her

Peter and Deborah Xu, partners in the gospel for many years, on the Great Wall of China

brother, and the two later became the most easily identifiable leaders of the Born-Again Movement. Peter says of his beloved sister: "I have always had a precious and close relationship with her. We have never argued or spoken harshly to each other. By the tender mercies of our Lord, Yongling grew up to become my close co-worker for the gospel."[20]

Later, when her brother was in prison, Deborah Xu was elected to lead the Born-Again Movement by its 15 regional leaders. At the age of 17 she had already made a firm commitment to the Lord to remain single for the rest of her life and to devote herself to His service. Over the years, her infectious zeal attracted many lost souls to Christ. Her brother recalled:

> Once, when Yongling was a teenager, I looked inside her Bible. She had written her vow to the Lord inside the cover, promising to remain married to the Lord Jesus for the rest of her life and to never give her body to a man. When I read those words, I was moved to tears and I told her I supported her decision. In the 1970s many single men were attracted to my sister because of her purity and holiness. They could see that she was a special lady, and numerous suitors tried to win her attention. They all failed, however, for her heart already belonged to another—the Lord Jesus.[21]

For more than four decades, Deborah Xu served God faithfully throughout China. Several times she was imprisoned, but her zeal for the lost never dimmed. She had the honor of being one of the first 17 evangelists sent to Sichuan in 1982, bringing revival to many areas.

Humble and self-effacing by nature, Deborah is reluctant to talk about herself, but she loves to talk about the Lord. She is an encyclopedia of testimonies of what God has done in China, and she often laughs heartily as she recalls events where He was clearly at work. In 2001, she shared some accounts of a Henan house church training school where the author was teaching. This establishment had gone undetected for years despite being located just down the street from a police station:

> We have held meetings here for eight years without any trouble from the authorities. We train as many as 80 believers at a time, for a period of three months.
>
> One day, a man who lives next door to the training school noticed large numbers of people entering the property, yet he never saw anyone leave. He was suspicious and started to record how many people came in and how many went out of the entrance. One day soon after he started doing this, the Lord struck him so that he was unable to count or write anymore!

> Another neighbor grew suspicious of what was happening in our training school so he climbed onto his roof to get a better view into the courtyard. He slipped and fell off his roof and broke his leg! Since then we have had no problems here.[22]

On January 24, 2004, Deborah Xu, who was then 58 years old, was arrested in Nanyang. She was sleeping on the second floor of her niece's home when two female officers burst into the house and seized her. She was taken to an undisclosed location and interrogated by the police, but Christians throughout China and around the world were mobilized to pray fervently for her, and she was released eight weeks later. The following year, she joined her brother and her sister-in-law as a religious refugee in America, where she continues to share the gospel among the Chinese community and to help many to know the Savior of the world.

Growth and fragmentation

From humble beginnings during the Cultural Revolution, the Born-Again Movement grew to encompass millions of believers by the end of the millennium.

There have been some wildly contrasting guesses on how many Christians the Born-Again Movement has numbered at its strongest point, with estimates ranging from just a few million, to ten million,[23] to 23 million.[24]

The reality is that even the leaders of the movement didn't know because they purposely didn't keep such records; they were afraid of incurring God's wrath by repeating the sin of King David, who conducted a census out of a sense of pride and fleshly ambition.[25] After probing by the author of this book, however, Peter Xu did shed some light on the massive size and scope of the Born-Again Movement when he shared the following information:

An outdoor house church meeting

Between April and November 1996, we held advanced training classes for many of our senior leaders. In that seven-month period we trained more than 4,000 house church leaders from various parts of the country. Many of those leaders were responsible for multiple numbers of fellowships. At the end of 1996, we calculated there were between 10,000 and 12,000 full-time leaders in our group. This figure only included evangelists and church leaders.

If local pastors, elders, deacons, and other workers are included, there were at least 30,000 leaders. However, in many cases one evangelist might be responsible for several congregations.

Finally, each of the seven regions we divided China into consisted of seven regional committees. This means there were 16,807 churches in each of the seven regions, or a total of over 117,000 churches nationwide. Of course, nothing ever works as smoothly as these numbers suggest, but this is the structure of our churches in China.

> These figures may sound impressive, but you need to realize there are now more than 2,800 cities, districts, and counties in China, with an average population of more than 500,000 people in each. There remains much work to do. Whatever growth has eventuated has all been the work of the Holy Spirit. No person can take any credit for what He has done. "The LORD has done this, and it is marvelous in our eyes" (Psalm 118:23).[26]

After Peter and Deborah Xu left China for the United States, it does appear that the Born-Again Movement, which formerly had a strongly centralized leadership, fragmented into numerous smaller church groups with no central structure. According to one publication, "the movement practically disintegrated overnight,"[27] while former *Time* reporter David Aikman claims that the movement "fell into turmoil after Xu's departure."[28]

Our inquiries reveal that while the millions of believers who once belonged to the Born-Again Movement continue to worship the Lord, they have since formed into numerous localized fellowships and loose networks. Some members of these groups feel deeply hurt by their past experiences and refuse to have any contact with foreign Christians.

The complex fragmentation of the Born-Again Movement means it is practically impossible for outsiders to gain a clear picture of its current size and activities—or even to grasp whether the movement still exists in any cohesive and recognizable form.

Information about the fate of this network has dried up over the years, although in early 2020 the Born-Again house church movement, which has played such a prominent role in Christianity in Henan and throughout the nation, made the news when 100 of its members were arrested in a large crackdown.

1980s

Henan Christians in the 1980s preach the gospel at the funeral of one of their members
RCMI

Choosing sides

Of all the provinces in China, perhaps nowhere is the division and hostility between the Three-Self Patriotic Movement (TSPM) and the unregistered house churches as stark as in Henan. Although the house church leaders recognize that millions of sincere Christians attend TSPM churches, many regard the politically appointed TSPM hierarchy as corrupt and morally bankrupt enemies of the gospel. As a result, the overwhelming majority of house churches in Henan have refused to register or unite with the TSPM in any way.

From the time the TSPM first emerged in Henan in 1980, its leaders issued statements that immediately placed it in a position that most house church Christians found unacceptable. Remarkably, the first leader of the TSPM, Wu Yaozong, went as far as to declare: "God has taken the key of salvation away from the Church and given it to the Communist Party."[1] Little wonder, then, that the majority of Christians in Henan and throughout China refused to submit to such an organization. Many house church leaders believe that registering would be tantamount to denying Christ, and they would rather die than compromise their spiritual freedom.

Fire and blood

The 1980s saw the continuation of both brutal repression and God-sent revival among the Henan house churches. Thousands of believers throughout the province were beaten, imprisoned, or maimed during the decade. The few examples shared in this book are representative of the widespread brutality inflicted throughout Henan. Only eternity will reveal the true scale of the terror, and of the obedience and dedication to Jesus Christ that millions of God's children displayed in the face of suffering.

The start of the 1980s brought a few years of relative calm for the house churches in Henan—compared to the excessive punishment meted out to them in the 1970s and then again in 1983. Christians were still under pressure, and countless arrests were made between 1980 and 1982, but these years are typically remembered as times of tremendous growth and revival in Henan. Unusual signs and wonders occurred that caused entire communities to turn to Jesus Christ. Brother Yun recalls:

> 1980 was a phenomenal year for the Church in Henan. We remember it as the year when God constantly did outstanding

miracles and divine healing, and the words of Jesus supernaturally came to many people. That wonderful year saw tremendous growth in the church. Later, many of the converts from 1980 became leaders of the body of Christ throughout China . . .

In one meeting in the Nanyang area hundreds of people—Christians and unbelievers alike—saw a vision of a beautiful boat floating on a sea of clouds above the meeting place. Many sinners repented and gave their lives to Christ as a result of this sign and wonder.

In Fen Shuiling . . . village, also in Nanyang, an unbeliever was dying from a protracted illness. His family had never heard the gospel, but one evening the Lord appeared to that man and said, "My name is Jesus. I have come to save you."

Fen Shuiling village is situated in a remote mountainous area where preachers had not yet visited. It had no church or pastor, so when I first visited there I was surprised to find the gospel had spread to many villages and that dozens of families had put their faith in Christ. Jesus himself had preached the gospel to them! These new believers were hungry to receive teaching from his Word.[2]

A chronic shortage of Bibles

Although house churches throughout Henan were growing rapidly, deep concerns were expressed at the lack of available Bibles. The Hong Kong newspaper *Pai Shing* reported in 1982:

Last August there were several tens of thousands of believers in one particular county, but only about 30 copies of incomplete Bibles. One old pastor and three seminary-trained missionaries were shared by more than 1,000 meeting points in the whole county. This kind of shortage is reaching a disastrous point. What makes the situation worse is the shortage of Bibles and doctrinal teaching, causing the emergence of heathenism in the mountain districts. Many witchdoctors practice witchcraft

> behind the name of Christianity, and this has caused a lot of internal disturbances inside the house churches.[3]

The reporter was nevertheless able to see a bright future for the gospel in China, and predicted that Christianity would one day become the dominant religion—a remarkable claim to make at the time. He wrote:

> Even though there are various kinds of difficulties and crises, Evangelicals in China today, whose main body is in the house churches, are growing rapidly. It has become an historical trend . . . [The house churches in China today] have gradually become the motivating power of millions of lonely, depressed and empty-hearted people. Evangelicalism will surely become the leading ideology among the Chinese people. Prospects are very bright.[4]

In 1981, at the height of need, a monumental event took place that gave a huge boost to the growth of the house churches in Henan and throughout China. On June 18, a large barge containing 232 tons of Chinese Bibles evaded Chinese naval patrols and unloaded its precious cargo onto a beach in Guangdong Province. The risky delivery, which was codenamed "Project Pearl" and directed by the American missionary Brother David, meant that multitudes of desperate believers received their first ever copy of God's Word.[5]

Tens of thousands of these Bibles found their way to the Christians in Henan Province. A letter of heartfelt gratitude from "the Church in Kaifeng" exclaimed:

> Thanks be to the Lord for His grace! Through many hardships and risks, you have brought us food, the Word of the Lord, to meet our needs. You perceived the great love of the Lord and knew our lack, and you satisfied our requests, helping our

spiritual growth and edifying us in the Word. Your Christ-like love is selfless, an example we should all learn from. Having God's Word, we are now able to distinguish between true and false, to discern the spirits, and to select the correct pathways. We treasure this Precious Book very much, for we know it did not come to us easily.

May the Lord Jesus Christ, the Father of glory, give us a spirit of wisdom and of revelation in the knowledge of Him, that we may fight a good fight. Your love has satisfied the hungry flock who thirst after righteousness. Your labor has not been in vain and will be blessed by God forever. Our cup overflows![6]

A powerful letter

After decades of silence, the 1980s brought a flurry of communications from Christians in Henan. In May 1982, a powerful letter from a Henan believer was received by a Hong Kong

A house church Bible study in Henan

ministry. Entitled "All Who Live Godly in Christ Jesus Will Suffer Persecution," it provides a wonderful insight into how Henan's Christians viewed discrimination and suffering, as well as detailing a brutal persecution that had recently taken place. It is worth quoting the letter at length:

> Dear brothers and sisters in Christ,
>
> On behalf of the brothers and sisters in Henan Province I send greetings to the members of the Body overseas!
>
> Today, the Church here is being greatly blessed by the Lord and the number of people being saved is increasing daily as the Good News of God is proclaimed more and more . . .
>
> The proverb, "When good is one-foot high, evil is ten-feet high," is true. Wherever the Church flourishes there are difficulties. The revival has grown up in such circumstances. If Jesus had not been crucified, nobody today could be saved. If there is no testing by fire, then true faith will not be apparent, and if the Lord does not train us, we will not become instruments fit for His use. If the rock was not split open, the living water could not have sprung forth in the desert. Difficulties are therefore the means for promoting life and revival in the churches.
>
> Recently the gospel here has once again been greatly promoted, because 10 brothers and sisters were imprisoned, beaten, and bound. They regard their sufferings for the Lord as more precious than the treasures of Egypt. They started to preach the gospel in the poorest and most barren areas, and then one day they went to a certain commune where they met those who attended a Three-Self church. Those people only believe in the four Gospels, and they tore up all other books of the Bible. They were not separate from the world.
>
> It was a confusing situation, so that when our co-workers preached the truth to them, no one listened or received it. The evangelists split up and went to different places to preach. As soon as they opened their mouths, the power of God came

forth. They preached with tears streaming down their cheeks, causing the passers-by and street merchants, Christians and non-Christians, to stand still and listen. Even the fortune-tellers were moved by the Holy Spirit and burst out crying. Many people, after hearing the Word of the Lord, forgot their food, their work, and even forgot to return home. This went on until the evening, and still the people had not dispersed. The brothers and sisters preached until they were exhausted, but the crowd would not let them leave . . .

The authorities made a move and seized the believers, dragging them away one by one. They bound them with ropes and tortured them with electric batons. They also slapped their faces with their shoes and knocked them unconscious, but when they came to, they continued to pray, sing, and preach to the bystanders. One little sister, just 14 years old, was beaten senseless.

When she revived, she saw that many people were sympathetic, so she continued to preach. Her words were few and her voice faint, but the people could not stop from crying out, and they repented and believed in Jesus. When the believers were bound and beaten, many noticed that their appearance was lively and gracious, and that they were smiling. People asked them why they did not feel ashamed, and many were led to faith in Jesus by their example . . .

The brothers and sisters in that area saw the young preachers bound and forced to kneel on the ground for more than three days without food or water, and beaten with sticks until their faces were covered with blood and their hands were black from the ropes. Yet they continued to pray, sing, and praise the Lord. The watching believers were cut to the heart and wished to be bound with them and cast into prison. In this area the flame of the gospel has spread everywhere. There has never been a revival like this before, and because of persecution, many have received the seeds of life . . .

> Dearly beloved brothers and sisters—in men's eyes this was all an unfortunate incident, but for Christians it was like a rich banquet. This kind of lesson cannot be learned from books, and this sweetness is not usually tasted by men in a comfortable environment. Where there is no cross, there is no crown . . .
>
> These saints who went down into the furnace, far from being harmed, now have glorified faces and their spirits are filled with power. They have greater authority to preach the Word and a far more abundant life. The Lord will have the final victory in their bodies, and will put Satan to shame. In fact, Satan could find no way to make them renounce their faith, and they were released . . .
>
> Emmanuel!
> From a weaker member of the Body,
> May 6, 1982.[7]

The Anti-Spiritual Pollution Campaign

In the summer of 1983 the Chinese government, concerned at the explosive increase of crime, launched a campaign to systematically eradicate "undesirable elements." Thousands of criminals—real and supposed—were rounded up and executed throughout the country. One source stated: "The rising crime rate resulted in perhaps one million arrests, and there were at least 10,000 executions. Many of these were held in public as a lesson for the people."[8]

Countless Christians were also caught up in the frenzy, with some paying the ultimate price for their faith in Jesus Christ. According to a report nearly one year later:

> In Henan Province alone, over 110 house church pastors and itinerant preachers are still in prison. Some of those arrested in July 1983 have now been sentenced to three to five years in

> prison . . . The local Public Security Bureaus are given quotas for arrests. To fill the quota, Christians conducting home meetings or doing evangelistic work were often arrested along with thieves and other criminals.[9]

The crackdown proved to be a catalyst for even more startling Christian growth, as multitudes of believers resolved to serve God more wholeheartedly and to value eternity more than this world. The bold witness of Henan's believers knew no limit. They were not afraid to witness to Communist Party officials, so that the Party magazine, *Red Flag*, was obliged to issue a stern warning reminding Party members that they were not permitted to believe in religion. Such warnings did nothing to slow the rate of conversions, however.

One Party Committee secretary in Henan was afflicted with cancer of the esophagus. After four months he was scarcely able to eat, and doctors told him he would soon die. The government paid him a sum of money and sent 500 bricks to his home so he could arrange for his grave to be built. The man's wife, however, had heard that many sick people had been healed by Jesus. She encouraged her husband to also believe in God, but he refused, saying, "I persecuted many Christians during the Cultural Revolution. Why should God help me?"

> His mother-in-law, a Christian, told him that the Lord did not come to call the righteous, but sinners to repentance. The man believed, and his mother-in-law gave him a bowl of soup in Jesus' Name, which he drank in faith. The next day he ate a bowl of noodles, and by the fourth day he was eating porridge and recovering rapidly.[10]

The Shi family's fiery trial

The most famous example of Christian martyrdom in 1983 involved the Shi family of Zunzhuang Village. Earlier that summer, a relative named Meichun had become sick and sought prayer from the Shi family, but several days later she died.

Because they were widely known to lead an illegal house church, the Shis were worried the authorities might use the death as an excuse to persecute them. Soon, several Public Security officers came to the house and arrested everyone except the youngest Shi children. The mother of the family, named Shi Lishi, and her son Wuting were charged with murder.

A remarkable scene ensued in the packed courtroom the next day. Shi Lishi was tried first. She spoke about Meichun's terminal illness, but when she told how they had prayed for her, it so incensed the judge that he instructed the guards to kick her to the ground. They then beat her with batons until she passed out. A bucket of cold water was thrown over her to revive her, but she still refused to confess to murder. In a rage, the judge sent her back to her cell. On the way, the bruised and bloodied woman passed some of her crying children, and she whispered to them, "Remain strong! We are considered worthy to suffer reproach for the Lord."

Next, it was Wuting's turn to be interrogated, followed by his brother Wuming. According to an eyewitness, "when the two brothers returned to the cell they were an unrecognizable mass of purple bruises and bloody wounds."[11]

Finally, three of the children were ordered to testify. To the astonishment of the judge and everyone present, each family member claimed responsibility for Meichun's death. The judge had never seen anything like it, as each new witness claimed to be the culprit. Such was the love the members of this family had for God and for one another, each of them preferred to take the punishment rather than to see their mother or another family member suffer for a crime that he or she didn't commit.

The public sentencing of the Shi family was scheduled for the morning of August 30, 1983. A theater in Shanzui Village was booked for the spectacle and the whole community was present. The assembled crowd gasped and shrieked as Shi Lishi and her eldest son, the 35-year-old Wuting, were sentenced to death. Shi's 24-year-old daughter, Meizhen, received a prison term of 15 years, while Meiying, the sister of the deceased woman, was given life in prison for her part in the "murder." The youngest son, Wuhao, was sentenced to ten years, Wuming four years, and 16-year-old Xiaoxiu was incarcerated for two years.

When the condemned Wuting passed his wife in the hallway, he said:

> My beloved wife, why are you crying? How can I not drink the cup that the Lord has given me? Don't you realize that we live for the Lord, and if we die, we die for the Lord? Therefore, whether we live or die we are the Lord's? I will be one step ahead of you. Before long, we will be together again, never to be apart. Don't be sad. Be strong and courageous. Whatever happens, you must live fully for the Lord. Don't waste any time.[12]

On September 14, 1983, Shi Lishi and Wuting were taken to a place known as "Frog Mountain." Wuting briefly saw his wife and told her, "I will go first, and will wait for you in our Father's house. Goodbye!" Both of the condemned Christians were perfectly calm and smiled to their friends and relatives. There was no fear. The house church historian Danyun recalled the moment when mother and son left this world for their heavenly reward:

> Mrs. Shi turned toward the soldier at her side and smilingly asked him, "May I be allowed to pray?" The soldier nodded his silent approval. Mother and son knelt down, lifted their eyes heavenwards and prayed to the Savior who created heaven and

> earth: "We ask you to forgive our country and our people for the sin of persecuting us. Save our country and the people. Forgive the sins of those who harmed us. Lord, we ask you to receive our spirits."
>
> Bang! Bang!
>
> Blood spurted out of Mother's head and her soul entered Paradise. Wuting, however, was not yet dead. He turned to look at the soldiers behind him and saw they were so frozen with fear that they could not fire a second time. But two other soldiers . . . raised their pistols and fired at Wuting. He slumped over, his brains and blood splattered all over the ground. Suddenly, there was a heavy downpour, with thunder and lightning flashing. But all the rain could not wash away the blood of the innocent that was spilled there on the execution ground.[13]

When family members collected the two martyrs' bodies for burial, they found a note in Shi Wuting's coat pocket, which said:

> It is now finished. Don't be sorrowful for me. I am only going to that place before you. Love the Lord fervently and hold steadfast to His Word. Later, you will also go to the Heavenly Father and meet me. He who endures to the end shall be saved. For my funeral, make it very simple. Take care of the two children and let them know that I died for the Lord.[14]

Meiying eventually received a reduction in her life sentence and was released in 1996. During the 13 years she spent in prison, Meiying often shared the gospel with the other inmates. She later said:

> The prison had about 500 inmates. After some time, more than 400 came to know the Lord. Some prisoners, who were so sick they couldn't work, were brought to the hospital and doctors said there was no hope—but then the Christians in prison prayed for the sick and they were healed . . . Consequently, even

> the officials had to stand back and watch—thus many people came to know the Lord.[15]

The brave witness of the Shi family continues to this day. They remain dedicated followers of Jesus Christ, and their courageous testimony has strengthened multitudes of believers throughout China.

A tidal wave of blessing

The months immediately following the persecutions in the summer of 1983 saw explosive revival across China, with an influx of new believers like a tidal wave. It was truly a time of great power, and there seemed to be few obstacles to people believing in God.

News of the tremendous revival in Henan reached believers throughout China and around the world. When a pastor from the south China city of Guangzhou traveled to Henan to see

Believers at a prayer meeting

for himself, he found churches in almost every village and was impressed by the believers' godliness, trusting faith, and Bible knowledge. He reported:

> One pastor told me, "It is God who is mightily at work today! We are doing nothing." That very morning he had baptized 114 people, a typical weekly event for him. It has been estimated that in recent years throughout the province up to 3,000 baptisms may have taken place every day of the year, and in all these groups young people were in the majority . . . Knowledgeable observers believe there may be as many as 10 million Christians in this province.[16]

In 1985, five Chinese Christians traveled around rural areas of Henan to witness the move of the Holy Spirit. They reported:

> Wherever we went, we felt that we were in the time of the apostles—filled with the Spirit, excited, and on fire. Signs and wonders also followed us and confirmed what we preached. Therefore many people came to the Lord.
>
> In those villages alone, more than 95 percent of the peasants have come to the Lord. The minimum attendance at each meeting is 400–500 people. Big meetings will have more than 1,700. All are held in the open air no matter if it rains or shines. We were so amazed to see their love for the Lord.[17]

As the house churches exploded in size throughout Henan, the need for Bibles became acute. A limited number were being printed for Three-Self church members, but house church believers found it difficult to access any copies, and were obliged to travel great distances to pick up bags of Bibles that had been smuggled across the border from Hong Kong by foreign Christians. One pastor lamented:

> The last time we came to Guangzhou we got 900 Bibles, mostly New Testaments. When we went back to Henan, there weren't

> even enough to give one copy to every group of several hundred believers! There were meeting places and evangelists to whom we couldn't even give one copy of the New Testament.[18]

A house church preacher named Zhu Baoshan was arrested in the spring of 1986 after the Three-Self Church accused him of preaching without permission. On the second day of his incarceration, Zhu asked the Lord why He had allowed him to be detained. According to one report:

> God told him he would be in prison for 20 days, and that he would lead 17 convicts to Christ.
>
> Brother Zhu shared the gospel faithfully, only to meet with ridicule and rejection from the other prisoners. On the 14th day of his imprisonment, a brawl broke out and one of the prisoners was killed in the skirmish. Because the jailers knew they would have to give an account for the incident, they said to Zhu: "We heard you Christians have power to pray for the dead and bring them to life."
>
> They promised Zhu: "If you pray for this dead prisoner and he comes back to life, you will be released. Otherwise we will sentence you to 15 years." The prisoner had been dead for seven hours and 20 minutes, but when Zhu prayed the man miraculously revived. When he was released six days later, Zhu had led 17 convicts to Christ just as the Holy Spirit had told him.[19]

Zhu Baoshan continued his ministry until he was rearrested in March 1987. During his year of freedom he led more than 3,000 people to Christ.

As the 1980s drew to a close, churches throughout Henan were crowded with worshippers, after a remarkable decade of both intense suffering and glorious revival in the province. Millions of desperate people had pressed into the kingdom of God, and church leaders were faced with the massive challenge of discipling the new converts and seeing them established in the faith.

Letters from Henan

We conclude this chapter by reprinting a selection of letters that were received from Henan by various Christian ministries during the 1980s. These precious communications reveal both the strengths and weaknesses of Christianity in the province, and provide insights into the daily lives and personal struggles of believers as they followed God. Their experiences also offer a fascinating snapshot of the ever-changing conditions experienced by the body of Christ at this time.

1982

Because of the ten-year Cultural Revolution and natural disasters, almost all our Bibles were lost. There were only a few copies left in the whole of our prefecture. We borrowed one Bible and copied it by hand day and night, until we finished copying the entire New Testament. It is really precious.

God has been reviving His churches here from the winter of 1980 onwards, and the number of believers is increasing daily. Our desire to have a Bible is much more important than our physical needs. When I visited a meeting in a remote area my deepest desire was fulfilled! I could not help shedding tears. Three co-workers and I wept over the Bible for more than an hour.

God uses His Word to direct and lead us. It is our light, our bread, and our strength. When we face Satan's temptations, God's Word is our weapon for victory. When we are weak, His Word is our strength. Our church is experiencing great revival, and we share the gospel widely, doing everything we can to help others know God. Sometimes we preach at weddings and funerals, and many people become believers.

The needs here are so great that even if we had a large truck full of Bibles it would barely touch our needs. We believe that God is rich and glorious, and He will meet all our needs. May His glory last forever! Amen.[20]

During the times before I had a Bible, I had nothing to do at home after work. I read novels, played cards, or chatted with my friends. Now I read the Bible as soon as I arrive home. My spiritual life has grown daily and the Lord is pleased with me more and more.

After I received the Bible, many brethren wanted to have a copy also. I told them that I only had one, but asked the Lord to provide a second one. It's not only me who has benefited from this Bible, but at least 5,000 other brothers and sisters have also benefited. Now tens of thousands of Christians are hoping that they too can have their own Bible.[21]

1983

The harvest is totally ripe but the laborers are so few. Young brothers and sisters thirst for the Lord's Word, but we have only three workers to serve tens of thousands of believers. The leaders feel very inadequate and exhausted. They don't spend enough time with the Lord, so they feel dry and have nothing left to feed the flock. When the preachers shared the Word of God with our brothers and sisters yesterday, they burst into tears, yet they remain very hungry. There is no spiritual food to eat.[22]

1984

The last days are drawing near. Angry waves are rising, and unrighteousness and lawlessness are on the increase. Even Christians are betraying and attacking each other. There is much disease and men's hearts are full of fear. The saints are facing tribulation . . . I am often in danger of imprisonment, but am not concerned about my bodily suffering. We must work for the Lord while it is still day, and I'm not afraid of suffering.

After our brethren were released from prison, they were despised and rejected by everyone, including their relatives and friends . . . One brother was injured when he was pistol-whipped while being interrogated by the Religious Affairs Bureau. They offered him money for his convalescence, but he refused to take it! He didn't want to be tempted by accepting money from the authorities, and he said would rather suffer and maintain his purity as a believer.[23]

1985

I am very busy. In Henan there are more than 100,000 believers in just a few counties. In the whole province there are dozens of Christian leaders on the run who cannot return home. There are still 36 believers in prison. I visited the relatives of 10 Christians who were behind bars for their faith. As I left, tears ran down my cheeks. I have spent 23 years in a prison labor camp, but I never wept. But when I saw the pitiful old mothers, wives, and the children of those imprisoned for the Lord's sake, I could not control my emotions . . . They were full of joy and thanksgiving. The local believers look after the families of those in prison more than they do their own families.[24]

1988

We were permitted to meet in a small village. Since then, our congregation has grown rapidly from 500 to 1,000. However, those who oppose Christ will not tolerate the spread of the gospel. Some sisters and I were thrown into jail. We prayed and sang like Paul and Silas, and after half a year we were all released. However, all my spiritual books including the Bible were confiscated. I asked God to prepare another copy for me. When I received another copy of God's Word I was so happy that I burst into tears.[25]

The Nanyang Church

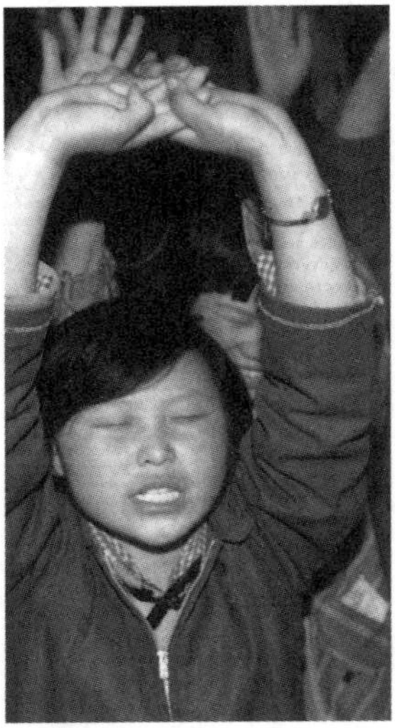

Prayer meetings in Nanyang are noted for their intensity

Nanyang—part of the Revival Triangle

Nanyang County is one of three adjacent areas in southern Henan that have experienced powerful and sustained revival since the late 1970s. These three areas—Tanghe and Fangcheng being the others—could be labeled China's "Revival Triangle." More than coincidentally, Nanyang was also the home base of Marie Monsen for most of her years in China from 1901 to 1932.

A house church movement known simply as "the Nanyang Church" emerged from this area and now extends throughout most of the country. Over the years, thousands of evangelists from Nanyang have been sent to every province in China, and even beyond its borders, as part of the Chinese missionary-sending initiative known as "Back to Jerusalem." Missionaries from Nanyang now serve God in at least a dozen other countries, and the area has produced some of China's outstanding Christian leaders of the twentieth and twenty-first centuries.

Of the three large house church networks to emerge from the Revival Triangle, the Nanyang Church is perhaps the least known and the most difficult to research. Its members tend to avoid contact with foreign Christians and have preferred to go about their work for the Lord quietly.

Unlike some of the other house church networks, the Nanyang Church tends to care little about whether or not Christians identify as part of its group. Its focus is simply on establishing the kingdom of God and seeing believers grounded in God's Word. As a result, it's difficult to estimate how many Christians in China "belong" to the Nanyang Church.

One official source in 1988 stated there were at least 100,000 Christians in Nanyang County at the time.[1] In 2007, however, an experienced missionary who works closely with the Nanyang Church said the movement may have grown to between seven and eight million believers nationwide.[2]

Persecution fuels revival

The Nanyang-based house churches have encountered decades of sustained persecution from the authorities, which has only served to strengthen their resolve and assist the spread of the gospel throughout China. When asked in 2001 what it is like to visit Nanyang, one house church leader replied:

> Thousands of homes have Scripture written around the door-frames, with phrases like: "The blood of Jesus saves." Many

Scriptures around the doorframe of a Christian home in Nanyang

> people quietly live their Christian lives, seeking to glorify the Lord. In some villages every person is a believer, while in others there are few Christians. In Nanyang County alone our church has more than 200,000 believers.[3]

Over the years, the Nanyang house churches have witnessed countless miracles. Their leaders tend to downplay these rather than publicize them, as they don't wish to draw attention to themselves. Instead, they prefer to point out that the greatest miracle is salvation and the wonder of seeing God change people's hearts on the inside.

Because of their humility, it sometimes takes years of developing trusting relationships before the Nanyang believers open up and share testimonies of some of the great things God has done in their midst. These include several clear-cut cases of dead people being raised back to life, a string of miraculous prison escapes, and countless examples of healing. Multitudes of people in Nanyang and beyond have witnessed such miracles and have surrendered their lives to Christ as a result.

On one occasion, the gospel was preached with great power in the village of Hongqiao in Xixia County. Even the students attending the state school sang worship songs during class time, and the children's infectious joy could not be contained. The teachers were amazed, for when the students in one classroom started to sing, those in the adjacent room also joined in worshipping the lover of their souls, Jesus Christ.

Because the teachers and school administrators couldn't suppress the children's desire to worship God, the police were called in. More than 300 Christians in Hongqiao Village were arrested out of a total population of just over 1,000 people. Those who were blessed to suffer for the Lord became even stronger in their faith, and they all committed themselves to full-time ministry. Now practically everyone in Hongqiao Village has been saved.

In a similar incident, one of the better-known evangelists from Nanyang, Brother Yun, remembers the enthusiasm and joy of a group of new Christians in Gao Village in 1974. Yun received a Bible after 100 days of prayer, and was immediately told by the Holy Spirit to go to the west and south to preach the gospel. When he arrived at Gao Village, the people pleaded with him to read the Bible to them. When he had finished the Gospel of Matthew, Yun said:

> I opened my eyes and saw how God's Word had captivated everybody. The Holy Spirit was convicting them of their sins. They all knelt down and repented with tears flowing down their cheeks . . . God poured His Spirit out on many desperate souls. Like thirsty men in the desert, they gleefully drank in the water of God's Word. Even though I was just a teenager, the Lord enabled me to lead more than 2,000 people to Jesus in my first year as a Christian . . .

When I first shared at Gao Village, the Lord gave me Scripture songs to sing before the people, and they wrote down the words so they could remember them. One of the songs was taken from the Gospel of Matthew where Jesus taught that if someone strikes us on the right cheek, we should turn our other cheek to him as well. Another song taught how we are to rejoice greatly when we are persecuted for the sake of the gospel. Yet another explained that we should never be like Judas and deny our Master.

After so many people came to the Lord at once, it caught the attention of the authorities. All the Christians in Gao Village were arrested and taken to the police station. The officers demanded: "Who brought the Name of Jesus to you? How did you all come to believe in this superstition?"

The believers were filled with overwhelming joy, and the only thing they would say was, "We won't be like Judas! We won't betray our Lord Jesus!"

The officers started to beat them and they rejoiced even more, saying: "Please, sir, hit us on the other side of the face as well!" The Christians were laughing and rejoicing.

The officers grew tired of beating them and finally said, "You Christians are all crazy!" After a final warning, they sent them all home.[4]

Miraculous provision

The extreme poverty of most Christians in Nanyang means that they have often faced financial challenges as they sought to spread the gospel. Many evangelists were sent out in faith, with no support from their congregations, simply because the church had no money to give them.

Yang Deling, the wife of Brother Yun, faced overwhelming struggles after her husband was imprisoned when she was pregnant with their first child in 1984. At home with only Yun's elderly mother to help with the farm work, she cried out to

God for help. They had to plant the crops that year, and were so poor that if the harvest failed they were likely to starve. Deling recalled:

> We had no clue what we were doing. We decided to plant sweet potatoes, but didn't know how to do it. I found out later that we should have planted the roots about two feet apart. I had planted them just a few inches apart!
>
> All summer long our neighbors who heard about my foolishness mocked and made fun of us! The news spread rapidly and I was the butt of many jokes.
>
> Then in autumn, all our neighbors started cursing because they had very poor yields from their harvest. Their sweet potatoes were only the size of tennis balls.
>
> When we pulled up our sweet potatoes, we found they were almost the size of basketballs! It was a great miracle and everyone knew that God had taken care of us.
>
> Our neighbors respected us more from that moment on and they didn't view my husband as a cursed criminal any more, but as a man who'd been unjustly incarcerated.[5]

Three years later, with Yun still in prison and no prospect of being released, a second miracle took place on the farm. Not knowing how to plant wheat seeds, Deling placed them so close together that they blanketed the soil. Later, just a week before the wheat harvest, a severe hailstorm struck the village. Deling remembers that she

> rushed outside when the hail started and some of our neighbors' wheat fields had been completely flattened by the storm. Yun's mother and I fell to our knees and cried out, "God, have mercy on us!"
>
> A great miracle happened. Our field was the only one protected by the Lord. All our wheat was standing upright, untouched by the hail. Every other field in the whole area had been obliterated.

People came out of their homes after the storm subsided and saw how the Lord Jesus had protected us. It was another powerful witness to them. While we enjoyed thick, healthy wheat that year, our neighbors had no harvest and were forced to use what was left of their crops to feed their animals.[6]

The man with two heads

In 1994, a well-known Nanyang doctor, an elderly man called Chen, developed cancer in the side of his face. The tumor grew to enormous proportions, so that from a distance it looked as though he had two heads. The ear on that side of his head moved a considerable distance from its normal position as fluids gathered and made his face bulge out. His appearance was so hideous that people often turned away in horror and disgust when he walked down the street. As his condition worsened, Chen suffered terrible pain and was unable to sleep.

He visited a specialist and was bluntly told there was nothing that could be done for him. He was instructed to go home, put his affairs in order, and prepare to die. The specialist gave some poison to Chen's 12-year-old grandson, and advised him to slip it into the old man's tea so that his life could be "ended mercifully."

Later that afternoon, as the boy walked down the street, he wept uncontrollably for his beloved grandfather. He knew he couldn't do what the doctor had urged him to do. His wailing attracted people's attention, including a house church evangelist who stopped the boy and asked what was wrong. After hearing the story, the evangelist said: "Whatever you do, don't put the poison in your grandfather's tea!" He wrote a note and told the boy: "Please bring your grandfather to this address at seven o'clock."

In intense pain and distress after barely sleeping for months, Chen made his way with his grandson to the address, not knowing what or who they would meet there. When they arrived, they found a house church meeting in progress, with the Word of God being taught. Despite Chen's shocking appearance, the preacher continued his message. When he had finished, he laid his hands on each of Chen's "heads" and prayed a simple prayer, asking God to heal him.

The old doctor returned home that evening with no apparent change in his condition, but he fell fast asleep and woke 13 hours later—the first good rest he had had in three months. He still had two "heads" and did not look any better, so Chen and his grandson rushed back to the preacher's house, who told them not to worry. They were assured that God had already healed him, but it would take a little time for his physical appearance to reflect the spiritual reality of what had happened.

Over the next few days, Chen's condition gradually improved, and a week later he had been completely healed and his appearance was restored to normal. His ear returned to its proper position and even the skin where his face had ballooned out now looked unscarred.

After Chen and his grandson became disciples of Jesus Christ, the doctor's conscience was troubled because for years he had deceived people by selling them fake herbal pills that had no medicinal value. Chen repented and immediately went to his clinic and threw the pills away. He kept the bottles, however, making new labels that said: "Whatever problem you have, believe in the Lord Jesus and you will be healed!"

Hundreds of people in Nanyang saw Chen's condition before and after his healing, and no one could dispute that a great miracle had taken place. The doctor became a bold evangelist, and by 1996 he had led more than 300 people to faith in Christ.

Elder Fu—the Elijah of China

One of the founders of the Nanyang house church movement is Elder Fu. Born in 1935 in Lushan County, Fu moved to Nanyang with his family when he was 31 years old. Over many decades he faithfully proclaimed the gospel and personally led tens of thousands of people to Jesus. During those years, he was arrested on countless occasions, and was severely tortured and mistreated in every conceivable way. As a mark of deep respect, some of his co-workers nicknamed him "the Elijah of China," although it was a name he would never use himself.

One of the cruellest forms of torture invented by the Chinese is known as the "water dance." Victims are stripped naked and placed in a room with a few inches of water covering the floor. The floor is also covered with hundreds of sharp tacks, nails, and shards of broken glass. An electric current is passed through the water, causing the victim to "dance" around to avoid the shocks—and as the person does so, his or her feet are shredded. The pain is unbearable, and many people have died or gone insane after undergoing this hideous and barbaric torture.

In 1983, the authorities arrested all of the Nanyang house church leaders and subjected them to the "water dance" in frustration at not being able to locate and arrest Brother Yun. When the ordeal was over, the men were taken outside and chained to trees, and the chief of police told them they would be released only if they revealed where Yun was hiding.

One of the men whispered to Elder Fu, "We are going to die because of Brother Yun," but Fu shouted back, "No! We're not suffering because of Brother Yun. We're suffering because of Jesus Christ!"

Elder Fu is a compassionate man of prayer, and tears often well up in his eyes when he prays. Here is a summary of the author's 2002 interview with "the Elijah of China":

I thank the Lord that all my five children serve the Lord. Today I cannot go home because the police are looking for me, so I'm always traveling around. The hardest times have been when I've been in prison, and also when I've been attacked by villagers as I tried to share the gospel with them.

I grew up in a non-Christian family, and I first believed the gospel in 1976 at the age of 41. My mother developed breast cancer, so we prayed and the Lord healed her. She then lost her sight for two weeks, so I prayed and God healed her again. The Lord used me even though I had only believed in Christ for a few weeks.

The Lord sent me to prison for five years from 1983 to 1988. During that time I led 40 inmates to Christ. Later, I was incarcerated in the Luoyang Prison labor camp from 1996 to 1998, and led 38 more prisoners to the Lord. I also led a warden to the faith. As punishment, the guards tied my hands behind my back for so long that I had no feeling in my hands and arms for two months.

After being released from prison I immediately resumed my ministry as an itinerant preacher. During the daytime I evangelize non-believers, and in the evenings and night-time I pray without ceasing for my fellow brothers and sisters. These days, I usually don't sleep more than one hour per night. I rise at 2 a.m. and pray till 7 a.m. Then I work for the Lord all day, and pray again in the evening and during the night. The Lord wants me to carry my cross every day and share the gospel with everyone I meet.

Because Jesus is in my heart I cannot help but share Him with everyone I meet. Each day I intercede for more than 60 different people whom the Lord has placed on my heart. I pray for each of them by name four times per day.[7]

A teenage girl is raised from the dead

In 1992, an 18-year-old Christian girl was raised from the dead in Nanyang. For weeks she had been sick with a fever, and she finally succumbed and died. Two days later, the family doctor happened to be passing through her village and saw people mourning at the house. He inspected the girl's body and issued a death certificate.

On the third day after she had died, her funeral was about to begin when Elder Fu arrived in the village with some of his house church colleagues. They asked for the coffin to be opened, and they stood around it, worshipping the Lord.

After three hours, Fu began to pray that life would return to the girl's body. The power of God came upon her and she sat up. Her astonished relatives helped her out of the coffin and gave her something to drink. Subsequently, the parents took their daughter and her death certificate and traveled around the border area between Henan and Hubei provinces, testifying that Jesus Christ had raised her from the dead. Six entire villages, numbering more than 6,000 people, repented and turned to God.

Fu went on his way, not wanting to draw attention to himself. His life has been full of so many incredible events that he struggles to recall specific miracles. When the author of this book had the privilege of interviewing him, some of Fu's co-workers suggested I should ask him about two other occasions when he saw dead people raised to life. His response was to hesitate, either because his deep humility made him reluctant to share such stories, or because even wonders such as these had slipped from his memory among thousands of other extraordinary incidents he has experienced. Like other house church leaders, he only looks forward and doesn't dwell in the past.

Brother Yun

One Christian who emerged from the Nanyang house church movement to become a blessing to the world is Liu Zhenying,

Brother Yun, a gift from Nanyang to the rest of the world
IMB

who is better known as Brother Yun. After meeting Jesus as a teenager during the Cultural Revolution, he became an outstanding evangelist, leading thousands of people to Christ in the midst of China's mighty revival.

On one occasion, the police surrounded a village where a house church meeting was in progress, and Yun was captured as he tried to flee. The officers demanded to know exactly where the meeting had been held so that they could arrest more Christians, but he refused to tell them. When they asked his name, Yun shouted at the top of his voice, "My name is Heavenly Man!" in an attempt to warn the other believers of the danger. They heard his shouting and fled. As a mark of respect, Yun was given the nickname "the Heavenly Man," which has stuck to this day—and became the title of his best-selling autobiography.[8]

Yun was finally arrested and sent to prison in 1984. Such was the brutality inflicted upon him by both the guards and other inmates, he decided it would be better to die than to risk revealing the names of his Christian brothers and sisters. Refusing to speak, he curled up in a corner of the cell and rejected both food and water.

God did not accept Yun's desire to die, however, and he supernaturally sustained his life. Many miracles took place during this period, and Nanyang was alive with talk of a "miracle man" in prison who continued to live even though he neither ate nor drank.

Finally, after 74 days, Yun's body was so shriveled that he weighed just 66 pounds (30 kg). The wardens were afraid they would have to give an account of how they had allowed a prisoner to starve to death, so they invited his family to the prison to try to get him to eat again. Even his own wife didn't recognize his tiny, battered, and bloodied body, and all his relatives thought it was a trick.

Only when his mother identified him by a birthmark did they believe that it was indeed Brother Yun.[9] He broke his long fast by taking communion with his loved ones. When he returned to his cell and spoke to his astonished cellmates, it was with such spiritual authority that those sin-hardened men all fell to their knees and repented.

Later, in March 1997, Yun attended a unity meeting of house church leaders, but the authorities were tipped off and were waiting for the participants to arrive. When Yun saw the situation he jumped out of a second-floor window, but there were officers waiting below, and as a result of the fall and the severe beating they gave him his legs were broken and he was unable to walk.

Yun was harshly tortured during the first few weeks in prison. He described it as the lowest point in his life and he complained to God, reminding Him of the call he had been given years before to preach the gospel. As he lay in solitary confinement, propping his legs up against the wall at night to lessen the pain, the guards mocked Yun and called him "the cripple."

On the morning of May 4, 1997, however, Yun stood up and walked out of the prison, oblivious to the pain of his broken legs. As he walked down the stairs and through a succession of iron gates, the armed guards along the route appeared unable to see him. He crossed the courtyard and went out through the main gate as other prisoners watched from the windows of their third-floor cells. When he reached the road outside, a yellow taxi-van immediately pulled up and the driver told him to get in. He was free.

Years later, Brother Yun recalled that the escape unfolded like a dream and he expected to be shot in the back at any moment. Local Christians hid him, and a number of guards lost their jobs after the authorities investigated how a "cripple" had managed to walk out of a maximum-security prison.

After Yun was reunited with his family, they kept a low profile as the authorities launched a manhunt to try to recapture him. Finding that many house churches were now too afraid to invite him to their meetings, Yun began to think of the possibility of moving out of China; he eventually went to Myanmar, but he was arrested while leaving that country and sentenced to seven years in prison for traveling with unofficial documents.

Hundreds of thousands of Christians around the world prayed fervently for Yun, and he was released from prison in Myanmar after just seven months and seven days behind bars.

After enduring more than 30 arrests and three lengthy prison sentences, Yun left China in 1997 and has since been traveling around the world, sharing his testimony and vision. His ministry continues to bless thousands of people, and God has uniquely gifted him to communicate to a Western

Brother Yun praying for people in Europe

audience. His gift for evangelism did not remain behind in China, and everywhere he goes he continues to lead people to the Lord.

Yun always has a fresh perspective on events in China, which sometimes shocks Christians who have not lived out their faith in a furnace of affliction. For example, in 2018 news reached the Christian world of thousands of church buildings in Henan and other provinces having the crosses torn from their roofs as the Communist authorities sought to destroy all visible evidence of faith.

When he was asked for his opinion on the matter by a group of pastors, they expected Yun to say how sad and dismayed he was because of the wanton removal of crosses. Instead, with a broad smile on his face, he replied:

> I am very happy that so many crosses have been torn down! The cross was never meant to be fixed to the roof of a building. Instead, the Lord Jesus called us to carry the cross on our shoulders and in our hearts. So, I completely agree with the government's decision to pull down all the crosses!

He went on to explain that Christians can grow lazy and start to let bricks and mortar carry the weight of the cross for us, but the words of Jesus have not changed. He said: "Whoever wants to be my disciple must deny themselves and take up their cross and follow me."[10]

Two resurrections from the dead

Brother Timothy is a key house church leader from Nanyang. When he was in his mid twenties, he was already leading a network of house churches spanning several provinces, with tens of thousands of believers.

When asked to share some testimonies, Timothy recalled two instances of people being raised from the dead. The first occurred in 1991 when a young boy named Li Baotang fell sick and became totally paralyzed. Timothy recalled:

> The boy died, and the nearest hospital was 19 miles [30 km] away. His uncle carried the dead body to our home, which also served as a house church. When he arrived at our door it was obvious the boy was completely dead. He had no heartbeat and his body had turned pale.
>
> Our church members immediately started to pray for him. After the first prayer, those standing near the boy thought he might have started breathing again. They laid hands on his body and prayed a second time and suddenly Li Baotang sat up, alive! This happened in my home and I witnessed it with my own eyes. He later became a pastor.[11]

Brother Timothy's second testimony was to an event that occurred two years later:

> In 1993, while I was speaking on the first day of a three-day meeting, I was asked to pray for a 50-year-old man named Chang, who was dying of mouth cancer. This unbeliever was very wealthy and was a well-known Communist Party leader.

By the time he reached the hospital his condition had deteriorated and he was close to death. The staff called Chang's wife to break the bad news that he would not recover.

Because the man was a public figure, visitors who wanted to see him at the hospital had to get permission beforehand. To help me gain access, I was given the man's name card. The next morning I went to the hospital, feeling nervous and not sure what the Lord's will was in all of this. At the hospital none of the staff paid any attention to me because I was just a poor farmer. Finally a nurse looked at me with disdain, and said, "You're too late. Chang died last night."

I was shocked to hear that he was already dead, and asked to see where his body was because I had promised his family I would pray for him. The nurse thought I was stupid, but said the corpse had been moved to the refrigerated morgue in the hospital basement. I went downstairs, and I told an attendant that I needed to pray for Mr. Chang. He gave me a strange look, but the man took me to a line of refrigerated boxes, located Mr. Chang, and opened the cover. His body slid out and I saw that he was truly dead. The blood had drained from his corpse, and his identification tag was tied around his big toe.

I felt afraid as his skin was frozen and ice cold. Despite the circumstances, I knew the Lord could do whatever He wanted. As I closed my eyes and prayed for Mr. Chang in a hushed voice, I leaned forward and said, "Mr. Chang, I know that you can hear me. I know that Jesus can bring you back from the dead because He wants to glorify His Name in your life." By now the morgue attendant had gathered several of his co-workers and they stood at a distance, snickering at the sight of a farmer praying for a dead Communist Party leader!

I had a very simple faith in God. I had read that both Jesus and Lazarus were resurrected after three days, so I thought if God was going to raise Chang I would need to return two more times.

I finished praying, thanked the workers for letting me pray for Mr. Chang, and told them I would be returning at ten o'clock the next morning to pray for him again. They laughed and looked at me like I was completely insane. News quickly spread around the hospital, and the next morning more than 20 staff members gathered to watch me pray for the corpse. They were all eager to witness the sight so they could have a laugh. Again his body was pulled out of the refrigerator and I closed my eyes and prayed for him. He had now spent one and a half days in the freezer and was still very much dead!

As I laid hands on the corpse I leaned forward and whispered, "Mr. Chang, if you are unable to talk, then I command you to move your eyes in the Name of the Lord Jesus Christ." I looked closely and it appeared his eyes twinkled a little! This greatly increased my faith because I knew that God was at work. Nobody else in the room was close enough to see his eyes move, however, and they thought the whole thing was a great joke.

I prayed Bible verses out loud and asked the Lord to prove that the Scriptures are true, and that He has power and authority over death. In a bid to reach others in the morgue, my prayer included a summary of the gospel. After a while the onlookers could feel the presence of the Lord and they became serious-minded and attentive. I announced that I would return again at ten o'clock the next morning, and would pray for the third and final time. His body was placed back in the refrigerator, the door was locked, and I walked up the stairs and returned to the place I was staying.

On the third morning I was amazed to find an even larger crowd had gathered to witness my prayer. It was difficult to get past everyone and into the basement. Dozens of people lined the stairs leading down to the morgue, and many more were crammed inside the room. People were talking among themselves, but everyone was watching closely to see what would happen.

The attendant again produced Mr. Chang's body and I prayed for him, asking the Lord to glorify His Name by healing this man and saving his soul, and the souls of the many witnesses in the room. Nothing appeared to change, so I thanked the attendants and left the hospital, as I had to make my way to the train station to travel across the country with a team of evangelists. I never saw what happened after I left the hospital, but a few days later the believers contacted me with an urgent message.

They said that about 20 minutes after I left, Mr. Chang suddenly sat up and started coughing. The terrified attendant and his co-workers watched as he coughed up a large ball of blood and pus from his mouth. The cancer spilled out of his mouth and onto the floor of the morgue.

Mr. Chang was healed and alive! He asked for food and water because he was hungry and thirsty. As you can imagine, news of the resurrection quickly spread to the upper floors of the hospital, and all those who had come to witness the prayer came rushing down to the basement to see if the report was true. All of the hospital staff saw Chang alive, and his grieving wife was called in to receive her husband back from the dead. Every person who saw this miracle dropped to their knees, repented of their sins, and confessed that Jesus Christ is truly the Son of God.

In the Lord's providence, I didn't personally witness Chang come back to life, but everybody told me about it later. I thank the Lord that I wasn't there because people might have thought it was due to my own power if he had sat up while I was praying for him. By raising him from the dead after I had left, everyone clearly understood that God Himself had performed the miracle, and all the glory and honor went to the Lord Jesus.

When I first heard what had happened, I was pleased but chose not to dwell on it. It was just an act of Almighty God. In those days the revival was burning so intensely that miracles took place at every meeting, and thousands of people were daily coming to Christ. Miracles were not something we focused on.

> They were merely evidences that confirmed the message we were preaching about Jesus was true.
>
> The whole Chang family came to Christ, and remained strong believers. Mr. Chang lived for many more years.[12]

Although some churches in Nanyang have struggled since the turn of the century because of the inrush of materialism, today the whole of Nanyang Prefecture contains an estimated 3.2 million Evangelical Christians,[13] and the influence of the Nanyang house church movement extends to all other parts of Henan Province and throughout the rest of China.

The China Gospel Fellowship

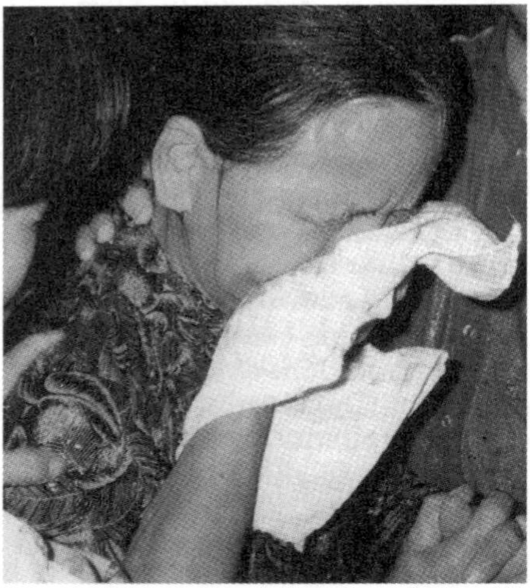

A woman sheds tears of repentance as she meets Christ

The China Gospel Fellowship (CGF) is a house church network that has grown to number at least several million members throughout China. It has its roots in Tanghe County in southern Henan, in the powerful Revival Triangle. The CGF grew out of the Tanghe house church movement in the early 1980s, as its founding pastor, Feng Jianguo, explained:

> The Tanghe Church and the China Gospel Fellowship are like father and son, while the Fangcheng and Nanyang networks are like brothers. In the 1980s, small house churches that had sprung up in Tanghe got into trouble for receiving Bibles from overseas. Under pressure, they joined together with us and so the CGF grew. Most of our leaders were forced to flee their

> homes and we were on the run for years. If we had comfortable lives, I'm sure the Lord would not have used us to spread his gospel in so many places.[1]

Over the years, the CGF has enjoyed a generally peaceful existence among its members, with few splits or controversies compared to some of the neighboring church networks. According to David Aikman, one reason for its harmonious internal relationships is that, "while Fangcheng tended to think of itself as a church with unified principles, the Tanghe Church, coming from a part of Henan with a greater variety of Christian traditions before 1949, thinks of itself as a loose-knit fellowship."[2]

Since its inception, the CGF has established churches in every province of China and has played a leading role in efforts to take the gospel beyond the nation's borders as part of the Chinese missionary movement. A leader of the CGF recalled what life was like for believers in Tanghe in the early 1980s:

> We didn't have Bibles, but many people with diseases came to our meetings and were healed. You could assume that when someone said, "I believe in Jesus!" they would be immediately healed. Some people who were sick said they heard a voice or saw a vision telling them to go to church. We called this period the "three-shedding period." We shed blood in persecution, we shed tears in our intercession, and we shed nasal mucus because we wept for such long periods of time.[3]

By the late 1980s, the CGF had saturated its home county with the gospel. Practically every person in Tanghe had heard about Christ and had been given an opportunity to either accept or reject God's offer of salvation. In 2001, the CGF founder Feng Jianguo said:

> In Tanghe County today, the proportion of Christians is as high as 80 percent, and in neighboring counties 30 to 40 percent.

> Every single village in Tanghe has at least one house church, and every person has heard the good news.[4]

The CGF began to look further afield, and adopted a zealous evangelistic strategy to take the gospel throughout the entire country. Their goal was to see people worshipping Jesus Christ in every city, town, and village, and among every ethnic minority group in China.

After much prayer, the CGF were led to set up a structure with national leaders at the top, and what they call the *chao hui* ("sending agency") level underneath. To qualify as a *chao hui*, a region must have at least 30,000 baptized believers and a certain number of qualified leaders and training centers. By the start of the new millennium there were 22 such agencies throughout the country.

Because of its highly organized structure and its uncompromising zeal to spread the gospel, the CGF has been severely persecuted by the Chinese authorities. On many occasions it has had dozens of its key leaders languishing in prison.

Feng Jianguo

Feng Jianguo (whose name can be translated "Establish God's Kingdom") has been described as "the most respected senior leader of the China Gospel Fellowship."[5] Born in Tanghe in 1925, his parents were committed Presbyterians who believed in Christ after being healed of an illness. Feng first placed his trust in Jesus when he was a small boy.

In 2001, Feng granted a rare interview to the author about his life and the development of his ministry, providing valuable insights into how the power of the gospel swept through Tanghe, touching and transforming multitudes of hungry people:

Feng Jianguo in 2001
Paul Hattaway

After the Japanese war ended I visited a few churches and shared the gospel with small groups. During that time people came to Christ very differently than today. Back then most Christians were elderly people who believed after they were healed of sickness. When we shared the gospel we usually just told testimonies. Then, after being healed, the recipients would receive Jesus and we taught them the Bible.

My sister had a powerful vision when she was just eight, in which she saw our Christian neighbors being received up to glory in heaven. Their clothes were glistening white, they had crowns on their heads, and their faces shone with overwhelming joy and peace. Then we heard that they had just died. This vision made such an impact on my sister that from that day forward she was a dedicated Christian. She shared the vision with many people and told them, "I have seen Christians in heaven. We must believe in Jesus immediately!"

In 1964 I received a clear vision from the Lord, where he showed me that I was to be a captain in His army. He gave me a sword which had my name written on it. When the Cultural Revolution began in 1966, I traveled around preaching the gospel. God gave me gifts of healing and the ability to cast demons out of people who were oppressed by the devil.

The authorities caught up with me in 1975 and branded me a "counter-revolutionary." I was imprisoned for five years, and during that time I met Zhang Rongliang, the leader of the Fangcheng Church. When I arrived in the cell, Zhang took my hand and asked, "Are you a Christian?" I excitedly replied, "Yes, I am!" The next day I found out there were other believers in the prison, and we secretly fellowshipped together and encouraged one another for five years.

In the labor camp we were given the task of working on a massive fruit farm, which covered an area of 2,000 acres. Two brothers smuggled a radio in for us, and every evening we gathered among the fruit trees to secretly listen to gospel broadcasts from overseas.

Once, we gave some visiting brothers apples to take back and share with the church members. During a service, each Christian was given a tiny piece of apple. They wept strongly as they remembered us in prison, and the pieces of apple helped them identify with us and share in our sufferings. Although we had some very difficult times in prison, the Lord showered us with His grace and presence, and we enjoyed intimate fellowship with Him.

In the early 1980s, the Three-Self Patriotic Movement visited me many times and tried to entice me to join them. I always asked: "How can an atheistic government lead the Church of God? Jesus Christ is the head of the Church. I will never join."[6]

Throughout the 1980s and 1990s, Feng Jianguo continued to lead the CGF as it expanded into a nationwide movement. He was highly respected for his godly wisdom and non-controlling style of leadership, which caused many young leaders to look up to him as a father figure in the faith. According to Feng, the revival burned most brightly in the early 1980s. He recalls that in those days:

> All the house churches were one in Christ. We didn't say "Here is this group" and "There is that group." We were all one, so when we were released from prison I joined Zhang Rongliang's team, even though I was from Tanghe and he was from Fangcheng. Just six months after we gained our freedom the authorities began searching for us again, so from 1981 to 1983 we fled together all around China, preaching the gospel and training believers everywhere we went.
>
> Once, in 1983, we were teaching more than a hundred Christians when a demon-possessed woman started shouting and violently disrupting the meeting. I asked two men to carry her to the front, and when we laid hands on her and prayed, she immediately calmed down and fell asleep like a harmless kitten! The believers told us she had often disturbed their meetings and sometimes climbed up the wall onto the roof of the building. After we cast the demons out she was no longer able to climb the wall!
>
> In those days if you didn't have the gift of casting out demons you would have trouble and continual disturbances at every meeting. It wasn't enough to preach the gospel with words only; you needed to preach with both words and a demonstration of the Spirit's power. I learned that we don't need to shout loudly for Jesus to hear us. He is closer than a brother, and He's there as soon as we whisper His Name. He will never leave us or forsake us.[7]

In early 1994, a large meeting was held in Tanghe at which 70 young evangelists were commissioned and sent to 22 of China's 30 provinces. Each worker was given 1,500 Yuan (about $180) by the local believers. Despite their poverty, farmers sold their chickens and eggs or worked on neighbors' farms to scrape together money to help spread the gospel throughout China.

God blessed the work of the evangelists, and when they all returned to Tanghe six months later, they reported how God had helped them to plant house churches and had miraculously provided for all their needs. One church movement that was birthed in Inner Mongolia later grew to include more than 100,000 believers.[8]

Two single women planted three churches with over 300 members in the six months they ministered in Heilongjiang Province, and by 2002 those churches had grown to more than 5,000 believers.[9] Feng fondly recalled those days:

> The 70 young workers had to sleep in the wilderness. They wept and prayed all night, and the Lord Jesus Himself provided for their needs. When they returned home and told us how God had used them, we all rejoiced greatly. Many of those evangelists made vows to the Lord to remain single, so they could devote themselves fully to winning souls and spreading the gospel.[10]

Between 1996 and 1999, Feng was again sentenced to a prison term after being labeled a "cult leader." During his incarceration the most painful part was knowing that his family was suffering. He recalled:

> My wife and children had to work in the fields just to survive. They were scheduled to face a public trial, but those who were planning to bring false accusations against them came under God's wrath. They all fell gravely ill and were unable to testify, so the case against them was dismissed.[11]

Feng was released early from this latest imprisonment due to health problems, but the government's opposition to the CGF reached a new level after the movement was placed on a list of "evil cults" because of its refusal to submit to the government-controlled Three-Self Patriotic Movement. The charge was ludicrous to those who knew the Chinese Church, for the CGF was recognized as one of the more conservative and biblically sound Evangelical movements in China.

Dozens of church leaders were arrested, and the eye of the storm was Xinyang City, where the house churches had grown by 10,000 believers in a single month during a mass evangelistic campaign in 1994.

Undeterred by the waves of brutal persecution, the China Gospel Fellowship redoubled its evangelistic efforts. In October 1999, it sent 200 new missionaries to every province in the country, including Tibet. Encouraged by the success God gave them, the movement expanded its vision and began to focus on even greater harvest fields in the Muslim, Buddhist, and Hindu nations beyond China's borders. One foreign Christian who was invited to share a Christmas message with a group of CGF believers had this to say:

> Their testimonies are laced with references to healing, visions, prophetic insight, and persecution. They also speak of being "filled with the Spirit," which enables them to face great hardships and adversity . . .
>
> When the service began, a sense of joy quickly permeated the small make-shift sanctuary . . . The service was filled with truly amazing and culturally authentic forms of worship. Small groups of believers, usually two or four, sang songs based on Scripture as they performed Christian folk dances. It was incredible—a wonderful form of worship which instructed and edified the entire congregation. Everyone entered in and the joy was almost tangible.[12]

The two Shens

Although Feng Jianguo was regarded as the founder and elder statesman of the China Gospel Fellowship, two younger men, Shen Yiping and his nephew Shen Xianfeng (whose name

Shen Xianfeng

means "Pioneer Shen"), rose to prominence in the 1980s as men of God and key leaders of the movement. Few people know of the events that led to their emergence, but in 2001 Feng told the author how God had promoted the two Shens to leadership positions:

> In the early 1980s we trained two young men, Shen Yiping and his nephew Shen Xianfeng. They lived only a short distance from my home. They attended a Three-Self church, but the preacher there didn't even use a Bible. He just read political messages and articles from the TSPM magazine.
>
> During Easter 1982, I went to their village to preach the gospel. By that time the two Shens were fed up with lukewarm Christianity, and they hungered to know the truth. They gave their lives to Christ with much rejoicing.
>
> Later, Shen Xianfeng, whose feet have been crippled since birth, came to my house and told me he was under great pressure. After praying with him, I felt we would be arrested at any moment, so we decided to flee together. We left my home at 11 p.m., and just moments later the police arrived to arrest us,

> but we were nowhere to be found. From that time, Shen Yiping and Shen Xianfeng became my fulltime co-workers. That's how the China Gospel Fellowship was founded, and within two years a loose network had formed of more than 200 house churches.[13]

In 1998, Shen Xianfeng and 16 other church leaders were seized and put behind bars. He recalled:

> We were constantly interrogated and beaten, stripped and exposed to the cold wind of electric fans during winter. When we could no longer bear the stinging pain and we cried out, our mouths would be stuffed with rags by our persecutors.[14]

For weeks no charges were laid against the detained leaders, until they were formally accused of "organizing a cult." Shen Xianfeng strongly protested their innocence and issued a public statement to Christians in China and throughout the world. It said:

> We are orthodox Christians, truly believing in Jesus. We are also against all cults and heresies . . . My belief is sound. I believe in the Triune God, and in Jesus who is both divine and human. I believe salvation is only through faith, and the Bible is the supreme authority on all matters . . . We conduct ourselves according to the principle of loving God and loving others, and we do not profit personally at other people's expense, nor do we demoralize society. Wherever the gospel is preached, society has improved. People turn from wickedness, broken families are restored, and the lazy become diligent. Whenever there is an increase in the Christian population, social harmony and unity also improves, as no true Christian is really against the government.[15]

Faced with such a compelling statement, the authorities admitted that what Shen said was true, but they reiterated that any church group that refused to submit to the Three-Self structure was a cult. After the director of China's Religious

Affairs Bureau, Ye Xiaowen, condemned all unregistered house church groups as "evil, illegal organizations that undermine social order,"[16] Shen and the other 16 Christians were sentenced to two to three years in prison with hard labor.

Shen's disability did not win him any sympathy from the authorities. On one occasion, the police seized his crutches and used them to beat him savagely. Other Christians "told of Shen being beaten up in prison by other inmates on orders from prison guards and tortured by electric shock."[17]

Although the CGF leaders know how far their movement extends throughout China, they tend to keep the figures to themselves to avoid being proud. Estimates by overseas Christians include a figure of three million believers in 2000,[18] while British author Tony Lambert noted in 2006:

> It has been stated as a fact that the CGF has 10 million followers. However, Brother Shen is on record as claiming that in 2004 the network had 23 districts, each with roughly 100,000 believers; so the real total is about 2.3 million.[19]

In the years since then, the CGF has continued to experience strong growth in many parts of China, and dozens of missionaries have been sent to other countries. Although the total number of believers in the movement remains unclear, it seems likely that the total now surpasses ten million believers.

To hell and back—kidnapped by a cult

In a tragic irony, while the Chinese government was concentrating on discrediting the China Gospel Fellowship and other house church groups as "evil cults," a truly evil cult was able to kidnap 34 CGF leaders and hold them captive for almost two months. News that the leaders had gone missing first emerged on April 17, 2002, and the immediate assumption was that they had been arrested by the authorities. It soon became apparent, however, that something even more sinister had occurred.[20]

The 34 CGF leaders had been systematically abducted in six different parts of China—Shanghai, Qingdao, Harbin, Hebei, Xi'an, and Zhongxiang—by members of the Eastern Lightning, which is noted for its acts of violence and for its belief that Jesus has already returned to earth as a woman named Yang Xiangbin, who reportedly lives in Henan Province.

Launching an elaborate plot that had taken more than a year to plan, cult members gained access to the CGF leaders by claiming they represented a reputable Bible training institution in Singapore. It later emerged that two female "spies" had circulated among CGF congregations for years, slowly winning their trust. After gathering church leaders together for their spurious Bible classes, the cult insisted that everyone hand in their mobile phones before the first lesson could begin. The CGF leaders knew at once that something was wrong, but the cult members were armed, and escape seemed futile.

One sister was able to get away, however, by climbing out of a bathroom window. She quickly alerted other church members to what had happened. But for her escape, the 34 kidnapped leaders would have likely disappeared without trace for a long time.

It appears the goal of the Eastern Lightning was to persuade the CGF leaders to join their cult, along with their millions of members. This was part of a wider plan to gain control over China and ultimately the whole world. They used psychological torture, physical abuse, drugs, and sexual enticement in an attempt to break the spirit of the captive Christians and destroy their resistance.

The CGF leaders were aware that members of the Eastern Lightning had not hesitated to maim believers in the past. They had cut off people's ears, noses, and limbs, and sometimes victims had their faces disfigured with acid. Adherents of the cult were known to have murdered some who refused to cooperate with them.

The Christians were subjected to daily brainwashing sessions, but the cult had not expected a powerful counter-attack. These senior church leaders, including Shen Yiping and Shen Xianfeng, had already spent extended periods in prison being tortured by the authorities. They were experienced warriors for Christ, and they countered the cult's attempts to brainwash them by vigorously disputing everything they were told and by preaching the gospel to their captors.

Aware that the food they were offered was laced with drugs, many of the believers refused to eat and began long fasts, dedicated to the Lord Jesus. In deep anguish of soul, one of the senior CGF leaders, Zhang, prayed aloud with great passion:

> Oh, God, please have mercy on us, and forgive us our ignorance! We have suffered enough all these years. Our co-workers have been persecuted over and over again, and have gone through continual hardships. Today we are trapped and kidnapped due to our innocence and eagerness to learn your Word.
>
> We can't see what lies ahead, or whether we will live or die. Now we are in the hands of the evil Eastern Lightning, who have absolutely no restraint. Shall we die in the hands of these wicked people? What if they seize the opportunity to deceive more churches in our names? Oh Lord, shall the fruit of our 20 years' labor be destroyed so quickly? If you still remember your glory, please protect all your servants and make a way out for us.[21]

Shen Xianfeng, who was one of those held in Shanghai, strongly denounced the cult leaders to their faces with the following words: "You gangsters! You are false Christs and anti-Christs. You are serpents cloaked in human skin. You are the scum and disgrace of our country. I will never give up my genuine faith or give in to your demonic teaching!"[22]

Meanwhile, millions of believers in China and around the world had been notified of the kidnappings, and fervent prayer was ascending to the throne of God, asking Him to intervene on behalf of His children. It was the first time that most Christians overseas had heard of the Eastern Lightning. Information began to circulate widely on the internet, drawing attention to the satanic origins of the cult and alerting believers so they would not fall prey to its deceptions.

In the United States, many Christians were angered to learn that the founder of the Eastern Lightning, Zhao Weishan, was living in their midst and was busily establishing the cult throughout North America, having been granted asylum by the US State Department as a victim of religious persecution.

When the hundreds of other CGF evangelists throughout China heard about the abductions, they returned to Henan from their far-flung fields to prayerfully decide what to do. They were in a quandary over whether or not to seek the government's help. For years the CGF had been outlawed and targeted as a cult itself, but after fervently seeking God's will, they decided to approach the authorities.

To its credit, the Public Security Bureau appreciated the gravity of the situation, and apparently its hatred of house church Christians did not compare with the utter loathing it felt for the Eastern Lightning.

The officers in the various cities where the kidnappings had occurred put pressure on known accomplices and relatives of cult leaders, and over the following weeks the Christians were released one by one, until the final pastor was freed on June 14, 2002.

Although the 34 CGF leaders had survived, they were in such a dreadful physical, emotional, and mental condition that it took more than a year of prayer and recuperation before they were back to normal. All except one brother from Shanxi Province had been able to resist the temptations and indoctrinations of the cult. Another brother fell into a coma after being poisoned, but he later recovered.

When they heard that their leaders had been set free, all the CGF evangelists gathered in Henan to meet with them face to face. It was an emotional reunion, with one report saying that when the co-workers first saw their beloved leaders they appeared

> weary and feeble, wan and sallow, standing on the platform heavily burdened, yet they still greeted and encouraged everybody with such loving kindness and steadfast strength. Tears burst out from the co-workers' eyes. Here were the teachers that they had been so worried about, yet despite the fact that they looked a bit older and feebler, their burden for missions and their love and concern for us had not been affected in the least way.[23]

For years the Eastern Lightning had been able to operate in the shadows, but God used the abductions to bring the cult's dirty deeds into the light. Many Christians prayed for the group's destruction, and hundreds of thousands of books were printed in China to warn believers of its tactics. Shen Xianfeng later issued a stern warning to believers around the world:

> On June 3, I was forced into a car by a few men and sent to the Shanghai train station. When I finally arrived home after 50 days' confinement, I was very pale, and as skinny as a stick. I hardly looked like a human after all the torment . . .
>
> We later held a denunciation meeting to profoundly expose and condemn the Eastern Lightning cult. Every one of the kidnapped co-workers shared their experiences during the confinement, disclosing the many vile and despicable methods employed by the cult, including lying, deceit, money,

> employment opportunities, women, mind-altering drugs, sexual stimulants, dreams, visions, pretending to be ghosts, abuse, spreading division, blackmailing, isolation, spiritual and emotional torments, and disrupting families . . .
>
> Let our stumbling be a warning to the Church in the rest of the world. May brothers and sisters be alert and watchful, standing guard and resisting the schemes of cults and heresies, and may we continually walk in the truth of the Lord.[24]

In the aftermath of the kidnappings, one lamentable consequence was that the trust between various house church networks was strained. Many church leaders were so shocked by the degree of sophisticated planning and deceit used by the cult that for some time they refused to meet any foreign Christians. Knowing that the Eastern Lightning often plants agents within house churches—sometimes waiting for years while they patiently win believers' trust before putting their plans into action—also shook confidence. Believers began to look more closely at one another, wondering if there were any spies in their midst.

The CGF, like all other house church movements in Henan, has had a tumultuous history. Thousands of its members have been imprisoned and tortured over the years, with 150 pastors arrested during a prayer breakfast at a Nanyang hotel as recently as January 15, 2019. During the raid, which was carried out by more than 100 armed agents, one pastor suffered a heart attack and numerous others required hospitalization.[25]

On July 14, 2018, hundreds of thousands of Christians throughout China were saddened to hear of the passing of Shen Yiping, who died at the age of 71. He had provided sterling leadership to the CGF for decades, experiencing the highs and lows of Christian life in China through many dark periods.

Despite the tremendous opposition and setbacks, the CGF has maintained a steady course over the years. Its members have faithfully proclaimed the truth without compromise, and thousands of churches have been established in previously unreached areas of China. Many evangelists have been sent to ethnic minority groups throughout China, and its work in the cities has also flourished.

The coronavirus pandemic, which started in the city of Wuhan in January 2020, deeply affected the work of the China Gospel Fellowship, and it spread across the Hubei border into Tanghe County, with many church members contracting the virus and more than a few dying.

After the threat subsided, the CGF leaders decided to stop holding public meetings due to increasingly brutal government interference, and at the time of this book going to press they were planning to conduct only online services for their members. With the Communist Party tightly controlling all websites and apps in China, this move may backfire badly, and it remains to be seen what form the CGF and other house church networks will take going into the future.

Today, the place where it all began, Tanghe County, has a population of 1.4 million people. Approximately 900,000 are estimated to be Evangelical Christians, making it one of the most densely populated Christian areas in China. God has greatly glorified His Name through these blessed and wholehearted disciples.

1990s

Christians in Henan boldly commemorate the death of a member despite warnings not to gather
RCMI

Preaching outside the prison gates

The first few years of the 1990s brought a relative respite for Henan's house churches. In many ways, China's leaders appeared to still be reeling from the impact of the Tiananmen Square demonstrations in June 1989, and for a while their focus was diverted from Christians to pro-democracy activists. The years following the massacre saw a great spiritual harvest of university students and intelligentsia across the country.

In April 1992, the authorities launched a new crackdown against the house churches. By June, one report said that in Henan, "hundreds of house church leaders and itinerant evangelists have been arrested for 'illegal religious activities,' including at least 80 house church members from Queshan County."[1]

In September of that year, another 120 house church believers and three foreigners were arrested when a training session in Wuyang County was raided by the authorities. Twelve of the detainees were released after paying fines, but "when they returned home, they found their houses stripped bare of personal belongings including Bibles, furniture, clothes and cooking utensils."[2]

The remaining 108 believers were "moved to a variety of locations, some in other provinces, and were repeatedly interrogated and beaten."[3] This mass arrest failed to achieve the desired results for the authorities in Wuyang, however, with one report stating:

> On the first day in prison, the 120 preachers were all together in the courtyard and began to sing and worship the Lord. This infuriated the officers who then dispersed the believers around the prison. This did not stop the worship, however, and when the believers were ordered to stop worshipping, they sang all the louder. According to [one sister]: "After all, we were already in prison, had lost all our earthly goods and were being beaten and tortured. What more could they do to us? Great boldness came upon us . . ."
>
> The Christian leaders involved in the incident have decided that they will no longer fear persecution. They have become very bold in preaching the gospel, even to the extent of preaching outside the prison gates upon their release.[4]

Many of the arrested believers were natives of Fangcheng County. After their release from prison, they

> went out and preached the gospel, encouraging other believers to do the same, and 16,200 people were saved in the space of 20 days in that county alone . . . Since that time many more

have believed, bringing their estimates of the number of new believers in the whole of Henan to tens of thousands.[5]

Miracles in prison

Although accounts of the experiences of Chinese Christians in prison are often sickening, there are also many wonderful testimonies of how God has worked miracles in even the darkest and most hopeless places. For example, in 1993 a young Henan house church leader named Joseph was arrested and thrown into prison. He received a savage beating from the guards, who knocked him unconscious and broke his collarbone and ribs. They then threw his battered and bloodied body into a cell that already contained about 30 prisoners.

This grim room contained just one bed and a single bucket for a toilet. In charge was a hardened criminal who had already established a protection system within the cell. No one was allowed to touch his bed. When the guards threw Joseph's unconscious body into the cell, however, even this unfeeling man had compassion, and he laid Joseph on the bed.

At around two o'clock in the morning, according to the testimony of the other inmates, a supernatural light appeared to hover over Joseph's body, and it shone on him for several hours. The other prisoners were terrified and backed into the opposite corner of the cell, crying out to the guards to let them out. The guards, too, saw the light and were afraid.

By sunrise, Joseph had regained consciousness. He had not seen the light at all, and considering the serious injuries he had received the previous night, he was much recovered and his broken collarbone and ribs appeared to be healed. Not surprisingly, the first question his fellow prisoners asked him was: "Who are you?"

He replied, "It doesn't matter who I am, but I believe in Jesus Christ."

Joseph led 28 of the other inmates to faith in Christ.[6]

Countless other signs and wonders took place throughout Henan as the revival continued. Peter Xu Yongze remembers one miracle that occurred in 1994:

> A Christian woman in Nanyang grew gravely ill and died. For two days she had stopped breathing and was certified dead. The Christians gathered around her, and with many tears they pleaded with God to bring her back. She was the life of her local church, and everyone loved her deeply. They couldn't imagine being without her joyous spirit in their midst. Suddenly, the woman came back to life and sat up straight!
>
> I visited her a few days after this miracle took place. She was so humbled by her experience that she couldn't speak. The Lord was eager to have this sister in heaven, however, and her return to the church was only temporary. About one year later she died and went to be with Jesus forever.[7]

The fear of God grips Henan

In 1995, the Chinese president Jiang Zemin admitted: "We are engaged in a secret struggle against the Church."[8]

Later that year, three female evangelists traveled to Xinye in southern Henan. Within a week, their preaching had prompted 1,100 people to repent of their sins, and many people had been healed. At one open-air meeting a man approached, blaspheming God and cursing the sisters at the top of his voice.

They tried to ignore his filthy remarks, and after the meeting, a group of unbelievers came up and asked how they could continue without lashing out at the vile man, and how they had even appeared to show compassion for him. The three women answered: "We leave this man in the hands of God."

At the very moment they said these words, the blasphemer fell to the ground and died. The fear of God fell on everyone who witnessed His judgment, and many more people repented and accepted the Lord.[9]

Throughout Henan, the fear of God gripped people's hearts, and thousands were swept into His kingdom. An old man who had worshipped idols for more than 70 years warned everyone to stay away from those who believed in Jesus, because there was "a group of people dressed in white who always follow the Christians wherever they go."[10]

During one meeting, a 22-year-old woman was suddenly seized by evil spirits and fell to the ground, foaming at the mouth. Bystanders examined her and established that she was dead, and they went to notify the authorities. A young evangelist, however, insisted on trusting God to perform a miracle. He later recalled:

> A spirit of worship fell in the meeting, and everyone began to praise and dance before the Lord for a long time. Eventually, she came to life and rose to her feet! We were so excited! Within an hour she was eating a bowl of noodles with us. What a mighty God we serve![11]

The systematic persecution of Henan's house churches continued in 1995, with more than 200 Christians arrested in three separate police raids in Zhoukou. At one of these raids, 42 Bible school students were captured. The officers were "very rough, hitting and kicking the believers, and slapping the sisters in the face so hard that some of them bled badly as a result."[12]

The reason for the persecution in Zhoukou, according to one church leader, was that the area had become one of the strongest Christian hubs in Henan. In 1995, church leaders had reported at least 33,000 known house churches in the prefecture.[13] God had also moved powerfully among the Three-Self churches in Zhoukou, and by 1999 the city contained 30,000 registered believers. Each service at the main church was attended by "2,000 to 3,000 people who eagerly share their testimonies before the sermon."[14]

Zhoukou had once been considered the most violent place in Henan, highly resistant to the gospel. Attempts to establish God's kingdom there had resulted in severe beatings, by both the citizens and the authorities. However, by persevering to the point of spilling their blood, God's people finally overcame the resistance with love, and great revival ensued.

Today, the entire Zhoukou Prefecture is home to more than eight million people. Of these, 1.6 million are estimated to be Evangelical Christians, comprising approximately 600,000 members of registered churches and one million house church believers.[15]

A hotbed of cults

While it's encouraging to read accounts of revival as millions of people have come to faith in Henan, the rapid growth of the Church and the lack of Bibles and solid teaching left many fledgling believers vulnerable to deception and abuse by cults.

In March 1990, a stranger walked into a sleepy village near Fangcheng in southern Henan, where he told several Christians he could take them to meet Jesus. Other villagers listened to the convincing visitor and his extraordinary offer. The impoverished farmers toiled in the fields from sunrise to sunset, so the prospect of meeting Jesus and being released from their daily struggles appealed to them.

After accepting money from the villagers, the man claimed that Jesus would appear to them on the banks of a nearby river. Dozens of people excitedly surged toward the river, where they waited patiently for the Savior to appear. The stranger, meanwhile, slipped away with the money. The day wore on until the shadows lengthened and the sun began to set. The believers grew increasingly agitated as the hours passed until finally:

> Unable to contain his frustration and desperate to see Jesus, one of the believers waded into the frigid waters. Some 19 others followed him, oblivious to the fact that they could neither swim nor withstand the strong current.
>
> The rest of the crowd stood silently on the river bank, staring gloomily into the gathering darkness. All night, they waited for their friends to return and, as the long hours passed, they feared the worst. When the morning dawned, their fears were confirmed. All 20, in their zealous haste, had drowned.[16]

Other reports tell of cases where people drowned while trying to walk on water as Jesus and Peter did, and there have been several cases of women "attempting to emulate the story of Abraham and Isaac by sacrificing their sons because of simplistic and literal interpretations of the Scriptures."[17]

Due to these grim stories and many others like them, as the 1990s progressed, church leaders in Henan placed an increased emphasis on training and grounding new believers in God's Word, in a bid to prevent more of the massive harvest in Henan being swept away by cults.

Revival in Zhumadian

In March 1994, several evangelists traveled to a remote Henan village where no one had ever heard the gospel before. One of the preachers began sharing the good news about Jesus, and a small crowd gathered around him. He taught for four hours, and the crowd increased in size until more than a thousand eager people pressed in to hear his every word. One of the participants reported that as the evangelist continued to proclaim the Scriptures:

> The people saw with their eyes scenes of the teaching. It was as if they were watching the life of Jesus being portrayed by video or a movie. However, there was no video or movie projector, no screen, and no electricity. But everyone saw the same thing.
>
> When he said, "Jesus was baptized in the Jordan River," they saw the scene of the baptism of Jesus. This went on right through the crucifixion and resurrection, at which time everyone fell on their knees and repented of their sins. They all said: "God is real and alive in our midst. What can we say but to thank Him and believe in Him?" . . .
>
> The biblical scenes went away, and we have not heard of such a thing being repeated anywhere else. It was so real that we tried to record it on our video camera, but unfortunately it was not working. God probably allowed this very unusual miracle to take place because many had been fasting and praying for this village where there was not a single Christian.[18]

Zhumadian is located in south-central Henan Province. Although in the early 1980s the government declared the prefecture to be "without religion," by 1996 Three-Self church leaders estimated there were at least 200,000 Evangelical believers in Zhumadian. House church leaders, however, claimed the true number of believers was at least half a million.

Local authorities, angered and embarrassed by the growth of Christianity, refused to register any more TSPM churches or meeting points, but the churches continued to grow anyway. Today, the number of Evangelical Christians in Zhumadian Prefecture has mushroomed to an estimated one million, out of a total population of just over seven million people.[19]

New levels of degradation

The extraordinary revival that swept Henan in the 1990s came at great cost to many of God's children, as the Communist authorities sank to new levels of violence and degradation.

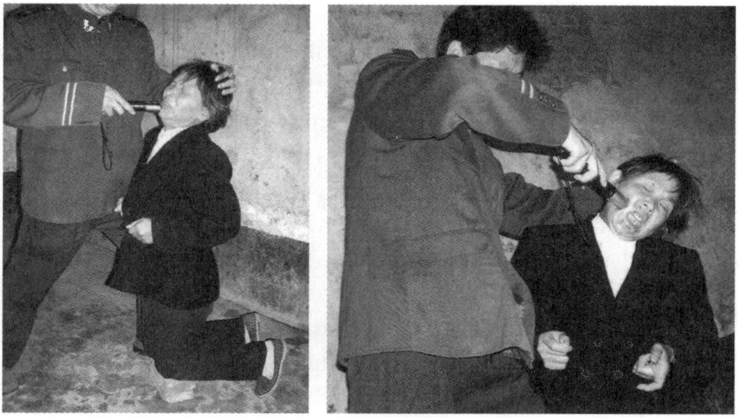

An elderly Christian woman, Miao Aizhen, is tortured with an electric baton at the Wenshu Village police station. The officer posed for pictures thinking they would enhance his prospects of promotion, but the photographer sent copies overseas before going into hiding
CIPRC

In January 1996, a pastor named Shi Yunchao perished after being severely tortured. Shi had previously spent four years in a prison labor camp and was leading a church meeting when officers broke in with handcuffs and batons. According to *Christianity Today*:

> One of the officers, a man named Yang Shoushan, shouted, "Old diehard! It is you again!" He handcuffed Shi, cursing, "You never change, even when the time of your death has come!" Shi was taken to the Qingfeng Jail. His howls and shrieks under torture rang out so far that those Christians locked in the jail could hear it clearly. He was released from prison, but his health was beyond repair. He died on January 17, 1996.[20]

On May 26, 1996, a 36-year-old woman named Zhang Xiuju also received a martyr's crown after being killed in Xihua County. She was dragged out of her home by PSB officers and died after being continually beaten throughout the night. The authorities returned the corpse to her parents and gave them 5,000 Yuan (about $600) in an attempt to keep the family quiet.[21] When officials in her hometown insisted she had died by jumping out of a car while in custody, local Christians disputed this claim, pointing out that the scars and rope marks around her wrists were consistent with torture techniques commonly used by the authorities.

By the late 1990s, house church leaders in Henan Province estimated that 40 percent of all prisoners serving terms in labor camps were there because of their faith in Christ. In early 1997, 50 out of the 126 inmates at the Henan Number One Prison labor camp were behind bars because of house church activities. According to Freedom House, approximately 300 house church believers were arrested and incarcerated in Luoyang Prison between July 1996 and June 1997.[22]

Just three weeks after the Chinese government signed the International Covenant on Civil and Political Rights—which upholds freedoms of speech, assembly, and religion—authorities arrested 70 house church leaders during a meeting on October 26, 1998 at Wugang in central Henan. The officers viciously beat and kicked the Christians, a number of whom managed to escape in the mayhem.

One of those arrested was a 26-year-old woman, Cheng Meiying, who lay unconscious for three days after receiving a severe beating. A Christian organization reported that Cheng was "lashed with a wet rope and hit repeatedly on the head with a baton. Although the authorities released Cheng when she regained consciousness, she had completely lost her memory and appears mentally disturbed."[23]

It was later confirmed that Cheng had suffered permanent brain damage. According to other believers, she had been a prominent evangelist who had "either directly or indirectly been involved in the establishment of several thousand house churches and the conversion of several hundred thousand people."[24]

Despite the tight security in Henan at the time, more than 140 key house church workers from different networks decided to meet in a factory owned by a Christian businessman in Nanyang on November 5, 1998. Five foreign Christians were also invited to participate in the meeting. The factory was surrounded by a high cement wall that blocked any view from the outside, and the only structure tall enough to overlook it was a water tower several hundred yards down the road.

At one stage, some of the believers saw men climbing to the top of the tower, and on the third night of meetings, as a Western missionary was giving a presentation on ministry to Tibet, the electricity to the building was suddenly cut. It was a moonless night and the factory was plunged into total darkness. The missionary gave an eyewitness account of what happened next:

> The Chinese pastors immediately realized that trouble was at the door, but before we had a chance to escape, hundreds of armed policemen and cadres charged into the complex, completely surrounding us. The darkness was lit up by streaks of gun-flash as officers fired their weapons. In the ensuing pandemonium, no one knew if the bullets were being aimed into the air or if Christians were being shot.
>
> Armed with loudspeakers and generator-operated floodlights, the chief Public Security officer screamed at the believers to remain on the floor or be shot dead. What followed was a most touching example of Christ's love. The police formed a tight circle around the Christians and mercilessly thrashed them as hard as they could. Old women were kicked in the head with steel-capped boots, and jaws and ribs cracked as batons were yielded with brute force. Through the dark room and surreal atmosphere, I could see the senior pastors

> shielding their flocks from the worst of the blows by placing their bodies between the officers and the defenseless believers. The shepherds were willing to lay their lives down for their sheep.[25]

When the chaos subsided, all of the participants were pushed into the back of army trucks and taken away for interrogation. They were all given heavy fines, and many received extra beatings while in custody. When the officials had identified everyone, they were delighted to discover that they had netted some of the "biggest fish" in the Chinese Church, some of whom had been on their "most wanted" lists for years.

The authorities in Nanyang tried to justify their actions with the ludicrous claim that people had been "hauled away only when they resisted. Some shot at the officers with home-made rifles."[26] The state-approved China Christian Council tried a different tack: It simply denied that any arrests had taken place at all.[27]

As the 1990s drew to a close, Christians in Henan looked back on another decade of harsh persecution, but also of extraordinary growth. The gospel had continued to flourish throughout the province, and most believers regarded the repression not as a curse, but as an opportunity to grow in Christ and share the gospel with needy men and women in prison.

Even official figures at the end of the 1990s revealed the tremendous Christian growth that had taken place in Henan. The conservative British researcher Tony Lambert had published a figure of just 800,000 registered Evangelical believers in the province in 1989,[28] but by the end of the following decade he had sharply increased his estimate to five million Evangelicals in Henan,[29] a more than sixfold jump in just ten years.

The Christian world had become aware that God was doing something extraordinary in this blessed province of central

China, with the 2001 edition of the authoritative mission book *Operation World* estimating an even higher number of 6,964,200 Evangelical believers in Henan.[30]

Letters from Henan

1992

> There are many believers in my village. Some believe in the Local Church,[31] and I attend the Three-Self Church, although most of us are not baptized. We do believe in the importance of baptism, but we think the baptism of the Spirit is more important. Is that correct? The people from the Local Church say that when the Lord comes again, they will be picked up first, numbering 144,000. Only after that will believers from the Three-Self be picked up. In my one year or so of being a Christian, I consider that to believe [in] Jesus Christ as our Savior, and to confess Him openly and believe in my heart, are all that is needed to be saved. I want to be saved, but I don't know which is better, the Local Church or the Three-Self Church.[32]

> Recently, a preacher from the north visited our village. His teaching was different than our pastor. He preached on the book of Revelation and said that the kingdom is near. I was very unhappy when I heard him. He said many "amens" when he prayed. I did not understand his message. Is he a false Christian? He doesn't face the cross when he prays, as he claims the cross is an idol![33]

1993

There is no church in our village, but my mother and other Christians attend the Three-Self church not far away. My aunt is a born-again Christian. She told my mother that she could only be saved if she went to her church, so my mother believed and went there with several sisters. When the Three-Self leaders realized that they no longer attend their church, they informed the Public Security Bureau, who put my mother and the sisters in prison. They were freed one week later after we paid a 200 Yuan fine [about $30] for each of them. Having seen their experiences, some seekers have decided not to believe in Jesus, while others lost their faith.[34]

One day our pastor's face was full of sorrow because he was being attacked. During [the] Christmas service, our congregation of 2,000 was raided by the local authorities. They recorded every believer's name, and then the villagers broke into our homes and stole our food. Our pastor was put into prison and the church was shut down. Anyone who tries to meet will be fined, so our church has remained closed until today.[35]

1994

Our situation is not good. The Public Security Bureau fines us without reason. They claim our meetings are illegal and that we disturb the society. The fines range from 300 to 500 Yuan [approximately $38 to $62], and they detain us until we make the payment. Nonetheless, the meetings here have carried on as usual. We hold all-night prayer meetings, discipleship training and Bible study classes, and we continue to serve the Lord as a team.[36]

1995

I converted to Jesus Christ in 1993, and I attended a meeting every Sunday evening. Later I was told by some Christians from Zhengzhou that my church belongs to the "Shouters" sect, so I left and joined a Three-Self church quite far from my home. Then someone warned me that this church was not led by Christ and the congregation will not inherit eternal life. Therefore I left the Three-Self church. Recently, a lady invited me to her church. She emphasized that they worship the true God who came into the world. I am puzzled. Which church is God's Body? I dare not go to any of the churches. I just want to preach the gospel.[37]

1996

I was baptized a long time ago but still have doubts. Sometimes I even wonder if I have been born again. Thus when I was asked to serve in my church, I hesitated. I am also worried about my poor health. My husband is an unbeliever, and one night when I was attending a meeting he came home and didn't see me, so he became very angry and tore my Bible into pieces. I was sad and blamed myself for not putting the precious Bible in a safer place. Since that time, whenever I come home late from church he loses his temper and scolds me. I want to serve the Lord, but the pressure from my husband and my own spiritual and physical weaknesses hinder me from doing so. I am confused and distressed.[38]

I used to be a Chinese opera singer who always skipped Sunday services to make money. After God disciplined me repeatedly, I finally gave up singing and have now joined a Christian team that preaches in villages. Since my family members are not Christians, they always urge me to return to the opera group.[39]

1997

Last month I suddenly fell ill. Half of my body was paralyzed, and I couldn't move or talk. I was taken to the hospital where I was diagnosed with having a blood clot in my brain. After staying in the hospital for one month, with the help of Almighty God and the care of doctors, I recovered well and was discharged . . . This is a blessing of God and a miracle of the Holy Spirit. I praise the Lord from the bottom of my heart. The grace of the Lord is surely abundant to me. When a person suffers a stroke at 70 years of age like me, it usually leads to death or being permanently paralyzed. I give thanks to the Lord, for it is true that in all things God works for the good of those who love Him. I have committed the rest of my life for God's use. I won't be ashamed when Jesus Christ comes again.[40]

1998

Maybe I am too critical, but I think the Christians in our village are not truly consistent in what they say and do. They talk a lot about faith and love, but don't show these in their actions. Daughters-in-law quarrel with their mothers-in-law, as do Christian husbands and wives. This kind of behavior is not only despised by non-believers, but it brings reproach to God. Nowadays, I would rather stay home and listen to the radio than go to church. Am I drifting away from the Lord?[41]

1999

I was miraculously saved from a severe electric shock in 1983. One year later my life changed when my wife and several Christian ladies in our village had a communion service. My friend and I went out to drink, and I arrived home before my wife and lost patience. I was so angry that I whipped her, telling her my anger would only subside when the belt I was using broke. Strangely, after a short while it did break! My wife wasn't resentful but remained calm. This made me feel ashamed and I was unable to sleep that night. I asked myself why I beat my wife, who had done nothing wrong. I cried painfully and woke her up to ask forgiveness. I thought of God but doubted if He would accept a bad person like me. She told me God loves me and is the Savior of all who believe in Him. I confessed my sins and prayed with her.[42]

The Fangcheng Church

Courageous house church evangelists in Henan
RCMI

Explosive growth in the "Jesus nest"

One of the largest house church networks to emerge from Henan is the Fangcheng Church, named after the county where it originated. In more recent years, after it expanded into every province of the country, the name "China for Christ" has been used to describe the larger church-planting organization. However, most of its members still refer to "the Fangcheng Mother Church" as the place where this tremendous movement began.

Compared with China's other major house church networks, the Fangcheng Church probably has the most contact with foreign Christians and has subsequently received the most publicity around the world.

The first Evangelical missionaries entered Fangcheng in 1886, but progress was excruciatingly slow, and by 1922 the county contained just 199 believers in seven churches.[1] By the time the People's Republic was founded in 1949, Fangcheng was home to 4,000 believers.[2] David Adeney was one missionary who labored in Fangcheng until his expulsion from China in the 1950s. He recalled:

> When the time came for our family to leave Fangcheng, we knew that the Lord had indeed established His Church in that area. We did not know about the ordeal that lay ahead—these Christians suffered terribly during the Cultural Revolution—but many years later, in 1979, we began to hear of great numbers of believers in the whole district. Fangcheng itself was called a "Jesus nest" by the Communists. Not only had the Church survived, it had grown and was sending out missionaries to other parts of China.[3]

In the decade following the end of the Cultural Revolution, Fangcheng experienced an explosive growth of Christianity, so that by 1985, 300,000 people in the county had reportedly become Christians.[4] This figure represented 43 percent of the total population of 700,000 at the time.

According to its own leaders, the Fangcheng house church network traces its origins to Gao Yongjiu, a captain in the Nationalist army who was converted in the 1940s. He proved to be a powerful evangelist, and many people throughout the county found Christ due to his preaching. In the 1950s, Gao and two other prominent church leaders were imprisoned for several years, and he was again incarcerated in 1966. On one occasion, Gao was paraded through the streets "wearing a thickly-padded cotton coat. The Red Guards beat him so hard with sticks that the cotton padding came flying out."[5]

The Fangcheng Church, which today boasts over ten million members, had its humble start in the village of Guan Zhuang. There were only six Christians there in the late 1960s, out of about 200 people. By 2002, however, 167 out of the 170 families in Guan Zhuang were followers of Jesus. Countless testimonies give glimpses into how God reached the village with great power. A woman named Chen Yurong was attending a prayer meeting while two of her nephews, aged five and nine, played near a well. Suddenly:

> She felt an intense urge to go to [the children], intuiting that one of her nephews might drown. As she approached, the nine-year-old cried in terror: his younger brother had fallen into the well. "Lord, save this boy! Let me die instead," Chen suddenly shouted out.
>
> Somehow, as other villagers gathered around to see what they could do, the boy spluttered to the surface. Ropes were let down and he was pulled out. "Did you swallow a lot of water?" someone asked anxiously. "No," said the boy. "There was a man in white holding me up."[6]

Many other miracles, especially healings, took place in this village in the late 1960s. A woman with breast cancer was completely cured, and people recognized that Jesus had the power to save. The gospel impacted many families and then spread to surrounding villages. Zhang Rongliang, the main leader of the Fangcheng Church, remembers the hunger believers had for God at the time:

> In the 1970s we were in great revival, and every Christian was engaged in fervent intercession for souls. If you walked through a village at night you would hear the weeping and pleading of many Christians on their knees crying out to the Lord.
>
> From 1972 to 1974, we organized three all-night prayer meetings every week. People were so hungry and desperate for the Lord. We had no teaching of the Scriptures because nobody had a Bible, so when we came together we just sang and prayed. People were so simple-hearted; they would believe the Lord for anything and everything. Messages from the Lord were

like honey dripping from heaven. The people were so eager for spiritual truth.[7]

The vital influence of Li Tian'en

The experienced Bible teacher Li Tian'en (who is regarded as one of the patriarchs of China's house churches) played a crucial role in giving early vision and direction to the Fangcheng Church. He was born in the county in 1928, although he spent most of his life living and ministering in Shanghai.

Li was imprisoned for ten years, from 1960 to 1970. Following his release, the authorities still had the man of God in their crosshairs and Li was imprisoned for another six years, after originally being sentenced to death. In 1980 the government placed him under house arrest for another decade, but he used that time to write several books, which proved to be a great blessing to believers in China.

During the times he was between imprisonments, Li visited Henan to train a new generation of church leaders there. In one meeting, "no less than an astonishing 4,000 attended a clandestine training session. The rapidly growing numbers of Christians made Fangcheng County a 'problem' county for Henan's officials."[8]

The formation of the Fangcheng Church

Like most of the other house church networks based in Henan, the Fangcheng Church came into existence as a structured fellowship in the early 1980s. Almost immediately, pairs of young evangelists were trained and sent to other parts of the province and beyond, and the movement began to expand rapidly. In 2002, Zhang Rongliang shared this account of their humble beginnings:

> In 1980 we had a secret prayer meeting in the mountains outside Fangcheng. The very next day eight young men believed in the Lord. The second day a young man was completely healed of cancer by the power of the Holy Spirit. This news spread rapidly among the villagers and many hundreds of people repented and surrendered their lives to Jesus. Because of the power of the Lord in answer to fervent prayer, the kingdom of God spread quickly.
>
> In 1980 we also received our first Bibles from outside China. We held them in our arms and kissed them delicately, with tears streaming from our eyes. They were the fulfillment of many years of desperate prayer and longing. Some elderly brothers and sisters had not touched a Bible for more than 20 years.
>
> Our church flourished and grew because many people denied themselves and followed Jesus wholeheartedly. In the beginning we were extremely poor. The whole church had a total of just 5 Yuan [less than $1] between us all! We know that what happened has truly been the work of the Lord, and not the efforts of men.
>
> One sister named Chen was desperate to serve God's people but had no money at all, so she went to the hospital and sold her blood, and used the money to purchase notebooks and pencils for our Bible class. The hospital paid just 2 Yuan [about 25 cents] for a liter of blood, but this was all she could do to serve God's people. She went back to the hospital frequently and sold her blood for us. Sister Chen is still serving the Lord today.[9]

A highly significant event in the history of the Fangcheng Church took place on China's National Day, October 1, 1981. Zhang organized a large prayer meeting that was attended by more than 400 house church leaders. The date was deliberately chosen in open defiance of the Communist authorities. A sheep was slaughtered for the evening meal, and the believers were enjoying rich fellowship together when more than 40 officers arrived in a string of police cars. A senior official addressed the church leaders and told them that the gathering was illegal and they must immediately disband. In reply, Zhang boldly declared that they would not stop until they were ready.

The officers were taken aback by this brazen challenge, and they stood by while the Christians enjoyed their dinner together. Then they moved in and started to arrest people, but Zhang managed to slip away. A house church historian said:

> This occasion was a turning point in the history of the Fangcheng Church. It moved from being underground to holding open meetings in front of the police. The evangelists became very bold. They traveled far and wide telling people to have nothing to do with the Three-Self.[10]

One of the senior Fangcheng leaders, Zheng Shuqian, recalled the pivotal event in an interview:

> The large crowd caught the attention of the Public Security Bureau and they came and surrounded our meeting place. Zhang Rongliang and I were told they had come to arrest us. I went to the head officer and sat beside him. I saw that he had a flashlight and a large knife attached to his belt, so I grabbed his flashlight and used it to read my songbook. All the believers then broke out in song, and then I declared: "Now the Lord's servant will preach!" The officers were stunned and waited before starting the arrests.
>
> Two minutes after Zhang Rongliang began to speak, the chief officer stood up and shouted, "Enough!" When he brandished his knife and threatened Brother Zhang, I stood up and proclaimed: "Let us protect our brother and keep him from falling into the hands of evil men!" Dozens of believers crowded around Zhang and carried him to safety. In the confusion and darkness the officers couldn't get near him and he escaped![11]

From 1980 to 1990 Zhang became a fugitive, unable to return home because the authorities were waiting for him. As he traveled throughout the country, he led many people to Christ. He also discipled and trained 80 men and women, who later became the core leaders of the Fangcheng Church. Zhang recalled the extreme devotion evident in the lives of many Christians at the time:

> Two of our young female co-workers were so committed to serving the Lord that they went to the hospital and had an operation so that they would never be able to have children. They didn't want to leave any chance at all that they might marry and share their devotion for the Lord with another.
>
> I remember a faithful brother who had only one leg. When he heard I was speaking in the area, he always tried to walk across the mountains to the meeting place on his one leg. Often he would walk for hours, but would arrive as everyone was leaving. That brother would get so mad! His devotion for the Lord was great, and he refused to let his disability stop him from knowing the Lord.[12]

A letter from Fangcheng

In 1985 a rare and insightful letter emerged from Fangcheng, addressed "To the brothers and sisters in other lands who bear the same burden of the Lord." The letter revealed both the bitter persecution and the powerful revival that was underway at the time:

> Fangcheng County in Henan is now receiving special blessing from the Lord. Among the 700,000 people in this county, there are at least 300,000 believers, and the number is increasing . . . The authorities call this place a "Jesus nest." The revival going on in Fangcheng today has arisen from more than 20 years of persecution. Most of the preachers are those who were released

> from prison in 1978–79. There is one senior pastor whose church had only several hundred people when he was first imprisoned, but it grew to several tens of thousands by the time he went to prison the second time.
>
> The authorities are thoroughly surprised. They can't understand why the more they persecute us, the faster we grow . . . Through suffering, God has deepened the faith of His children. We have come to know God more profoundly, and we are able to perceive the ways of the devil. We have also learned to entrust ourselves completely into the hands of the faithful and trustworthy God . . .
>
> Praise the Lord that we are able to overcome suffering. Satan has been shamed and forced to retreat. Although men are weak, by relying on the Lord we are able to triumph over Satan.
>
> Emmanuel![13]

In the mid-to-late 1980s, the Fangcheng Church began to come under the influence of the Hong-Kong-based American missionary Dennis Balcombe, and since that time it has been identified as one of the most overtly Pentecostal house church networks in China.

On one famous occasion in September 1992, Balcombe was smuggled from one village to another inside a coffin. The Public Security Bureau was dispatched to the village after reports of the presence of a foreign preacher, but the believers staged a mock funeral and walked right past the officers to safety. Balcombe tells the story:

> I was asked to speak the first evening to 160 leaders . . . The next day I was told the police were coming up the road. Several brothers immediately put me in a cart that is usually used to transport very sick people or corpses, put a lid on the top, and took me out of the village. They had only gone a few yards when they met a large group of PSB officers on the dirt road coming to arrest me . . .

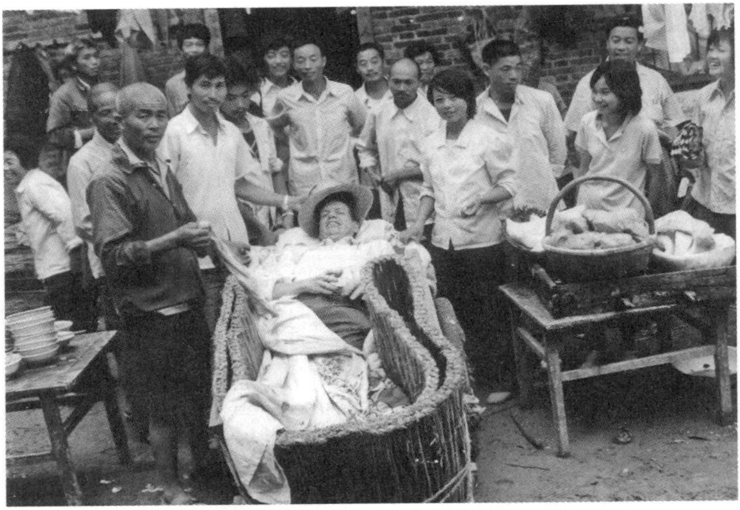

Dennis Balcombe in the coffin he was carried in to avoid arrest in 1992
RCMI

> This was obviously a very precarious situation, for once they saw me, I would have been arrested and the 160 leaders also would have gone to prison. But the Lord gave one of the brothers the right words to say. He told the head officer, "You should know that he had a very severe case of HIV/AIDS." This was the early 1990s, when many believed the AIDS virus could be easily transmitted by simple contact, or even through the air.
>
> The officer said: "Don't you dare open that coffin! At any rate I am going to arrest a criminal and have no time to speak with you. Get out of here!" Though I could not see anything because I was totally covered up, I felt the "coffin cart" moving at top speed over the bumpy trails. I said to myself, "This is great! If I had not believed in Jesus I would never have these exciting experiences."[14]

Through the years, the ministry of the Fangcheng Church has been marked by extraordinary signs and wonders that have attracted multitudes of people to Jesus Christ. In 1997 an evangelist, Brother Yang, went to a village where several hundred people came to hear the gospel. Some gangsters caused a disturbance to try to stop the meeting, but Yang said:

> I prayed and asked God to perform a miracle. God told me there were deaf people in the meeting. A sister brought a deaf woman, and when I prayed for her, she was immediately healed. I then asked all the deaf to come forward that night and they were all healed one by one . . . The gangsters looked on in amazement as they beheld the miracles. Then they returned to their homes and brought their sick family members to the meeting. Among them were eight paralytics, six of whom were healed instantly. Because of the miracles, the whole village including the gangsters believed in Jesus.[15]

The Gospel Month

The single most crucial factor in the explosive growth of the Fangcheng house churches was the "Gospel Month" initiative launched in the early 1990s. A fellowship with about 200 members came up with the idea in 1992. Between Christmas and the Chinese Lunar New Year—which is actually more than a month later—each of its members was required to lead at least three people to the Lord, while leaders were expected to reach at least five people.

The timing of the Gospel Month also contributed to its success. Being in midwinter and between two major national holidays, people were generally less busy than at other times. This was especially true in rural areas, where the demands of the harvest dominated people's time and strength for the rest of the year.

The Gospel Month initiative quickly spread to many other churches in Fangcheng, and soon thousands of Christians were mobilized to win their neighbors. The results were nothing short of incredible. After the Lunar New Year celebration in 1993, 13,000 new believers were baptized—and they were trained to take part in a similar outreach the following year. By that time, however, the Christians had realized there was no point confining their soul-winning efforts to just one month each year, and many became evangelists during the other 11 months as well. At the conclusion of the Gospel Month in early 1994, the house churches conducted a total of 123,000 baptisms throughout Henan. The leader of the Fangcheng Church, Zhang Rongliang, reflected on those extraordinary days:

> We saw God move in a mighty way. Churches everywhere experienced great revival and many people were saved daily. The things we experienced were beyond anything we had even thought possible. During the Gospel Month in 1994, in a period of a little over 50 days, there were more than 120,000 confirmed conversions to Christ in Henan alone.
>
> Previously, during our open-air meetings, few people would pay attention. Now, everywhere we went, crowds of people stopped whatever they were doing to listen. As we preached, many cried out: "We have never heard such good news in all our lives. Why has nobody told us this before?" The people put aside all their plans and activities and remained for hours to hear the gospel. This was God's work, and the Holy Spirit confirmed His Word with signs and wonders.[16]

Since 1994, the number of people saved each year as a result of the Gospel Month has grown too large to keep track of. Fangcheng has one of the highest concentrations of Christians of any place in China, and they have sent thousands of evangelists to all parts of the country. Remarkably, by God's providence, the formerly small, impoverished farming area of Fangcheng has earned the reputation as an engine room for mighty revival throughout China.

Unusual miracles attract many to Christ

The miracles that occurred during the Gospel Month campaigns are far too many to recount. A few examples shared by leaders of the Fangcheng Church will have to suffice here.

In Zhoukou during the 1994 Gospel Month, a Christian with a gift of healing saw God completely heal 26 deaf people. Another man had been born with severe mental disabilities. Everyone in the area despised him and called him an "idiot." After being prayed for, he was completely restored. God gave him a brilliant mind, excellent speech, and many talents, which astonished all who knew him. As a direct result of this miracle, 83 people believed in the Lord.

There had been about 5,000 house church Christians in Xinye County before the 1994 Gospel Month. By the end of it, 15,000 new converts had been baptized, quadrupling the number of believers in a single month. Zhang Rongliang recalled a remarkable incident that occurred in Xinye:

> So many people gathered on the road to hear the gospel that the traffic was blocked. The police arrived with their sirens blazing

Three generations of a family listening intently to the gospel

> to see what the commotion was. They were enraged to find thousands of people pressing in to hear the gospel. The chief of police got out of his car and stretched out his hand, commanding us to stop as we were under arrest.
>
> Just like King Jeroboam in the Old Testament [1 Kings 13:4–6], the police chief could not pull his arm back in once he stretched it out! The people carried him back to his car and put him inside, but he was still unable to pull his arm back in. Everyone knew this was God's judgment on him for persecuting God's children, and hundreds more people opened their hearts to the Lord.
>
> Advisers told the chief that he must ask Christians to pray for him and that he should treat believers with respect. He called some local church leaders to his home, had his wife prepare a nice meal for them, and when they prayed for his arm he was instantly healed. He repented from his sins and attended a Bible study.[17]

During the 1995 Gospel Month, five young ruffians disrupted an evangelistic meeting, shouting obscenities and challenging everything the preacher said. When the time came for prayer, the preacher asked Jesus to teach the five men a lesson. When he prayed, "Lord, please bind them!" the men immediately knelt down on the ground and put their hands behind their backs as though they were bound with a tight rope. People tried to help them up, but they were as heavy as rocks and could not be moved. Several strong men were unable to lift even one of the thugs to his feet.

Curiously, the young men were still able to speak even though they were otherwise immobilized. They offered the preacher money and cigarettes if he would pray for their release, but he said, "No way! Jesus wants your hearts. If He doesn't loosen you, nobody in the world will be able to help you." More than a hundred people repented and were saved after witnessing this sign—and all the five men gave their lives to Jesus Christ.

In 2002, Zhang Rongliang reflected on the Gospel Month campaigns. Speaking with a childlike awe, he said:

> At times, the police recognized the power of God was at work, and they were too afraid to do anything to us. In some places, officers were dispatched to meetings not to arrest us but to ensure the crowd was orderly.
>
> It was amazing to see how the Lord put such expectancy in people's hearts during the Gospel Month campaigns. I have seen people climb onto the roofs of their homes or hang onto tree branches in order to hear the gospel.
>
> We witnessed entire communities invigorated and transformed by the power of Jesus Christ. In 1994, I visited one county where nobody knew me. I had to repair my shoes, and while I was waiting the repairman shared the gospel with me and tried to lead me to the Lord. Later that day I went to a barber shop for a haircut, and while I was in the chair the barber shared the gospel with me. I was the founder of the Gospel Month, but now I had become a target for evangelism!
>
> Once I caught a train and noticed that one man had a Bible, so I asked if he was a Christian. He said yes, and we enjoyed rich fellowship together. I thought the man sitting between us was an unbeliever, so I asked if he would mind changing seats so I could talk with the brother during the journey. The man in the middle objected, saying he also was a Christian so we should all fellowship together![18]

Zhang Rongliang

Zhang Rongliang, the founder and principal leader of the Fangcheng Church, was born in 1951. He became a Christian at the age of 12, largely due to the godly influence of his grandfather. In 1969, Zhang became a member of the Communist

Zhang Rongliang in the 1980s

Party, but five years later the government learned that Zhang secretly followed Christ and he was arrested. When he refused to abandon his faith, he was severely beaten with blows to his head and body. He was sentenced to seven years in the Xihua Prison labor camp, where he met Feng Jianguo, the founder of the Tanghe Church, and other believers who later played key roles in the Henan house church revivals. Zhang recalls:

> The labor camp was a place of mental and physical torture. Often we had to carry heavy loads on our backs for 16 hours per day. The believers soon realized we had to help one another; otherwise the experience would be impossible to bear.
>
> Deng Xiaoping became the president of China while I was in prison, and all inmates were offered freedom if they would renounce their "crimes." I prayed about it and decided I would rather stay inside than seek an early release, as it was better to suffer with my fellow believers than compromise my faith.[19]

Only two days after finally regaining his freedom in 1980, Zhang decided to visit some of the house churches he had established before his confinement. As he enjoyed fellowship with the believers, the police arrived and rearrested him, shattering the hopes of his wife, Chen Hongxian, that their family might enjoy a more settled life. Zhang shared some of the struggles his family have endured over the years:

> My wife has been a great warrior for the Lord, and she gradually accepted the call the Lord has placed on my life. I have not been able to return home for Chinese New Year for 27 years. During that time I have been in prison or on the run from the authorities, or with believers somewhere else in the country. I appreciate her support and faithfulness over many difficult years.[20]

Sacrificial love

Anyone who spends time with the core leaders of the Fangcheng Church will soon recognize how much Zhang means to them. He is greatly honored for the sacrifices he has made. One of the movement's founding leaders, Sister Mei, told the author:

> Today, most of the main leaders in Fangcheng are those who were part of the original group of 80. We love and respect Zhang Rongliang because he is always willing to give up his own rights to follow the Lord. For example, in 1984 we were extremely poor. We didn't have any money or possessions at all. We didn't even have bicycles, so we had to walk everywhere.
>
> One day the leadership team was asked to attend a meeting in another county. There was no way we could walk that far, and we didn't have any money. Although Zhang owned just one cow, he sold it and gave the money to us so we could attend the meeting. This showed us the depth of his dedication and service. His way of life is consistent with Jesus' example. God blessed him and his ministry because he was willing to deny himself, take up his cross, and follow Jesus.[21]

Extraordinary boldness

Zhang's ministry has always been marked by extraordinary boldness. He has refused to bow to intimidation, believing that China should be a country where Christians openly worship God and preach the gospel. He expects China to conform to God's will, rather than the Church conforming to China's will.

His boldness has included openly giving interviews to foreign journalists. In 1998, a reporter from the American newspaper *The Oregonian* asked Zhang at the start of an interview what concerns he had for his security. He replied: "If you don't write, they'll come to get us. If you do write, they'll come to get us. But the difference is that the people outside will know what's happening to the Church here."[22]

Streetwise and adaptable, Zhang is noted for his casual appearance as well as his complete lack of fear. After mobile phones became available in China, he was rarely seen without one in his hand, keeping in constant contact with his church leaders. "Wearing sandals and khaki shorts with a frequently ringing cell phone in his pocket," wrote the reporter from *The Oregonian*, "Zhang Rongliang didn't look like the founder of one of the world's largest underground Christian networks, much less a threat to the Chinese Communist government."[23]

Zhang's freedom again came to an abrupt end on August 23, 1999, when he was arrested with 31 other leaders from four different house church networks. After being violently beaten and kicked, all but six of the arrested leaders were released after paying fines. The remaining six, including Zhang, were charged with "using an evil cult to undermine the law" and were sentenced to between one and three years in prison.

On February 3, 2000, just five and a half months into his prison term, Zhang was released early on account of poor health. He immediately resumed his itinerant ministry, but was careful not to stay in the same place for more than four consecutive days to reduce the risk of arrest.

Zhang's overseas travels

In 2002, Zhang Rongliang began to preach in churches throughout Asia and the West. This development surprised many people both inside and outside China. No one could understand how a man with his criminal record was able to obtain a passport. The truth about how he managed it would later hurt him.

During his travels to various countries, Zhang was approached by well-meaning Christians who wanted to help him settle in America, where he could live in relative peace and quiet. He turned down the offers, saying: "For my family and for my safety, I wish I could be in the United States, secure in

Zhang Rongliang in 2002
Paul Hattaway

that wonderful land. But for my church and for God's people, I have to go back to China."[24]

On December 1, 2004, Zhang was imprisoned for the sixth time in his life. For six months little was heard of his whereabouts, until he finally appeared in court on June 6, 2005. Many of his supporters hoped he would be let off, but it soon became clear that Beijing had taken an interest in his case and a heavy sentence was likely.

In court, Zhang was charged with "obtaining a passport through cheating and illegal border crossing."[25] He was sentenced to seven and a half years in prison. Later, when the official court documents were released, it was revealed that he had obtained a total of 13 passports under false names, using them to make 15 trips overseas.[26]

Some Western mission organizations distanced themselves from him after hearing the reason for his sentence, but others said the fact he had been denied the freedom to travel was itself a form of persecution. Christian Solidarity Worldwide stated:

> The case would not have arisen if it were not for the discrimination faced by religious figures in the issuing of passports, freedom of movement and freedom of association with co-religionists abroad, all of which are in violation of international standards. The sentencing of Pastor Zhang demonstrates how the persecution of religious believers can be disguised by other seemingly unrelated charges.[27]

Zhang's sixth time in prison was the most difficult of his life. Five chronic diseases, including high blood pressure and advanced diabetes, caused him to be admitted to the hospital several times. One witness reported seeing Zhang handcuffed and chained to his hospital bed.[28]

Finally, on August 31, 2011, Zhang Rongliang was released from prison. Since that time he has kept a lower profile than in previous years, quietly leading what remains of the Fangcheng Church still under his authority.

In 2016 and 2017, Zhang was one of a small group of senior Chinese house church leaders summoned to Beijing for face-to-face meetings with President Xi Jinping. Although the contents of those meetings have been kept confidential, a tidal wave of persecution broke out against the house churches shortly afterward. Most commentators believe the pastors were offered one last chance to register their churches with the government, and the subsequent crackdown reveals the non-compliance by Zhang and the other leaders.

Without doubt, God has greatly used the courageous Zhang Rongliang. He has been hugely influential, and a vast network of house churches containing millions of believers throughout China emerged under his leadership. Journalist David Aikman has said of him:

> It is hard to think of any house church leader in China who has been more visionary or entrepreneurial in evangelizing not only his own country but anywhere in the world. Zhang is the most influential Christian leader today in the Church in China. Of the leaders of the five main groups, he has been the most mature, the wisest, and the most tolerant. He has a strong influence on all of the people. He is the person all the leaders look up to.[29]

Ding Hei

One of the key women to emerge from the Fangcheng house church movement is Ding Hei, who was born in 1961. The respected author David Aikman, who is not given to hyperbole, remembers the first time he met her in 1999:

> Taller than most Chinese women, slim, attractive, shorthaired, and with a ready smile, she would have been striking in any

Sister Ding Hei

> professional environment. Within just a few minutes of conversation she was demonstrating . . . vivid narrative skills, a keen analytical mind, obvious charm, and dazzling self-confidence. She was used to being a leader and she was also used to having everyone around her know that she was good at it.[30]

Ding's mother became a secret follower of Christ in the late 1960s after being healed from an eye disease. She kept her faith private because her husband was a leading Communist cadre in the village and was responsible for persecuting religious believers. Ding Hei first placed her trust in Christ at the age of 13. She was the only Christian in her school, but within six months 40 of her classmates also became believers.

When an intense persecution broke out against the Fangcheng Church in 1974, Ding was still in school, but she remembers watching the trial of Zhang Rongliang on a television in the classroom as her teachers taught the students what happens to "Christian criminals." Little did Ding know that she would later become one of the key leaders of the church movement led by Zhang.

In the mid 1970s, Ding's father discovered that both his wife and daughter were secret Christians. He frequently beat them, and destroyed the pages of Scripture they had meticulously copied by hand from a borrowed Bible. Despite this, Ding Hei refused to be intimidated and continued to attend meetings, only to return home and face another beating. These stressful times helped to prepare the teenager for the many persecutions that would later mark her ministry for Christ.

After years of fruitful evangelism throughout China, Ding was finally captured in October 1989. She was interrogated 123 times as the authorities sought to learn everything they could about the Fangcheng Church and its contact with foreigners. After Ding refused to betray any of her co-workers, she was sentenced to three years in a labor camp near Zhengzhou. Her gifts soon emerged in the prison, and within weeks she was promoted to cell-block leader of 189 female inmates.

Ding was released in March 1992. In the following year she was rearrested, but managed to escape in time to attend her own wedding. In 2001, she told the author about her role in the Fangcheng house church movement and expressed her concerns for the future of the Chinese Church:

> We have 21 main teams of workers, which are separated into five regional units. I am responsible for the north China team: Inner Mongolia, Shandong, Hebei, Liaoning, Jilin, Beijing, Tianjin, and the northern part of Henan Province north of the Yellow River. This responsibility means I travel frequently to many different provinces.
>
> Today, I am worried that the younger generation of house church believers are not as committed as previous generations.

> They haven't had to cling to the cross as tightly as we did. Twenty years ago our only options were to serve the Lord or face a life of struggle and hardship on the farm. We figured we might as well experience hardship while serving the Lord! There are many new distractions and temptations for young believers today.
>
> I have faced the daily pressure of being hunted by the Public Security Bureau. Zhang Rongliang is their number one target, and I am number two. If they catch him I will be upgraded to their number one target. Please pray for us.[31]

A few years after this interview, Sister Ding retired from her exhausting itinerant ministry, choosing to spend more time with her family and lead a more settled life. She spoke of her deep desire to mentor a new generation of house church leaders:

> We see our founders as heroes . . . always in and out of prisons. We don't mind arrests, or imprisonments. But in all other areas our leaders did not mentor us. They were far too busy. Or they themselves didn't know how to mentor us to face the new challenges of today.[32]

From her new home base, Sister Ding Hei continues to be a great blessing to those who have contact with her.

Lu Xiaomin

It is clear that in Henan, instead of using strong, qualified workers to do His work, God has often chosen to use many lowly and uneducated followers who have hearts willing to submit to the Holy Spirit. No greater example of this truth can be found than the remarkable testimony of Ruth Lu Xiaomin, a shy young woman from Fangcheng who obeyed God's call and became a great blessing to the whole Church in China.

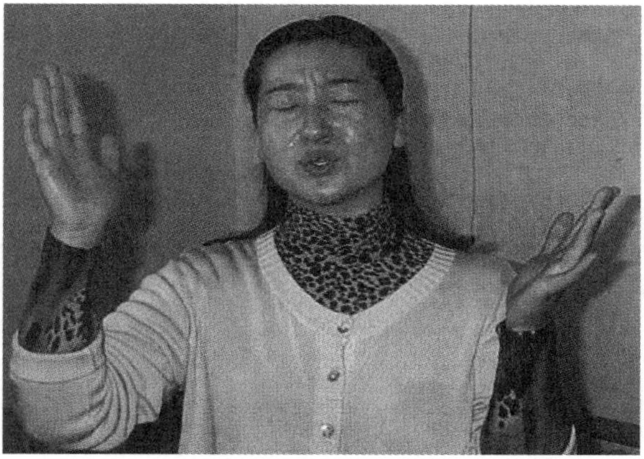

Sister Lu Xiaomin

Born in 1970, she grew up with a limited education. Her family belonged to the Hui ethnic minority group, whose members are the descendants of Muslim traders and soldiers who migrated to China many centuries ago. Xiaomin first heard the good news as a teenager when her aunt shared it with her, and she responded immediately.

After attending a worship meeting in 1989, Xiaomin was lying in bed when the words and melody of a song came to her mind. She had never studied music and was surprised at what had occurred. Not wanting to appear proud, the only person she shared the song with was another young girl from her village. She, in turn, began to sing the song and her parents asked where she had learned it. When Xiaomin was questioned as to how she had composed the song, she simply replied that she had received it from the Holy Spirit.

Over the following months, many more songs were given to her by the Lord. Often the words were inspired by the beauty of nature, and at other times the hymns reflected the struggles and suffering of the Chinese Church. She faithfully wrote the words down, and later a Christian recorded the 23 songs Xiaomin had composed by that time. Something about the simplicity and holiness of her songs touched all who heard them, and they were soon disseminated widely by evangelists who heard them while visiting Fangcheng and took them back to their mission bases around the country.

In 1992, Xiaomin was arrested and imprisoned for more than two months after a house church meeting was raided by the police. While she was incarcerated she wrote another 14 worship songs, and by the mid 1990s she was composing a new song every few days, and a system had been established where the words and melodies would be recorded and transcribed by others, and then taught in house churches the length and breadth of the country. One writer explained:

> Xiaomin is unschooled in music or musical theory. When she writes a song, she does not think in terms of music beat, tempo, and rhythm. When the Spirit moves her to write songs, she just sings out the melody and lyrics that impress her. After a few rounds of practice, she has the song recorded. She then passes the recorded work to someone to write out the musical notes.[33]

Now married and with children, Xiaomin has largely remained in her home area in Fangcheng and seems reluctant to travel far, despite many requests. She has composed nearly 2,000 songs, and her music has featured in television documentaries and has even been performed by professional orchestras.

The "Songs of Canaan," as they came to be known, also made their way into Three-Self and Catholic churches, while many unbelievers who heard them have been attracted to Jesus. Well over one million songbooks containing her compositions have been printed and distributed throughout China and overseas.

God has used this humble farming girl, whose ancestors were Muslims, to touch the lives of millions of people and direct them to Jesus. She is motivated by a deep love of God and her nation, and once declared: "Even if there is only one drop of blood left in me, I will spill it for China. Even if there is just one breath left in me, I will devote it to China."[34]

While many people have desired to know the "secret" behind Lu Xiaomin's remarkable ability to compose so many beautiful and anointed worship songs, she remains unassuming and offers no explanation except that it is a supernatural gift, by the grace of God.

A challenging future

The number of Christians associated with the Fangcheng Church nationwide is believed to have increased from five million in the early 1990s[35] to ten million in 1999.[36]

A major split in 2002–3 caused a number of Fangcheng Church leaders to leave and start a new group, which has been referred to as the "New Fangcheng Church." This group is primarily responsible for local believers in the Fangcheng area, rather than the nationwide movement. Some claim the split was caused by issues of unresolved sin and oppressive control by Zhang Rongliang and other leaders, while others believe that foreign money induced second-level leaders to usurp their elders.

Since the start of the new millennium the Fangcheng Church has continued to grow, though perhaps at a slower rate than during the height of revival in the 1980s and 1990s.

Since its inception, the expansion of the Fangcheng Church has been truly spectacular. It has been a genuine work of God, implemented through the humble sacrifices of many men and women. Although there have been problems along the way, and controversies surrounding some of its leaders, God has unquestionably blessed and empowered the Fangcheng Church in a mighty way, and as a result millions of people throughout China have become His children.

2000s

A huge crowd of believers attending a Three-Self church in Henan

Sheep without shepherds

Astonishing church growth continued to occur throughout Henan at the start of the new millennium. Although they are considered illegal, the house church movements had one major advantage over their Three-Self counterparts in that they aren't bound by religious and political restrictions. As the registered TSPM churches also grew, their progress was affected by a chronic shortage of pastors and church workers to take care of the new converts. The Henan Seminary, located in Luoyang, had graduated more than 1,000 theology students since its inception in 1989, but the impact had been little more than a drop in the bucket in a province where even the authorities acknowledged 3.5 million TSPM members in 1996.[1]

Even if every seminary graduate had ended up serving God's flock in Henan, each one would have to take care of 3,500 Christians. Unfortunately, many of those who graduated from the seminary did not remain long in the ministry. Church leaders reportedly "found themselves trapped in a spiral of ever-worsening poverty, until they finally had no choice but to leave home and become migrant workers."[2]

Some of the official statistics from Henan were deeply alarming. In 1996, the 50,000 TSPM Christians in Gushi County were served by a single pastor, while Zhumadian Prefecture—with an estimated 200,000 registered believers—had just two pastors and nine elders.[3]

By 2001, there were a mere 100 TSPM pastors serving churches in the whole of Henan Province, along with 394 elders and 3,000 evangelists.[4] With 1,100 registered churches and 5,000 meeting points at the time, each pastor in Henan was responsible for an average of 61 congregations and 35,000 believers![5]

Misguided Westerners

At the dawn of the new millennium, certain Western church and mission leaders ignorantly claimed that persecution of Christians in China was a thing of the past and that believers now enjoyed religious freedom. In making such unenlightened claims, those leaders shamefully denied the sacrifices of thousands of suffering Chinese brothers and sisters who love Jesus Christ.

In 2005, the well-known Argentine-American evangelist Luis Palau even issued a statement urging all Chinese believers to register with the Three-Self Patriotic Movement, saying:

Four Henan gospel warriors in 2002: Brother Yun, Enoch Wang Xincai, Zhang Rongliang, and Peter Xu Yongze. Together they have spent 47 years in prison for their faith in Jesus Christ
Paul Hattaway

"You can't get away with defying order. I feel that registering is a positive thing for the followers of Jesus. Believers should live in the open."[6]

Stung by a chorus of criticism, Palau reconsidered his statement and said ten days later:

> It's not my role as an evangelist to suggest that churches in China should register . . . It would pain me deeply if any of my comments would provoke any kind of trouble for God's saints in the People's Republic of China. And I pray our Sovereign Lord would not allow it.[7]

The following year, yet another Western church leader displayed his ignorance when Dr. Rowan Williams, the Archbishop of Canterbury, said: "China's a long way past the Cultural

Revolution—a long way past a situation where there is a systematic attempt to block out or extirpate religion."[8]

On the ground in Henan, meanwhile, more than 300 leaders of the Born-Again house church movement alone were behind bars for the sake of the gospel at the dawn of the new millennium, and several of Henan's house church networks provided Asia Harvest with a list of more than 1,000 Christians who had been crippled or badly injured during torture sessions while in detention.[9]

In the first months of 2000, things seemed relatively quiet in Henan, but in August a fresh wave of persecution broke over the churches. It was noted: "In that single month, another 142 believers were arrested in Henan as authorities continued their crackdown on unregistered churches."[10]

On August 10, a dozen members of the China Gospel Fellowship were arrested in Yucheng County, and a few weeks later on August 26—ironically at exactly the time a delegation of Chinese religious leaders were traveling throughout the United States trying to convince politicians and church leaders that there was complete religious freedom in China—130 believers affiliated with the Fangcheng Church were arrested in Xihua County, after 50 Public Security officers swooped on their meeting. Many of the detainees later testified that they had been mercilessly tortured.

The martyrdom of Liu Haitou

Yet another Christian was added to the long list of Henan's martyrs at the start of the twenty-first century. The 21-year-old Liu Haitou died on the night of October 15, 2000, in Xiayi, after being severely beaten by the authorities. Liu was arrested on September 4 when the police raided a house church meeting he was attending. Subjected to daily beatings and weakened by

Liu Haitou, martyred for Christ in 2000

the prison's poor hygiene and barely edible food, he developed a high fever and started vomiting.

Liu's parents were notified of their son's arrest on September 28, three and a half weeks after he was taken into custody. They were ordered to come down to the local police station and pay 5,000 Yuan (approximately $600) for his release, but as a poor farming family they had no way to raise this sum. Liu was harshly beaten with sticks and other tools, causing him to faint on several occasions.

The other Christians in the prison pleaded with the guards to give him medical attention, but their requests were ignored until October 15, when, realizing Liu was dying, officers took him to the prison hospital, where they tried to evade responsibility by releasing him. One report stated:

> When Haitou's father carried him for emergency medical treatment, the weighty leg irons still bound him, right up to six hours before his death. Haitou never complained. There were

> no struggles with death. He left quietly and peacefully in the middle of a dark night, amid his mother's tearful prayers.[11]

That night, Liu's face radiated peace and joy as he told his mother, "I am very happy. I am fine. Mother, persist in our belief and follow Him to the end. I am going now. Pray for me."[12]

As he lay cradled in his mother's loving arms, his final word as he left this world was "Amen."

Liu Haitou had been a Christian for only 18 months, but had gained a reputation as a young man who loved God with all his heart. In prison, he had shared his meager food rations with his fellow inmates, hoping they might see the goodness of Jesus in his life. His commitment is summed up in this excerpt from a letter he wrote before his arrest:

> By His unlimited great love, the Lord saved me. He leads me to eternal life and entitles me to become a son of God. How can I ignore His salvation and freely accept His grace without doing something for Him in return? More than 90 percent of people in China don't know God. My heart is broken. If the Lord is going to use me, I am ready to give my life to Him and start the journey of serving Him.[13]

The struggle continues

Shocking pictures of the actual persecution of Christians emerged from China in 2002, after a police photographer was so disgusted by what he saw that he smuggled the images out of the country before going into hiding. Although it is painful to look at pictures of fellow believers being treated so cruelly, many house church members were glad the images were smuggled out of China because they revealed the stark reality of their long struggle with the Communist Party. Chinese believers had long been amazed to hear that many Christians around the

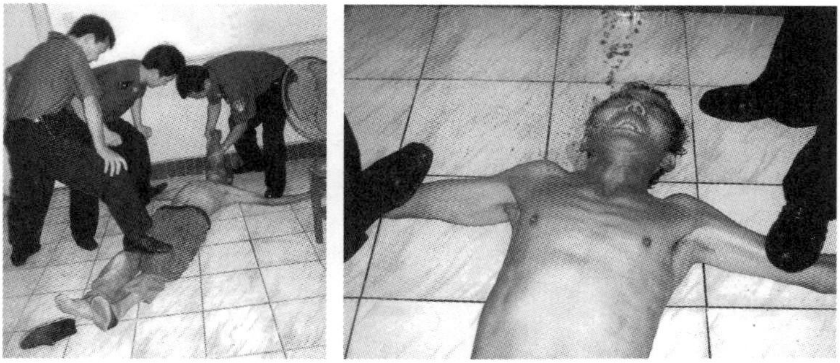

Cai Xiangdong being tortured by the police in Xiayi in August 2002
CIPRC

world believed the lie that there is no persecution in China. The pictures made it more difficult for church leaders in the West to make such ignorant and reprehensible claims.

As the much-persecuted Brother Yun said after leaving the country:

> The government and the Three-Self Patriotic Movement have fooled many Christians around the world by insisting there is freedom of religion in China; freedom for people to choose. They boldly claim Christians are no longer persecuted for their faith.
>
> My own personal experiences—as well as those of thousands of other house church believers—are quite the opposite. On one occasion when I was arrested the authorities let me choose whether I wanted to be shocked with an electronic baton or whipped with a rope. They mocked me and said, "This is your free choice."
>
> There is "freedom" of religion in China only if you're willing to do, say, live and worship exactly as the government instructs you. Anyone who desires to live a godly life and obey Jesus' teachings will soon find out how much freedom there really is.[14]

The harrowing photographs that were smuggled out of China included images of the ordeal of a female house church Christian named Jiang Dongyun, who was seized in Qingfeng County in north-east Henan. She was taken to the local Public Security office and abused for three hours by a 30-year-old officer called Lu Dengkun, who stamped on her ankles before sexually assaulting her. Jiang later testified that the wicked man "stood on my feet and ground them in a rolling action. As I screamed in pain, he took a piece of cloth, which was full of shoe polish, and stuffed it into my mouth."[15]

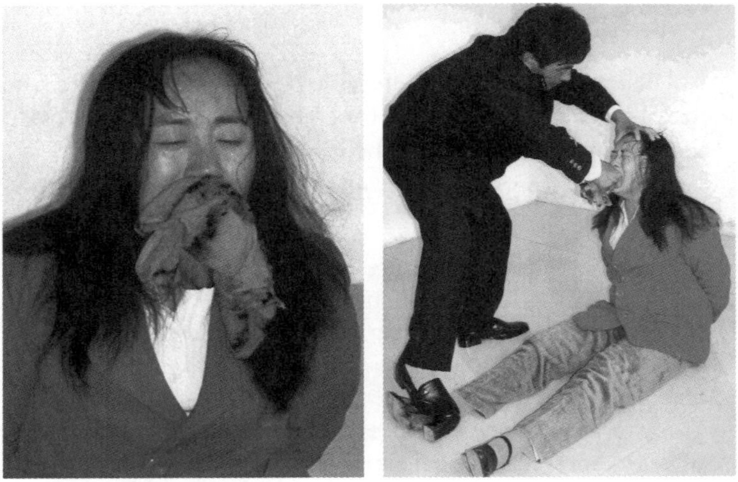

Jiang Dongyun being tortured in Qingfeng in 2002
CIPRC

Revival spreads to the cities

Since the majority of Henan's house church believers come from rural farming areas, it has long been assumed that they were incapable of carrying the revival into the more sophisticated cities. This has clearly proven to be untrue, however, and churches have also grown exponentially in major cities since the turn of the century.

In April 2000, a foreign Christian attending an urban house church felt impressed by the Lord that there was someone in the meeting who had not obeyed God's call to be a missionary. After he asked the assembly seven times whether anyone present had disobeyed a specific call, a young woman came forward and revealed that a few years earlier the Holy Spirit had clearly told her to be a missionary to Myanmar, but she had become immersed in her studies and God's call on her life was pushed aside.

After an intense time of prayer and worship, the young woman was prayed for and commissioned by those present. The meeting ended just before midnight, at which point the young woman left and the foreigner assumed she had gone home for a good night's rest. The next day, he noticed she was absent and asked where she was:

> "Oh, she left this morning," one of the other students replied.
>
> "Left? Where to?" the visitor asked.
>
> "Well," someone said, "she was called to the mission field last night, so she lined up a partner and they left on the bus at 4:00 a.m. this morning. They have gone to Myanmar!"[16]

Letters from Henan

2001

> Since 1997 we have witnessed the preachers of our mother church twisting the truth. Though we have shared God's Word with them on numerous occasions, the situation has not changed. At the end of 1998 they made a public proclamation: "One cannot be saved by trusting the Bible but only through

our preaching. All intercessory prayers are censured and all meetings are to be stopped. The number of people called by the Lord has been met so there is to be no more sharing of the gospel." This decree has truly deceived many believers. We have determined to break relations with this church. Is this the right thing to do?[17]

Our church has a youth fellowship for teenagers and 20-year-olds. Praise God, since it started with two members in 1998 it has grown to several dozen! Now many more lost souls are being gathered in! They join us and become children of God! I know that being a Christian is not just repenting in one's heart, but there must also be a change in one's conduct, speech and life. Even if we suffer for the Lord, we are blessed! No one has suffered more than our Lord suffered for us.[18]

2003

I am a 20-year-old man born in a small mountain village in Henan. I grew up knowing God's love, and my father was a leading Christian worker . . . Last year, I attended a Bible school run by a teacher from South Korea. He had great faith and set up two classes. The teacher said he could never abandon his 100 students because they were the future hope of the Chinese house churches.

But last November, the school was discovered by the Public Security Bureau after our meetings were reported by some church leaders. We never imagined that they would betray their own people! My Korean teacher was sent home and not allowed to return to China. Several other students and I were detained by the police for a day.

When we were released, many of our fellow students were waiting for us, and we wept as we embraced one another. Thus our Bible school was brought to an end. Now I am at home quietly waiting on the Lord. I long for the time when there will be another opportunity for theological training. This is the desire of the other 100 brothers and sisters. Please pray for us.[19]

2006

Today we have 30 churches in Zhengzhou City, but only ten full-time leaders—the harvest is great but we are short of workers. We are especially lacking Bible teachers, and have to beg other churches to send their teachers to us. Please pray for us, and may God send some teachers and workers to our midst. If you know some believers who are gifted teachers, please send them to us. Let's serve the Lord together![20]

2007

Thank you so much for blessing our fellowships by providing Bibles to us. The growth in numbers and in spiritual strength that our fellowships have experienced in recent years is in large part due to our members having the Bible to feed upon daily. In the past we were very happy to share one Bible for an entire group; some of our churches didn't have even a single Bible and they had to borrow from others. Just to meet the current need within our church network alone, 2,138,000 Bibles are required.

Please pray we will be strong in the Holy Spirit as we face opposition and persecution because of our faith. It is truly an honor to share the sufferings of our Lord Jesus Christ. Thank you so much for sharing God's precious Word with us![21]

2008

We received the 4,100 Bibles and 650 study Bibles from your contact. Praise the Lord! In the past 12 months the Lord has graciously enabled us to reach more than 60,000 souls for Jesus, and we are now praying and striving to nourish these newborn babes in Christ. Without God's Word this is impossible. The Scriptures you sent were received like hungry children longing for good and satisfying food. Please pray we will receive at least 50,000 more Bibles from the hand of the Lord, so that none of our new believers would be without a copy of God's holy Word.[22]

2010s

The Cultural Revolution revisited

At a time when many voices are trumpeting China's supposed improved human rights record to the world, house church believers in Henan continue to be brutally persecuted for their faith, throughout the 2010s and until the present day. Once China had successfully hosted the Olympic Games in 2008, the nation's leaders felt confident that it had now emerged onto the world stage as a respectable power, and they altered the methods they employed to crush God's children. The government drove the persecution into the dark, far from the world's gaze.

After closing all the dreaded prison labor camps in 2014, China secretly shifted the places where it conducts torture to "black jails"—secure facilities constructed inside abandoned warehouses, old junkyards, and the like. Thousands of Chinese Christians were forcibly taken to such locations, and many were never heard from again. When someone is taken to a black jail, his or her family members are not given any formal notification of arrest, and local officials deny any knowledge of the person's whereabouts. The victim simply disappears, but the very few who have managed to escape tell of the horrendous and inhuman treatment meted out to people.

Buried alive for Christ

Not all attacks on the body of Christ in Henan were conducted in shadowy places, however. On April 18, 2016, a sickening

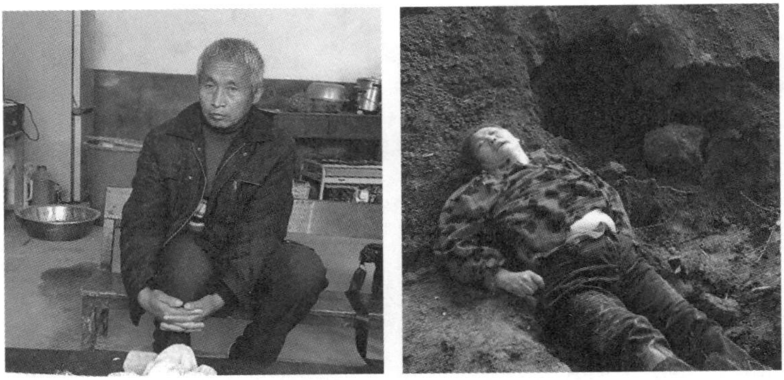

Li Jiangong and the body of Ding Cuimei
China Aid

incident occurred in Zhumadian when a house church leader, named Li Jiangong, and his wife Ding Cuimei were buried alive by the head of a government construction unit.

The diabolical story began when the authorities ordered the destruction of the Beitou Church. Bulldozers were sent to demolish the building and claim the land, which was legally owned by the local Christians. Li and Ding protested vehemently, with dozens of their church members looking on. The China Aid Association reported:

> On April 1st, a government-backed company dispatched personnel to bulldoze Beitou Church in Zhumadian, after a local developer wished to take control of the church's valuable property. Li Jiangong and his wife, Ding Cuimei, stepped in front of the machinery in an attempt to stop the demolition.
>
> "Bury them alive for me!" a member of the demolition team said. "I will be responsible for their lives."
>
> Subsequently, a bulldozer shoved Li and Ding into a pit and covered their bodies with soil. Crying for help, Li was able to dig his way free, but Ding suffocated before she could be rescued.[1]

Photographs and video of the horrific event were taken by church members and uploaded to the internet, shocking people around the globe.

In the aftermath of this cruel and barbarous act, the Chinese government seemed more concerned about the worldwide publicity the murder had attracted than the brutal slaying itself. Criminal charges were brought against the construction manager, and Li was told the government's case against the church property had been dropped and he could continue to occupy the land.

Less than a week after Ding Cuimei was buried alive in Henan, the Chinese president Xi Jinping spoke at a national conference on religion in Beijing. *Christianity Today* reported:

> He called on leaders to take the initiative in reasserting Communist Party control over religion . . . His speech directed religious groups to "dig deep into doctrines and canons that are in line with social harmony and progress . . . and interpret religious doctrines in a way that is conducive to modern China's progress and in line with our excellent traditional culture."[2]

Xi's determination to rid China of all religious belief outside governmental control increased in 2017 and subsequent years, with millions of believers throughout Henan forced to return to practices not seen since the Cultural Revolution in the 1960s and 1970s.

Against all expectations, the Church in Henan was again forced underground. Facing a firestorm of brutal persecution, congregations of hundreds—and even thousands—of believers suspended their large gatherings. Small prayer and Bible study meetings of four or five believers became the norm again throughout the country.

Christian families faced harsh discrimination, and the children of believing parents found their paths to higher education blocked. Countless church buildings were demolished and hundreds of pastors and evangelists arrested.

The government stepped up its use of new technology to identify and disrupt clandestine Bible production, and Bible apps and websites were blocked, leading to a famine of God's Word in the land.

The same dark spirits that had caused the authorities to try to bury the Chinese Church throughout the centuries resurfaced. Many believers were beaten and targeted just for displaying a cross or a Christian poster in their homes.

Trouble for the Three-Self

For decades, most people associated with the registered churches in China felt relatively safe from the threat of persecution, and

A crane removing the cross from a church at Lankao, Henan, in September 2018
China Aid

some Three-Self church members arrogantly looked down upon the unregistered house churches and chastised them for being rebellious. During Xi Jinping's purge of Christianity, however, the lines between the two groups were blurred, as the government sought to degrade all Christianity by tightening control over the Three-Self Church.

Communications from the registered churches suddenly ceased, and the Amity News Service was disbanded after 19 years of reporting on the Three-Self churches in China. Thousands of foreign Christians who were legally working in China had their visas revoked and were expelled.

By 2018, the level of persecution against Henan's Christians had escalated to the worst point since the Cultural Revolution. President Xi Jinping's drive to control and crush God's children reached new heights, with hundreds of registered Three-Self churches throughout the province being demolished or forced to close.

The authorities launched a "cross removal campaign," and by March 2019 more than 4,500 crosses had been taken down from church buildings in Henan, as the nation's atheist rulers sought to destroy all visible evidence of religious fervor.[3] Many Christians who opposed the removal of the crosses were arrested and beaten.

In Zhengzhou, a registered church with a building worth approximately 10 million Yuan ($1.5 million) was seized by the authorities in May 2019 after the congregation refused to stop meeting. Despite evidence that the church had every legal permission to function, the government seized the building and converted it into a hotel.[4]

Earlier that year Song Yongsheng, the chairman of the TSPM in Shangqiu City, committed suicide by jumping from the fifth floor of a church building to protest increasing government repression. Song, who came from a long line of Christians and who had taught the Bible for 23 years, had grown increasingly distressed by being constantly harassed by the authorities, who had forced him to preach patriotic sermons extolling the virtues of Confucianism and the Communist Party.

Finally, when the cross was torn down from the roof of his beloved Shengtongxin Church, Song could take no more. He left a suicide note saying: "I don't have the mental or physical strength to handle so many complicated things anymore. I'm willing to be the first martyr."[5]

On one occasion, the Qiaobei Three-Self Church was forced to close after video cameras installed by the local authorities captured footage of a child inside the building—in violation of new regulations designed to clamp down on Christianity. In fact, the child was the one-year-old granddaughter of a church volunteer, who had brought her along to keep her occupied for a short time.

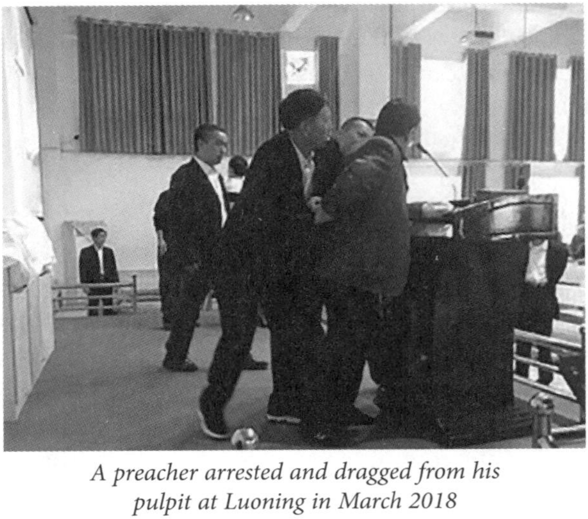

A preacher arrested and dragged from his pulpit at Luoning in March 2018
China Aid

In December 2018, the dreaded United Front Work Department—whose members operate as the henchmen of the Communist Party—ordered the permanent closure of the Qiaobei Three-Self Church, claiming the land was needed for a renovation project. On December 4, the authorities blocked the streets and a cordon was set up around the property. Before church members had a chance to respond, the church was turned into rubble by dynamite.[6]

War on the house churches

Although Three-Self churches experienced an unprecedented level of persecution at the hands of the government they had agreed to submit to, the unregistered house churches throughout Henan bore the brunt of persecution, with many pastors presumed to have been killed in "black jails" after they vanished from their homes.

A house church pastor named Zhang Yongcheng disappeared after being seized on September 24, 2019. Zhang had

A cross being replaced by posters of Xi Jinping and Mao Zedong
China Aid

refused an order to demolish his church in Tanghe County. He was taken into police custody and not seen again, and the church building was duly knocked down.[7]

As part of President Xi's massive persecution of Christians, he ordered the removal of all religious pictures, crosses, and other items from church buildings and even people's homes. In their place were hung portraits of himself and Chairman Mao, and the national flag.

Interestingly, in some places where posters of the Ten Commandments hung, the authorities did not remove them all but just scratched out the first commandment: "You shall have no other gods before me." They did not object to any of the other nine commandments, but the first one upset them. One source noted:

> Those who do not comply with the regulations are subject to harassment and arrest. Church attendees tried arguing with the authorities, but the government agents scolded them, saying, "Xi Jinping is against the commandment" and anyone who didn't cooperate was fighting against the country as this action is national policy.[8]

Impoverished and disabled Christians were threatened with the removal of their state subsidies unless they renounced their faith, and to justify the authorities' bullying tactics an official in the Hebi area of northern Henan held a meeting for Communist Party members which was titled "Christianity's Enormous Harm to China's Security." Attendees were instructed to fight against Christian belief wherever they found it, and to prevent its spread.[9]

Pastor Li Juncai, the leader of the Zhongxin house church in Yuanyang, was imprisoned in 2019 after he refused to change a slogan in his church that said "Love God and people" to "Love the country and religion." He was charged with "disrupting public peace" on February 20, 2019, and at the time of writing he was still in custody.[10]

The authorities, meanwhile, tore down the slogan and replaced it with the national flag. The Zhongxin church had long angered the authorities as it had originally been a Three-Self church, before the believers could no longer tolerate the corruption and compromise of the religious authorities. After renouncing their registration in 2013 and merging with a local house church, they quickly grew to a weekly audience of 700 to 800 believers.

In November 2013, Zhang Shaojie, the pastor of the Nanle County Christian Church, was arrested and charged with fraud and "gathering a crowd to disturb public order." In reality, the local authorities had wanted to seize the land the church was situated on. When he opposed them, the government had him beaten and charged. Zhang was sentenced to 12 years in prison, and he remained behind bars when this book went to press.

Zhang Shaojie, imprisoned since 2013

China Aid

In 2019, Zhang's daughter Esther Yunyun was able to flee to the United States, where she advocated for her father's release. She expressed concern that he had been force-fed unknown medicine by prison doctors, which had severely reduced his physical and mental well-being.[11]

Many house church leaders went into hiding, turning off their phones and other electronic devices due to China's invasive surveillance capabilities. Dark times had returned, and many believers felt the current persecution would be more difficult to overcome than any others endured by God's people in the past, due to the government's use of powerful new technologies to identify believers and destroy the Church.

With house church leaders under massive pressure and generally unwilling to receive foreign visitors, most news of what was happening to China's Christians dried up. Letters from the province became rare, and the scene was set for the body of Christ in Henan to enter what promises to be another long and protracted period of struggle against the forces of darkness.

Finally, in early 2020 the Born-Again house church movement, which has played such a prominent role in Christianity in the province, made the news when 100 of its members were arrested in a large crackdown. The movement had been largely out of sight since Peter Xu Yongze moved to the United States, but the arrest proved that many of its members were continuing to worship Christ throughout Henan and other parts of China.

Letters from Henan

2010

We have been greatly blessed to receive the Bibles that you provided. Our current outstanding need for Bibles is 283,731, so that each believer in our fellowships would have their own copy. This does not include seekers who also wish to read God's Word. Our churches have been expanding into new areas and it seems there are never enough Bibles to go around, especially for new believers. We have experienced many police raids over the last three years, and the authorities have confiscated and destroyed our Bibles on each occasion. Some of our meetings that were raided had Bibles from the Three-Self Church, and we pleaded with the police not to destroy them, to no avail. We cannot control what evil people do, but we thank our Heavenly Father that He has been providing our need for His Word through you! May God continue to bless your ministry![12]

2014

I was a full-time worker and I served 350 churches. I thank God for His love. Even when I was in prison, He cared for me. After I was released, I suffered cerebral paralysis, but God still uses me to preach the gospel to many lost sheep. The prison guards also broke my arm, but I know that Jesus cares for me. Sometimes the local believers help by giving me eggs or vegetables because they can see I'm in need. Other times I just tell the Lord I'm fasting because there's no food. Although I cannot travel freely now, I find a constant flow of brothers and sisters coming to my door for prayer and counsel.[13]

The future of the Church in Henan

The home of Jesus' disciples

It has been said that Henan is "the Galilee of China"—the place where Jesus' disciples come from. The province boasts the largest number of Christians in China today, and over the past 50 years it has experienced more powerful and sustained revival than probably any other part of the country.

Over the years, Henan's Christians have gone into the furnace of affliction numerous times, but have always emerged as refined gold. Their love for the Lord and zeal to reach people for Christ is exemplary.

The accounts of persecutions and injustices against Christians that are mentioned in this book are but a few of all that has occurred in Henan. If the outrages detailed in these pages were all that has happened to believers it would be bad enough; but they are just a tiny sample of the many thousands of incidents of torture and detention that have taken place over the years. Many are simply too gruesome to put into print. God keeps a thorough record of all things, however, and one day He will avenge all the brutal treatment that evil human beings have meted out to His children.

Few of the early missionaries in Henan—such as Jonathan Goforth, Whitfield Guinness, Alphonso Argento ("the man who refused to die"), and Marie Monsen—ever imagined that in the latter half of the twentieth century and the early twenty-first, Henan would be at the very epicenter of China's mighty revival, sweeping millions of people into the kingdom of God.

As this book went to press, the Church in Henan had again entered a dark period of persecution and repression. Once more, believers have been forced to cling to Jesus Christ for their very survival—but just as He has done on numerous occasions throughout history, God will stamp His will on proceedings.

When the body of Christ emerges from this dark tunnel, it will be no surprise if God's people are more committed, and even more numerous, than before. This pattern has invariably been the experience of the Church in Henan. God has gained much glory for Himself in this blessed province, and He will continue to do so until the very end.

A tribute

After spending considerable time getting to know the house church Christians of Henan, I was once unexpectedly asked in a meeting to describe the main thing I've learned from them and to identify their main characteristic in one word.

Having been put on the spot, I quickly thought about the horrific persecution they have endured, but I realized that was just one part of their story. Then I thought about the extraordinary miracles that are a regular part of believers' lives, but again, that was just another part of their identity. As I thought back on my times in Henan and the many unforgettable moments of fellowship with God's children there, it suddenly dawned on me what their main characteristic is.

Love.

The believers in Henan are full of love.

They love Jesus Christ, they love people, they love their persecutors, and they love China.

And they have loved me.

I thank my brothers and sisters in Henan, and I appreciate their help in this feeble attempt to portray Christianity in their blessed province.

Appendix

Table 1 Evangelical Christians in Henan (1875–2020)

(Both Three-Self and house churches)

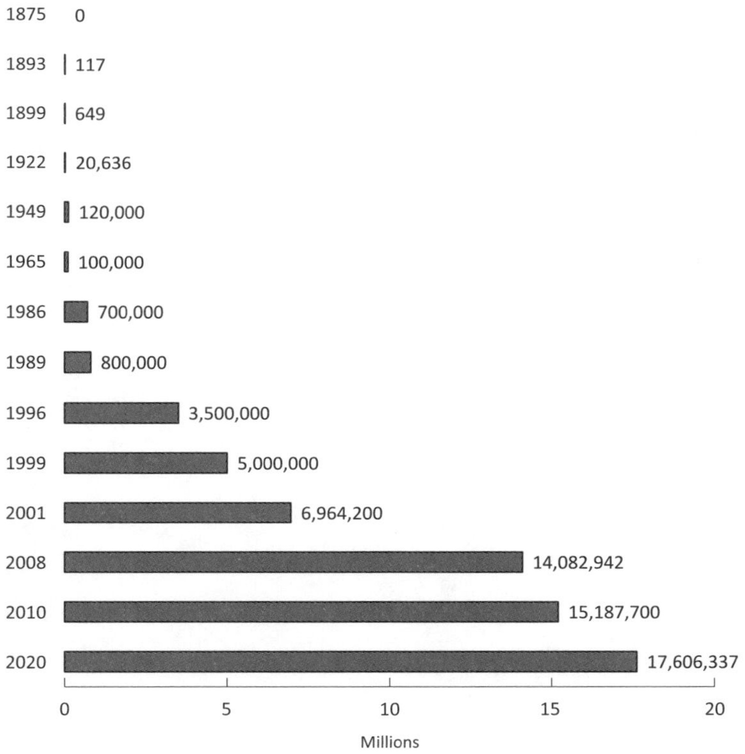

Sources:

0	(1875)
117	(1893 – Guinness, *The Story of the China Inland Mission*)
649	(1899 – Austin, *China's Millions: The CIM and Late Qing Society*)
20,636	(1922 – Stauffer, *The Christian Occupation of China*)
120,000	(1949 – *China Study Journal*, August 1994)
100,000	(1965 – Lambert, *China's Christian Millions*)
700,000	(1986 – *Bridge*, September–October 1986)*
800,000	(1989 – Lambert, *China's Christian Millions*)*
3,500,000	(1996 – Amity News Service, March 1996)*
5,000,000	(1999 – Lambert, *The Resurrection of the Chinese Church*)*
6,964,200	(2001 – Johnstone and Mandryk, *Operation World*)
14,082,942	(2008 – Hattaway, *Fire and Blood, Vol. 2: Henan*)
15,187,700	(2010 – Mandryk, *Operation World*)
17,606,337	(2020 – Hattaway, *The China Chronicles*)

* These sources may only refer to registered church estimates. Three-Self figures typically only count adult baptized members.

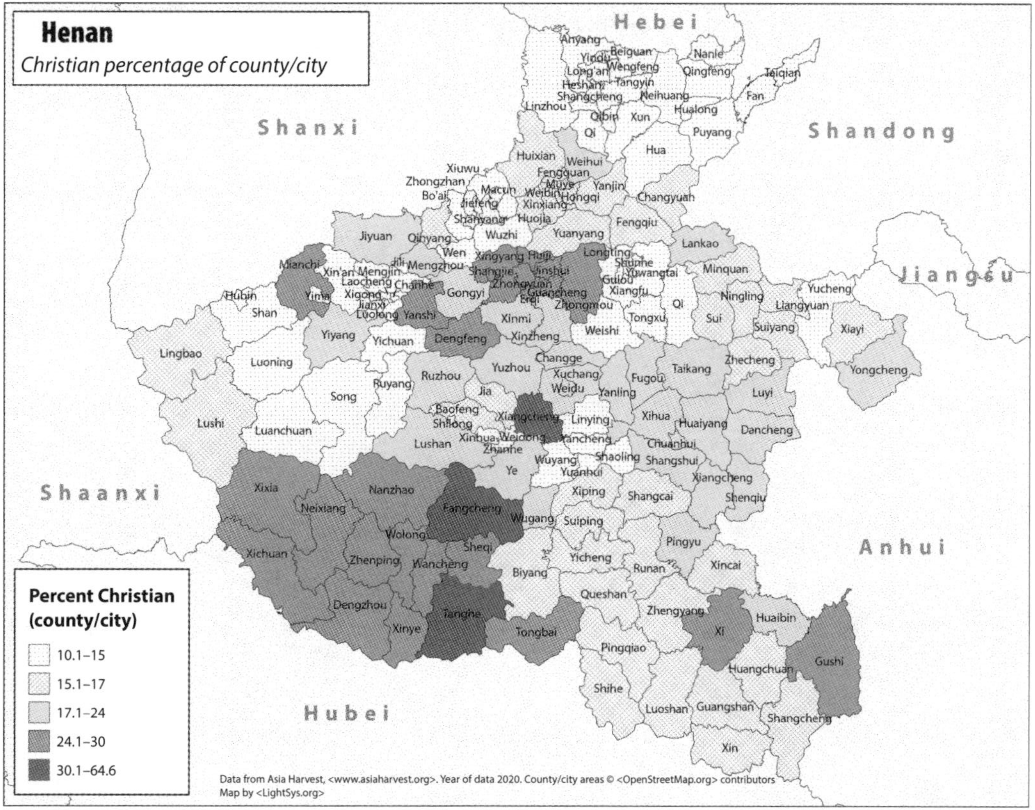

Map of Christians in Henan

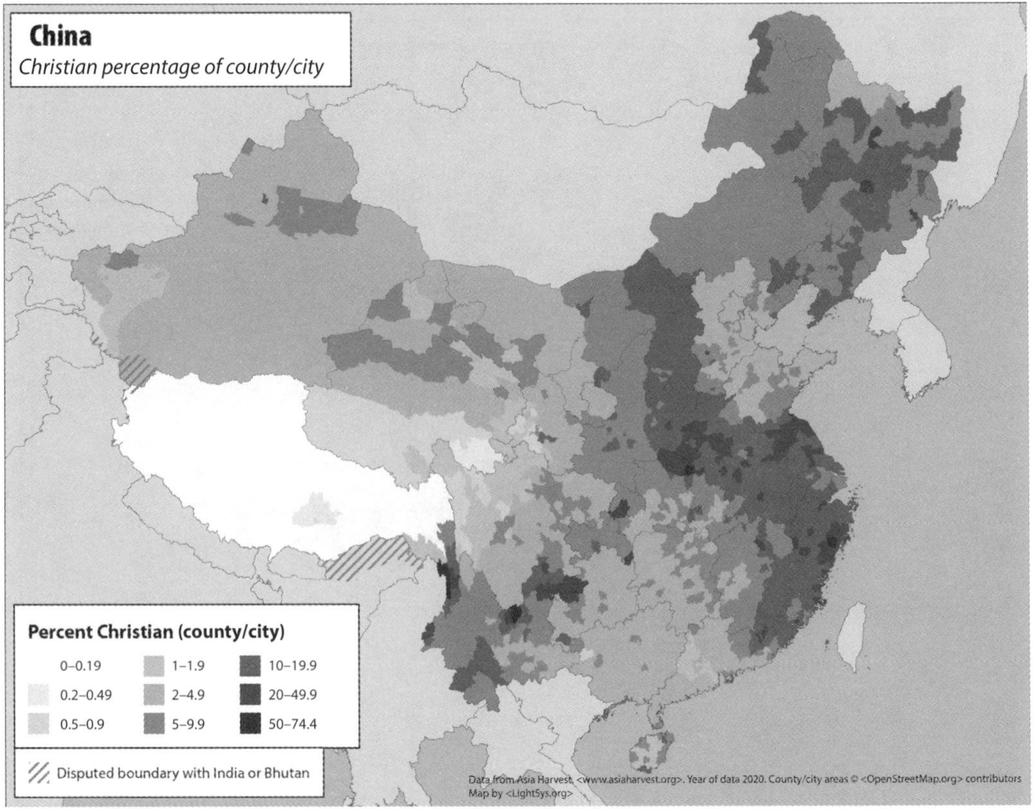
China
Christian percentage of county/city
Percent Christian (county/city)
0–0.19
1–1.9
10–19.9
0.2–0.49
2–4.9
20–49.9
0.5–0.9
5–9.9
50–74.4
Disputed boundary with India or Bhutan
Data from Asia Harvest <www.asiaharvest.org>. Year of data 2020. County/city areas © <OpenStreetMap.org> contributors
Map by <LightSys.org>

Map of China's Christians

A survey of Christians in China

For centuries, people have been curious to know how many Christians live in China. When Marco Polo made his famous journey to the Orient 750 years ago, he revealed the existence of Nestorian churches and monasteries in various places, to the fascination of people back in Europe.

Since I started traveling to China in the 1980s, I have found that Christians around the world are still eager to know how many believers there are in China. Many people are aware that God has done a remarkable work in the world's most populated country, but little research has been done to put a figure on this phenomenon. In recent decades, wildly divergent estimates have been published, ranging from 20 million to 230 million Christians in China.

Methodology

In Table 2, I provide estimates of the number of Christians in Henan. Full tables of the other provinces of China can be found at the Asia Harvest website (see the "The Church in China" link under the Resources tab at <www.asiaharvest.org>). My survey provides figures for Christians of every creed, arranged in four main categories: the Three-Self Patriotic Movement; the Evangelical house churches; the Catholic Patriotic Association; and the Catholic house churches. I have supplied statistics for all 2,370 cities and counties within every province, municipality, and autonomous region of China.

The information was gathered from a wide variety of sources. More than 2,000 published sources have been noted in the tables published online, including a multitude of books, journals, magazine articles, and reports that I spent years meticulously accumulating. I have also conducted hundreds of hours of interviews with key house church leaders responsible for their church networks throughout China.

Before entering data into the tables, I began with this assumption: that in any given place in China there are no Christians at all, until I have a figure from a documented source or can make an intelligent estimate based on information gathered from Chinese Christian leaders. In other words, I wanted to put aside all preconceptions and expectations, input all the information I had, and see what the totals came to.

A note about security

None of the information provided in these tables is new to the Chinese government. Beijing has already thoroughly researched the spread of Christianity throughout the country, as shown by high-ranking official Ye Xiaowen's 2006 announcement that there were then 130 million Christians in China. In December 2009, the national newspaper *China Daily* interviewed scholar Liu Peng who had spent years researching religion for the Chinese Academy of Social Sciences. Liu claimed the "house churches have at least 50 million followers nationwide." His figure at the time was consistent with my research.

After consulting various house church leaders in China, I was able to confirm that all of them were content that this information should be published, as long as the surveys focus on statistics and avoid specific information such as the names and locations of Christian leaders.

The Chinese Church in perspective

All discussion of how many Christians there are in China today should be tempered by the realization that more than 90 percent of the population faces a Christless eternity. Hundreds of millions of individuals have yet to hear the gospel. Church leaders in China have told me how ashamed and burdened they feel that so many of their countrymen and women do not yet know Jesus Christ. This burden motivates them to do whatever it takes to preach the gospel among every ethnic group and in every city, town, and village—to every individual—in China, and to do whatever necessary to see Christ exalted throughout the land.

May we humbly give thanks to the Living God for the great things He has done in China. We are privileged to live in a remarkable time in human history, like the days prophesied by the prophet Habakkuk:

> Look at the nations and watch—and be utterly amazed. For I am going to do something in your days that you would not believe, even if you were told.
>
> (Habakkuk 1:5)

Table 2 Christians in Henan

Henan 河南		POPULATION					CHRISTIANS							
							Evangelicals			Catholics			Total Christians	
Location		Census 2000	Census 2010	Growth	Growth (percent)	Estimate 2020	TSPM	House church	TOTAL Evangelicals	CPA	House church	TOTAL Catholics	TOTAL	Percent of 2020 population
Anyang Prefecture	安阳市													
Anyang County	安阳县	1,116,162	849,057	-267,105	-23.93	581,952	29,098	48,971	78,069	1,164	1,629	2,793	80,862	13.90
Beiguan District	北关区	185,724	245,624	59,900	32.25	305,524	15,276	25,710	40,986	611	855	1,467	42,453	13.90
Hua County	滑县	1,182,162	1,263,289	81,127	6.86	1,344,416	67,221	113,133	180,353	2,689	3,764	6,453	186,807	13.90
Linzhou City	林州市	982,254	789,702	-192,552	-19.60	597,150	29,858	50,250	80,108	1,194	1,672	2,866	82,974	13.90
Long'an District	龙安区	249,294	214,456	-34,838	-13.97	179,618	8,981	15,115	24,096	359	503	862	24,958	13.90
Neihuang County	内黄县	678,730	693,498	14,768	2.18	708,266	35,413	59,601	95,014	1,417	1,983	3,400	98,414	13.90
Tangyin County	汤阴县	432,806	430,803	-2,003	-0.46	428,800	21,440	36,084	57,524	858	1,201	2,058	59,582	13.90
Wengfeng District	文峰区	150,360	442,885	292,525	194.55	735,410	36,771	61,885	98,655	1,471	2,059	3,530	102,185	13.90
Yindu District	殷都区	183,614	243,874	60,260	32.82	304,134	15,207	25,593	40,800	608	852	1,460	42,259	13.90
		5,161,106	**5,173,188**	12,082	0.23	**5,185,270**	207,286	348,863	**556,149**	10,371	14,519	**24,889**	**581,038**	11.21
Hebi Prefecture	鹤壁市													
Heshan District	鹤山区	140,130	131,421	-8,709	-6.21	122,712	6,381	10,739	17,120	245	344	589	17,709	14.43
Qibin District	淇滨区	115,476	272,332	156,856	135.83	429,188	22,318	37,561	59,879	858	1,202	2,060	61,939	14.43
Qi County	淇县	249,986	269,149	19,163	7.67	288,312	14,992	25,232	40,224	577	807	1,384	41,608	14.43
Shangcheng District	山城区	239,730	230,968	-8,762	-3.65	222,206	11,555	19,447	31,001	444	622	1,067	32,068	14.43
Xun County	浚县	656,550	665,338	8,788	1.34	674,126	35,055	58,997	94,051	1,348	1,888	3,236	97,287	14.43
		1,401,872	**1,569,208**	167,336	11.94	**1,736,544**	90,300	151,975	**242,276**	3,473	4,862	**8,335**	**250,611**	14.43
Jiaozuo Prefecture	焦作市													
Bo'ai County	博爱县	419,228	436,319	17,091	4.08	453,410	23,124	38,918	62,041	907	1,270	2,176	64,218	14.16
Jiefeng District	解放区	273,823	295,695	21,872	7.99	317,567	16,196	27,258	43,454	635	889	1,524	44,978	14.16
Macun District	马村区	128,842	139,533	10,691	8.30	150,224	7,661	12,894	20,556	300	421	721	21,277	14.16
Mengzhou City	孟州市	354,302	367,113	12,811	3.62	379,924	26,215	44,119	70,334	760	1,064	1,824	72,158	18.99
Qinyang City	沁阳市	446,404	447,701	1,297	0.29	448,998	27,389	46,095	73,484	898	1,257	2,155	75,640	16.85
Shanyang District	山阳区	233,639	324,121	90,482	38.73	414,603	21,145	35,587	56,731	829	1,161	1,990	58,721	14.16
Wen County	温县	404,621	421,796	17,175	4.24	438,971	22,388	37,678	60,066	878	1,229	2,107	62,173	14.16
Wuzhi County	武陟县	642,544	713,945	71,401	11.11	785,346	40,053	67,409	107,461	1,571	2,199	3,770	111,231	14.16
Xiuwu County	修武县	274,418	287,814	13,396	4.88	301,210	15,362	25,854	41,215	602	843	1,446	42,661	14.16
Zhongzhan District	中站区	110,995	106,064	-4,931	-4.44	101,133	5,158	8,681	13,838	202	283	485	14,324	14.16
		3,288,816	**3,540,101**	251,285	7.64	**3,791,386**	199,532	335,812	**535,343**	7,583	10,616	**17,713**	**553,056**	14.59
Jiyuan Prefecture	济源市													
Jiyuan City	济源市	626,478	675,757	49,279	7.87	725,036	52,203	87,857	140,060	1,450	2,030	3,480	143,540	19.80
		626,478	**675,757**	49,279	7.87	**725,036**	52,203	87,857	**140,060**	1,450	2,030	**3,480**	**143,540**	19.80

Henan 河南		POPULATION					CHRISTIANS							
							Evangelicals			Catholics			Total Christians	
Location		Census 2000	Census 2010	Growth	Growth (percent)	Estimate 2020	TSPM	House church	TOTAL Evangelicals	CPA	House church	TOTAL Catholics	TOTAL	Percent of 2020 population
Kaifeng Prefecture	开封市													
Gulou District	鼓楼区	132,587	143,175	10,588	7.99	153,763	5,351	9,006	14,357	461	646	1,107	15,464	10.06
Jinming District	金明区	268,030	262,258	-5,772	-2.15	256,486	8,926	15,022	23,948	769	1,077	1,847	25,794	10.06
Lankao County	兰考县	718,177	677,826	-40,351	-5.62	637,475	43,348	72,955	116,303	1,912	2,677	4,590	120,893	18.96
Longting District	龙亭区	87,411	127,784	40,373	46.19	168,157	5,852	9,849	15,701	504	706	1,211	16,911	10.06
Qi County	杞县	1,002,592	956,533	-46,059	-4.59	910,474	31,684	53,325	85,010	2,731	3,824	6,555	91,565	10.06
Shunhe District	顺河回族区	188,800	232,296	43,496	23.04	275,792	9,598	16,153	25,750	827	1,158	1,986	27,736	10.06
Tongxu County	通许县	552,363	567,495	15,132	2.74	582,627	20,275	34,124	54,399	1,748	2,447	4,195	58,594	10.06
Weishi County	尉氏县	812,150	879,713	67,563	8.32	947,276	32,965	55,480	88,446	2,842	3,979	6,820	95,266	10.06
Xiangfu District	祥符区	705,080	698,799	-6,281	-0.89	692,518	36,011	60,606	96,617	2,078	2,909	4,986	101,603	14.67
Yuwangtai District	禹王台区	119,343	130,604	11,261	9.44	141,865	4,937	8,309	13,246	426	596	1,021	14,267	10.06
		4,586,533	**4,676,483**	89,950	1.96	**4,766,433**	198,947	334,828	**533,776**	**14,299**	**20,019**	**34,318**	**568,094**	11.92
Luohe Prefecture	漯河市													
Linying County	临颍县	632,427	710,845	78,418	12.40	789,263	41,042	69,073	110,115	2,368	3,315	5,683	115,798	14.67
Shaoling District	召陵区	477,340	477,340	477,340	0.00	477,340	24,822	41,775	66,597	1,432	2,005	3,437	70,033	14.67
Wuyang County	舞阳县	498,970	538,447	39,477	7.91	577,924	30,052	50,578	80,630	1,734	2,427	4,161	84,791	14.67
Yancheng District	郾城区	493,680	493,680	0	0.00	493,680	25,671	43,205	68,876	1,481	2,073	3,554	72,431	14.67
Yuanhui District	源汇区	323,954	323,954	0	0.00	323,954	16,846	28,351	45,197	972	1,361	2,332	47,529	14.67
		2,262,404	**2,544,266**	595,235	26.31	**2,662,161**	138,432	232,982	**371,414**	7,986	11,181	**19,168**	**390,582**	14.67
Luoyang Prefecture	洛阳市													
Chanhe District	瀍河回族区	167,069	177,939	10,870	6.51	188,809	9,440	15,888	25,329	566	793	1,359	26,688	14.14
Jianxi District	涧西区	455,611	619,221	163,610	35.91	782,831	39,142	65,875	105,017	2,348	3,288	5,636	110,653	14.14
Jili District	吉利区	70,593	69,076	-1,517	-2.15	67,559	3,378	5,685	9,063	203	284	486	9,549	14.14
Laocheng District	老城区	141,571	163,176	21,605	15.26	184,781	9,239	15,549	24,788	554	776	1,330	26,119	14.14
Luanchuan County	栾川县	312,838	342,848	30,010	9.59	372,858	18,643	31,376	50,019	1,119	1,566	2,685	52,703	14.14
Luolong District	洛龙区	323,375	523,726	200,351	61.96	724,077	36,204	60,931	97,135	2,172	3,041	5,213	102,348	14.14
Luoning County	洛宁县	422,972	421,262	-1,710	-0.40	419,552	21,817	36,718	58,534	1,259	1,762	3,021	61,555	14.67
Mengjin County	孟津县	418,065	414,637	-3,428	-0.82	411,209	20,560	34,603	55,164	1,234	1,727	2,961	58,124	14.14
Ruyang County	汝阳县	397,833	408,009	10,176	2.56	418,185	20,909	35,190	56,100	1,255	1,756	3,011	59,110	14.14
Song County	嵩县	527,768	507,052	-20,716	-3.93	486,336	24,317	40,925	65,242	1,459	2,043	3,502	68,744	14.14
Xigong District	西工区	333,461	372,941	39,480	11.84	412,421	20,621	34,705	55,326	1,237	1,732	2,969	58,296	14.14
Xin'an County	新安县	481,740	470,198	-11,542	-2.40	458,656	22,933	38,596	61,529	1,376	1,926	3,302	64,831	14.14
Yanshi City	偃师市	816,026	666,696	-149,330	-18.30	517,366	47,598	80,107	127,705	1,552	2,173	3,725	131,430	25.40
Yichuan County	伊川县	708,387	756,669	48,282	6.82	804,951	40,248	67,737	107,984	2,415	3,381	5,796	113,780	14.14
Yiyang County	宜阳县	650,356	636,491	-13,865	-2.13	622,626	38,603	64,969	103,571	1,868	2,615	4,483	108,054	17.35
		6,227,665	**6,549,941**	322,276	5.17	**6,872,217**	373,651	628,854	**1,002,505**	20,617	28,863	49,480	1,051,985	15.31

Henan 河南		POPULATION					CHRISTIANS								
							Evangelicals			Catholics			Total Christians	
Location		Census 2000	Census 2010	Growth	Growth (percent)	Estimate 2020	TSPM	House church	TOTAL Evangelicals	CPA	House church	TOTAL Catholics	TOTAL	Percent of 2020 population
Nanyang Prefecture	南阳市													
Dengzhou City	邓州市	1,290,656	1,468,157	177,501	13.75	1,645,658	143,337	241,236	384,573	7,405	10,368	17,773	402,346	24.45
Fangcheng County	方城县	886,230	922,467	36,237	4.09	958,704	83,503	250,509	334,012	4,314	6,040	10,354	344,366	35.92
Nanzhao County	南召县	561,784	557,153	-4,631	-0.82	552,522	48,125	80,994	129,118	2,486	3,481	5,967	135,086	24.45
Neixiang County	内乡县	583,233	575,210	-8,023	-1.38	567,187	49,402	83,144	132,546	2,552	3,573	6,126	138,671	24.45
Sheqi County	社旗县	580,280	633,786	53,506	9.22	687,292	59,863	100,750	160,613	3,093	4,330	7,423	168,036	24.45
Tanghe County	唐河县	1,151,733	1,282,262	130,529	11.33	1,412,791	179,566	718,263	897,829	6,358	8,901	15,258	913,087	64.63
Tongbai County	桐柏县	403,359	393,942	-9,417	-2.33	384,525	33,492	56,367	89,859	1,730	2,423	4,153	94,012	24.45
Wancheng District	宛城区	785,943	887,234	101,291	12.89	988,525	86,101	144,907	231,008	4,448	6,228	10,676	241,684	24.45
Wolong District	卧龙区	798,772	924,578	125,806	15.75	1,050,384	91,488	153,975	245,464	4,727	6,617	11,344	256,808	24.45
Xichuan County	淅川县	641,327	685,683	44,356	6.92	730,039	63,586	107,016	170,602	3,285	4,599	7,884	178,487	24.45
Xinye County	新野县	629,106	629,210	104	0.02	629,314	54,813	92,251	147,064	2,832	3,965	6,797	153,861	24.45
Xixia County	西峡县	412,988	444,414	31,426	7.61	475,840	41,446	69,753	111,199	2,141	2,998	5,139	116,338	24.45
Zhenping County	镇平县	852,360	859,564	7,204	0.85	866,768	75,495	127,059	202,554	3,900	5,461	9,361	211,916	24.45
		9,577,771	10,263,660	685,889	7.16	10,949,549	1,010,217	2,226,223	3,236,441	49,273	68,982	118,255	3,354,696	30.64
Pingdingshan Prefecture	平顶山市													
Baofeng County	宝丰县	473,287	490,269	16,982	3.59	507,251	30,435	51,222	81,657	1,522	2,130	3,652	85,309	16.82
Jia County	郏县	533,168	571,524	38,356	7.19	609,880	36,593	61,586	98,178	1,830	2,561	4,391	102,570	16.82
Lushan County	鲁山县	822,541	789,901	-32,640	-3.97	757,261	45,436	121,904	167,340	2,272	3,180	5,452	172,792	22.82
Ruzhou City	汝州市	923,245	927,934	4,689	0.51	932,623	74,610	125,568	200,178	2,798	3,917	6,715	206,893	22.18
Shilong District	石龙区	53,499	54,912	1,413	2.64	56,325	2,816	4,740	7,556	169	237	406	7,962	14.14
Weidong District	卫东区	274,444	302,603	28,159	10.26	330,762	16,538	27,834	44,372	992	1,389	2,381	46,753	14.14
Wugang City	舞钢市	313,089	313,828	739	0.24	314,567	22,649	38,118	60,767	944	1,321	2,265	63,032	20.04
Xinhua District	新华区	337,733	389,866	52,133	15.44	441,999	22,100	37,194	59,294	1,326	1,856	3,182	62,477	14.14
Ye County	叶县	838,691	777,203	-61,488	-7.33	715,715	58,689	98,773	157,462	2,147	3,006	5,153	162,615	22.72
Zhanhe District	湛河区	235,227	286,661	51,434	21.87	338,095	16,905	28,451	45,355	1,014	1,420	2,434	47,790	14.14
		4,804,924	4,904,701	99,777	2.08	5,004,478	326,770	595,389	922,159	15,013	21,019	36,032	958,191	19.15
Puyang Prefecture	濮阳市													
Fan County	范县	479,818	469,874	-9,944	-2.07	459,930	23,916	40,251	64,168	1,610	2,254	3,863	68,031	14.79
Hualong District	华龙区	448,290	655,674	207,384	46.26	863,058	44,879	75,531	120,410	3,021	4,229	7,250	127,660	14.79
Nanle County	南乐县	468,360	458,487	-9,873	-2.11	448,614	23,328	39,261	62,589	1,570	2,198	3,768	66,357	14.79
Puyang County	濮阳县	1,081,832	1,046,654	-35,178	-3.25	1,011,476	52,597	88,520	141,117	3,540	4,956	8,496	149,613	14.79
Qingfeng County	清丰县	654,160	635,927	-18,233	-2.79	617,694	32,120	54,058	86,178	2,162	3,027	5,189	91,367	14.79
Taiqian County	台前县	325,872	332,124	6,252	1.92	338,376	17,596	29,613	47,209	1,184	1,658	2,842	50,051	14.79
		3,458,332	3,598,740	140,408	4.06	3,739,148	194,436	327,235	521,671	13,087	18,322	31,409	553,080	14.79

Henan 河南		POPULATION					CHRISTIANS							
							Evangelicals			Catholics			Total Christians	
Location		Census 2000	Census 2010	Growth	Growth (percent)	Estimate 2020	TSPM	House church	TOTAL Evangelicals	CPA	House church	TOTAL Catholics	TOTAL	Percent of 2020 population
Sanmenxia Prefecture	三门峡市													
Hubin District	湖滨区	288,746	325,628	36,882	12.77	362,510	14,754	29,508	44,262	1,450	2,030	3,480	47,743	13.17
Lingbao City	灵宝市	722,890	721,049	-1,841	-0.25	719,208	41,714	70,205	111,919	2,877	4,028	6,904	118,823	16.52
Lushi County	卢氏县	356,439	352,449	-3,990	-1.12	348,459	19,514	32,842	52,355	1,394	1,951	3,345	55,700	15.98
Mianchi County	渑池县	328,947	346,434	17,487	5.32	363,921	21,835	65,506	87,341	1,456	2,038	3,494	90,835	24.96
Shanzhou District	陕州区	343,863	343,679	-184	-0.05	343,495	13,980	23,529	37,509	1,374	1,924	3,298	40,807	11.88
Yima City	义马市	136,543	144,779	8,236	6.03	153,015	7,758	13,056	20,814	612	857	1,469	22,283	14.56
		2,177,428	**2,234,018**	56,590	2.60	**2,290,608**	119,555	234,646	**354,201**	9,162	12,827	**21,990**	**376,191**	16.42
Shangqiu Prefecture	商丘市													
Liangyuan District	梁园区	674,502	787,984	113,482	16.82	901,466	52,195	87,844	140,039	3,155	4,417	7,572	147,611	16.37
Minquan County	民权县	805,063	703,428	-101,635	-12.62	601,793	34,844	58,642	93,486	2,106	2,949	5,055	98,541	16.37
Ningling County	宁陵县	562,794	523,403	-39,391	-7.00	484,012	28,024	47,165	75,189	1,694	2,372	4,066	79,255	16.37
Sui County	睢县	757,080	711,136	-45,944	-6.07	665,192	38,515	64,820	103,335	2,328	3,259	5,588	108,922	16.37
Suiyang District	睢阳区	754,481	748,408	-6,073	-0.80	742,335	42,981	72,337	115,319	2,598	3,637	6,236	121,554	16.37
Xiayi County	夏邑县	1,033,519	915,291	-118,228	-11.44	797,063	46,150	77,670	123,820	2,790	3,906	6,695	130,516	16.37
Yongcheng City	永城市	1,264,607	1,240,382	-24,225	-1.92	1,216,157	87,563	131,345	218,908	4,257	5,959	10,216	229,124	18.84
Yucheng County	虞城县	1,025,261	954,785	-70,476	-6.87	884,309	42,358	71,289	113,648	3,095	4,333	7,428	121,076	13.69
Zhecheng County	柘城县	876,537	778,158	-98,379	-11.22	679,779	39,359	66,242	105,601	2,379	3,331	5,710	111,311	16.37
		7,753,844	**7,362,975**	-390,869	-5.04	**6,972,106**	411,990	677,355	**1,089,344**	24,402	34,163	**58,566**	**1,147,910**	16.46
Xinxiang Prefecture	新乡市													
Changyuan County	长垣县	765,740	809,535	43,795	5.72	853,330	49,408	83,153	132,561	2,987	4,181	7,168	139,729	16.37
Fengqiu County	封丘县	719,510	743,837	24,327	3.38	768,164	44,477	74,854	119,331	2,689	3,764	6,453	125,784	16.37
Fengquan District	凤泉区	100,132	144,298	44,166	44.11	188,464	10,912	18,365	29,277	660	923	1,583	30,860	16.37
Hongqi District	红旗区	330,170	391,290	61,120	18.51	452,410	26,195	44,085	70,280	1,583	2,217	3,800	74,080	16.37
Huixian City	辉县市	776,326	740,435	-35,891	-4.62	704,544	41,498	69,841	111,338	2,466	3,452	5,918	117,256	16.64
Huojia County	获嘉县	381,227	402,950	21,723	5.70	424,673	24,589	41,383	65,971	1,486	2,081	3,567	69,538	16.37
Muye District	牧野区	141,856	317,994	176,138	124.17	494,132	28,610	48,151	76,761	1,729	2,421	4,151	80,912	16.37
Weibin District	卫滨区	203,783	193,506	-10,277	-5.04	183,229	10,609	17,855	28,464	641	898	1,539	30,003	16.37
Weihui City	卫辉市	464,371	495,744	31,373	6.76	527,117	33,683	56,688	90,371	1,845	2,583	4,428	94,799	17.98
Xinxiang County	新乡县	424,138	339,942	-84,196	-19.85	255,746	14,808	24,921	39,729	895	1,253	2,148	41,877	16.37
Yanjin County	延津县	457,771	469,280	11,509	2.51	480,789	27,838	46,851	74,689	1,683	2,356	4,039	78,727	16.37
Yuanyang County	原阳县	642,409	659,380	16,971	2.64	676,351	39,161	65,907	105,068	2,367	3,314	5,681	110,750	16.37
		5,407,433	**5,708,191**	300,758	5.56	**6,008,949**	351,785	592,055	**943,840**	21,031	29,444	**50,475**	**994,315**	16.55

Henan 河南		POPULATION					CHRISTIANS							
							Evangelicals			Catholics			Total Christians	
Location		Census 2000	Census 2010	Growth	Growth (percent)	Estimate 2020	TSPM	House church	TOTAL Evangelicals	CPA	House church	TOTAL Catholics	TOTAL	Percent of 2020 population
Xinyang Prefecture	信阳市													
Guangshan County	光山县	649,578	585,353	-64,225	-9.89	521,128	30,173	50,782	80,955	1,824	2,554	4,377	85,332	16.37
Gushi County	固始县	1,188,599	1,023,929	-164,670	-13.85	859,259	75,529	127,115	202,644	3,007	4,210	7,218	209,862	24.42
Huaibin County	淮滨县	569,829	570,197	368	0.06	570,565	38,741	65,202	103,943	1,997	2,796	4,793	108,736	19.06
Huangchuan County	潢川县	679,278	630,376	-48,902	-7.20	581,474	33,667	56,662	90,329	2,035	2,849	4,884	95,214	16.37
Luoshan County	罗山县	574,100	504,577	-69,523	-12.11	435,054	25,190	42,394	67,584	1,523	2,132	3,654	71,238	16.37
Pingqiao District	平桥区	694,088	635,651	-58,437	-8.42	577,214	33,421	56,247	89,668	2,020	2,828	4,849	94,516	16.37
Shangcheng County	商城县	570,181	495,526	-74,655	-13.09	420,871	24,368	41,012	65,381	1,473	2,062	3,535	68,916	16.37
Shihe District	浉河区	561,662	594,391	32,729	5.83	627,120	36,310	61,110	97,420	2,195	3,073	5,268	102,688	16.37
Xin County	新县	269,773	275,304	5,531	2.05	280,835	16,260	27,366	43,627	983	1,376	2,359	45,986	16.37
Xi County	息县	770,280	793,802	23,522	3.05	817,324	63,670	170,825	234,495	2,861	4,005	6,866	241,360	29.53
		6,527,368	**6,109,106**	-418,262	-6.41	**5,690,844**	377,330	698,716	1,076,045	19,918	27,885	47,803	1,123,848	19.75
Xuchang Prefecture	许昌市													
Changge City	长葛市	646,306	687,130	40,824	6.32	727,954	60,202	101,320	161,521	2,548	3,567	6,115	167,636	23.03
Weidu District	魏都区	373,387	498,087	124,700	33.40	622,787	45,277	76,201	121,477	2,180	3,052	5,231	126,709	20.35
Xiangcheng County	襄城县	679,863	671,315	-8,548	-1.26	662,767	74,694	125,710	200,404	2,320	3,248	5,567	205,971	31.08
Xuchang County	许昌县	737,384	767,449	30,065	4.08	208,168	17,215	28,974	46,189	729	1,020	1,749	47,938	23.03
Yanling County	鄢陵县	564,477	551,611	-12,866	-2.28	538,745	44,554	74,985	119,539	1,886	2,640	4,525	124,064	23.03
Yuzhou City	禹州市	1,122,669	1,131,896	9,227	0.82	1,141,123	94,371	158,826	253,197	3,994	5,592	9,585	262,782	23.03
		4,124,086	**4,307,488**	183,402	4.45	**3,901,544**	336,313	566,014	902,327	13,655	19,118	32,773	935,100	23.97
Zhengzhou Prefecture	郑州市													
Dengfeng City	登封市	609,085	668,637	59,552	9.78	728,189	64,153	107,970	172,124	3,277	4,588	7,864	179,988	24.72
Erqi District	二七区	557,300	712,646	155,346	27.87	867,992	76,470	128,699	205,169	3,906	5,468	9,374	214,544	24.72
Gongyi City	巩义市	777,202	807,911	30,709	3.95	838,620	69,605	117,146	186,751	3,774	5,283	9,057	195,809	23.35
Guancheng District	管城回族区	348,513	645,932	297,419	85.34	943,351	83,109	139,873	222,982	4,245	5,943	10,188	233,170	24.72
Huiji District	惠济区	149,852	269,579	119,727	79.90	389,306	34,298	57,723	92,021	1,752	2,453	4,205	96,226	24.72
Jinshui District	金水区	878,308	1,588,716	710,408	80.88	2,299,124	202,553	340,896	543,449	10,346	14,484	24,831	568,280	24.72
Shangjie District	上街区	77,014	131,549	54,535	70.81	186,084	16,394	27,591	43,985	837	1,172	2,010	45,995	24.72
Xingyang City	荥阳市	619,840	613,804	-6,036	-0.97	607,768	53,544	90,115	143,660	2,735	3,829	6,564	150,223	24.72
Xinmi City	新密市	779,014	797,256	18,242	2.34	815,498	66,871	112,544	179,414	3,670	5,138	8,807	188,222	23.08
Xinzheng City	新郑市	609,173	758,128	148,955	24.45	907,083	75,288	126,710	201,997	4,082	5,715	9,796	211,794	23.35
Zhongmou County	中牟县	673,058	727,440	54,382	8.08	781,822	68,879	115,923	184,801	3,518	4,925	8,444	193,245	24.72
Zhongyuan District	中原区	578,400	905,491	327,091	56.55	1,232,582	108,590	182,758	291,348	5,547	7,765	13,312	304,660	24.72
		6,656,759	**8,627,089**	1,970,330	29.60	**10,597,419**	919,755	1,547,948	2,467,703	47,688	66,764	114,452	2,582,155	24.37

Henan 河南		POPULATION					CHRISTIANS							
							Evangelicals			Catholics			Total Christians	
Location		Census 2000	Census 2010	Growth	Growth (percent)	Estimate 2020	TSPM	House church	TOTAL Evangelicals	CPA	House church	TOTAL Catholics	TOTAL	Percent of 2020 population
Zhoukou Prefecture	周口市													
Chuanhui District	川汇区	323,738	505,171	181,433	56.04	686,604	49,435	98,871	**148,306**	2,746	3,845	**6,591**	**154,898**	22.56
Dancheng County	郸城县	1,151,994	1,003,910	-148,084	-12.85	855,826	61,619	123,239	**184,858**	3,423	4,793	**8,216**	**193,074**	22.56
Fugou County	扶沟县	666,779	625,819	-40,960	-6.14	584,859	42,110	70,871	**112,981**	2,339	3,275	**5,615**	**118,595**	20.28
Huaiyang County	淮阳县	1,229,357	1,089,699	-139,658	-11.36	950,041	68,403	115,122	**183,525**	3,800	5,320	**9,120**	**192,646**	20.28
Luyi County	鹿邑县	1,068,984	910,251	-158,733	-14.85	751,518	54,109	91,066	**145,175**	3,006	4,209	**7,215**	**152,390**	20.28
Shangshui County	商水县	1,093,686	940,792	-152,894	-13.98	787,898	56,729	95,474	**152,203**	3,152	4,412	**7,564**	**159,767**	20.28
Shenqiu County	沈丘县	1,079,278	983,583	-95,695	-8.87	887,888	63,928	107,591	**171,519**	3,552	4,972	**8,524**	**180,042**	20.28
Taikang County	太康县	1,254,680	1,102,952	-151,728	-12.09	951,224	68,488	115,266	**183,754**	3,805	5,327	**9,132**	**192,885**	20.28
Xiangcheng City	项城市	1,052,468	1,003,698	-48,770	-4.63	954,928	68,755	115,714	**184,469**	3,820	5,348	**9,167**	**193,636**	20.28
Xihua County	西华县	820,319	787,918	-32,401	-3.95	755,517	54,397	91,551	**145,948**	3,022	4,231	**7,253**	**153,201**	20.28
		9,741,283	**8,953,793**	-787,490	-8.08	**8,166,303**	587,974	1,024,764	**1,612,738**	32,665	45,731	**78,397**	**1,691,135**	20.71
Zhumadian Prefecture	驻马店市													
Biyang County	泌阳县	813,273	810,409	-2,864	-0.35	807,545	46,030	77,469	**123,499**	2,423	3,392	**5,814**	**129,313**	16.01
Pingyu County	平舆县	842,250	748,398	-93,852	-11.14	654,546	47,127	79,315	**126,443**	1,964	2,749	**4,713**	**131,155**	20.04
Queshan County	确山县	553,157	406,021	-147,136	-26.60	258,885	14,756	24,835	**39,592**	777	1,087	**1,864**	**41,456**	16.01
Runan County	汝南县	784,005	769,995	-14,010	-1.79	755,985	43,091	72,522	**115,614**	2,268	3,175	**5,443**	**121,057**	16.01
Shangcai County	上蔡县	1,198,534	1,084,210	-114,324	-9.54	969,886	55,284	93,042	**148,326**	2,910	4,074	**6,983**	**155,309**	16.01
Suiping County	遂平县	547,541	493,930	-53,611	-9.79	440,319	25,098	42,240	**67,338**	1,321	1,849	**3,170**	**70,509**	16.01
Xincai County	新蔡县	918,237	851,362	-66,875	-7.28	784,487	44,716	75,257	**119,972**	2,353	3,295	**5,648**	**125,621**	16.01
Xiping County	西平县	767,214	700,152	-67,062	-8.74	633,090	36,086	60,733	**96,819**	1,899	2,659	**4,558**	**101,377**	16.01
Yicheng District	驿城区	338,036	721,723	383,687	113.50	1,105,410	63,008	106,043	**169,051**	3,316	4,643	**7,959**	**177,010**	16.01
Zhengyang County	正阳县	690,505	645,034	-45,471	-6.59	599,563	34,175	57,517	**91,692**	1,799	2,518	**4,317**	**96,009**	16.01
		7,452,752	**7,231,234**	-221,518	-2.97	**7,009,716**	409,372	688,973	**1,098,345**	21,029	29,441	**50,470**	**1,148,815**	16.39
Totals		**91,236,854**	**94,029,939**	**2,793,085**	3.06	**96,823,024**	6,305,848	11,300,489	17,606,337	332,705	465,786	798,491	18,404,828	19.01

Notes

The China Chronicles overview

1 R. Wardlaw Thompson, *Griffith John: The Story of Fifty Years in China* (London: Religious Tract Society, 1908), p. 65.

Introduction

1 Sichuan formerly held the distinction of being the most populated province in China, but the 1997 creation of the Chongqing Municipality reduced Sichuan's population by approximately 30 million, and plunged Sichuan from first to fourth behind Henan, Shandong, and Guangdong. Since that time, the populations of Guangdong and Shandong have overtaken Henan.

2 Erleen J. Christensen, *In War and Famine: Missionaries in China's Honan Province in the 1940s* (Montreal: McGill-Queen's University Press, 2005), p. 9.

3 Christensen, *In War and Famine*, p. 10.

4 Theodore H. White and Annalee Jacoby, *Thunder Out of China* (New York, NY: William Sloane, 1946), p. 133.

5 Archibald Gracie, "The Province of Ho-nan," *China's Millions* (July 1902), p. 92.

6 Leo J. Moser, *The Chinese Mosaic: The Peoples and Provinces of China* (Boulder, CO: Westview Press, 1985), p. 62.

7 Moser, *The Chinese Mosaic*, p. 63.

8 *China Daily* (June 19, 2007).

The Jews of Henan

1 See Lewis C. Walmsley, *Bishop in Honan: Mission and Museum in the Life of William C. White* (Toronto: University of Toronto Press, 1974), p. 138.

2 Vincent Cronin, *The Wise Man from the West* (New York, NY: E. P. Dutton, 1955), p. 220.

3 Arthur Christopher Moule, *Christians in China before the Year 1550* (London: Society for Promoting Christian Knowledge, 1930), p. 1.

4 Cronin, *The Wise Man from the West*, pp. 224–5.

5 Cronin, *The Wise Man from the West*, p. 226.

6 In the nineteenth century the London Jews Society visited the Kaifeng synagogue and examined the ancient manuscripts. They found that while the main body of text was written in Hebrew, many of the rubrics and notes were in Persian, suggesting a Middle East connection. Another source specifically states that the Chinese Jews came from Persia and Yemen between 1,000 and 1,500 years ago. See Nancy Ryan, "Jews in the Far East Have Rich and Varied Roots," *Chicago Tribune* (January 23, 1987).
7 See Moule, *Christians in China before the Year 1550*, p. 2, n. 4.
8 Cited in Moule, *Christians in China before the Year 1550*, p. 5.
9 Michael McCabe, "The Jews of China," *San Jose Mercury News* (November 17, 1984). Also see Oliver Bainbridge, "The Chinese Jews," *National Geographic* (October 1907), p. 627.
10 McCabe, "The Jews of China."
11 D. J. Mills, "Ho-nan Province: An Eventful Itineration," *China's Millions* (April 1891), p. 47.
12 The three volumes were later reprinted as a single volume, 700 pages in length. See William White, *Chinese Jews: A Compilation of Matters Relating to the Jews of Kai'-feng Fu* (Toronto: University of Toronto Press, 1966). A recent book on the Chinese Jews is Jordan Paper and Alex Bender (eds), *The Chinese Jews of Kaifeng: A Millennium of Adaptation and Endurance* (Lanham, MD: Lexington Books, 2017).
13 Etan Smallman, "Can the Jews of Kaifeng, China, Survive Xi Jinping, as They Have 1,400 Years of Floods, Revolution, and Intermarriage?" *South China Morning Post* (March 8, 2020).
14 Lela Gilbert, "Tiny Kaifeng Jewish Community Faces Orwellian Future," *The Jerusalem Post* (February 15, 2019).

Early Christians in Henan

1 See Table 2: "Christians in Henan."
2 We will examine the Nestorian Stone in the Shaanxi volume of the China Chronicles, as well as investigating the fate of the Nestorian movement itself in various volumes.
3 Nicolas Standaert (ed.), *Handbook of Christianity in China, Vol. 1: 635–1800* (Leiden: Brill, 2001), p. 28.
4 Arthur Christopher Moule, *Christians in China before the Year 1550* (London: Society for Promoting Christian Knowledge, 1930), p. 5.
5 Moule, *Christians in China before the Year 1550*, p. 6.
6 Kenneth Scott Latourette, *A History of Christian Missions in China* (New York, NY: Macmillan, 1929), p. 183.

7 Evangelical missionaries' memorandum to Sir Rutherford Alcock, July 14, 1869, in *Parliamentary Papers* (1870), Vol. 69, no. 9, p. 4.
8 Latourette, *A History of Christian Missions in China*, p. 238.
9 *China's Millions* (December 1875), p. 81.
10 Koen De Ridder (ed.), *Footsteps in Deserted Valleys: Missionary Cases, Strategies and Practice in Qing China*, Louvain Chinese Studies 8 (Leuven: Leuven University Press, 2000), p. 58.

1870s and 1880s

1 Milton T. Stauffer (ed.), *The Christian Occupation of China* (Shanghai: China Continuation Committee, 1922), p. 80.
2 M. Henry Taylor, "The First of the Nine," *China's Millions* (July 1875), p. 2.
3 M. Henry Taylor, "Tidings from the First of the Nine," *China's Millions* (August 1875), p. 24.
4 M. Henry Taylor, "Missionary Journeys: Pioneer Work in Ho-nan," *China's Millions* (November 1875), pp. 60–1.
5 *China's Millions* (December 1875), p. 80.
6 Evangelical missionaries' memorandum to Sir Rutherford Alcock, July 14, 1869, in *Parliamentary Papers* (1870), Vol. 69, no. 9, p. 26.
7 Archibald Gracie, "The Province of Ho-nan," *China's Millions* (July 1902), p. 92.
8 G. W. Clarke, "Eighty Days in Ho-nan: From the Diary of Mr. G. W. Clarke," *China's Millions* (March 1877), p. 31.
9 "Providential Deliverances," *China's Millions* (October 1876), p. 210.
10 A. J. Broomhall, *Hudson Taylor and China's Open Century, Book Six: Assault on the Nine* (London: Overseas Missionary Fellowship, 1988), p. 294.
11 See "Honan," *China's Millions* (September 1892), p. 121.
12 Gracie, "The Province of Ho-nan," p. 93.
13 Gracie, "The Province of Ho-nan," p. 93.
14 *China's Millions* (July 1896), p. 168.
15 See J. J. Coulthard, "The First Church Founded in Ho-nan," *China's Millions* (March 1888), pp. 27–8.
16 J. J. Coulthard, "Power over All the Power of the Enemy," *China's Millions* (March 1890), p. 30.
17 *Bridge* (March 1998).
18 See Table 2: "Christians in Henan."
19 Geraldine Guinness, *In the Far East: Letters from China* (London: Morgan & Scott, 1890), p. 158.

20 Guinness, *In the Far East*, p. 159.
21 Stauffer, *The Christian Occupation of China*, p. x.
22 Consisting of approximately 68,000 Three-Self Church members and 115,000 Christians belonging to unregistered house churches. See Table 2: "Christians in Henan."
23 Marshall Broomhall, *The Bible in China* (London: China Inland Mission, 1934), p. 146.
24 Broomhall, *The Bible in China*, pp. 146–7.
25 "Christians in Northern Henan Province," *Bridge* (September–October 1986), p. 4.
26 "The Puzzle of the New: Open-Door Economics and a Search for Spiritual Renewal," *Time* (March 18, 1985), p. 40.
27 According to a prayer calendar published in 2002 by the Three-Self Patriotic Movement (TSPM), a network of churches registered and approved by the Chinese government.
28 See Table 2: "Christians in Henan."

1890s

1 Milton T. Stauffer (ed.), *The Christian Occupation of China* (Shanghai: China Continuation Committee, 1922), p. 34.
2 *China's Millions* (1900), p. 102.
3 Miss B. Leggat, "A Year of Hard Work and Great Blessing," *China's Millions* (October 1903), p. 133.
4 Marshall Broomhall (ed.), *The Chinese Empire: A General and Missionary Survey* (London: Morgan & Scott, 1907), p. 161.
5 Cited in George Sweeting, *More Than 2,000 Great Quotes and Illustrations* (Waco, TX: Word, 1985), p. 184.
6 *China's Millions* (October 1898), p. 148.
7 M. Geraldine Guinness, *The Story of the China Inland Mission* (London: Morgan & Scott, 1893), p. 147.
8 See Paul Hattaway, *Fire and Blood, Vol. 1: China's Book of Martyrs* (Carlisle: Piquant, 2007), for inspirational accounts of more than 1,000 Christian martyrs in China, including hundreds from the Boxer Rebellion.

1900s

1 Marshall Broomhall (ed.), *Martyred Missionaries of the China Inland Mission: With a Record of the Perils and Sufferings of Some Who Escaped* (London: Morgan & Scott, 1901), pp. 209–10.

2 F. S. Joyce, "Address by Mr. F. S. Joyce (Ho-nan)," *China's Millions* (July 1901), p. 96.
3 Broomhall, *Martyred Missionaries*, pp. 213–4.
4 Broomhall, *Martyred Missionaries*, p. 231.
5 "The Supreme Sacrifice: In Memoriam—Alphonso Argento," *China's Millions* (August 1917), p. 89.
6 Broomhall, *Martyred Missionaries*, p. 238. The same account also appeared in *China's Millions* (November 1900).
7 Broomhall, *Martyred Missionaries*, p. 240.
8 Broomhall, *Martyred Missionaries*, p. 242.
9 Broomhall, *Martyred Missionaries*, p. 242.
10 Alphonso Argento, "Spared to Serve," *China's Millions* (July 1902), p. 100.
11 "The Supreme Sacrifice," p. 89.
12 "The Supreme Sacrifice," p. 89.
13 See Table 2: "Christians in Henan."
14 Intercessors for China, *The Persecuted, the Poor and the Pioneer Missionaries* (2001 prayer calendar).

Jonathan Goforth

1 Rosalind Goforth, *Goforth of China* (Grand Rapids, MI: Zondervan, 1937), p. 29.
2 Goforth, *Goforth of China*, p. 33.
3 Goforth, *Goforth of China*, p. 30.
4 Ruth Tucker, *From Jerusalem to Irian Jaya: A Biographical History of Christian Missions* (Grand Rapids, MI: Zondervan, 1983), p. 189.
5 Alvyn J. Austin, *Saving China: Canadian Missionaries in the Middle Kingdom* (Toronto: University of Toronto Press, 1986), p. 44.
6 Rosalind Goforth, *Chinese Diamonds for the King of Kings* (Toronto: Evangelical Publishers, 1945), p. 92.
7 Eugene Myers Harrison, *Giants of the Missionary Trail: The Life Stories of Eight Men Who Defied Death and Demons* (Three Hills, Canada: Prairie Bible Institute, 1973), p. 189.
8 Rosalind Goforth, *Climbing: Memories of a Missionary's Wife* (Grand Rapids, MI: Zondervan, 1940), p. 41.
9 Goforth, *Climbing*, p. 203.
10 Dave and Neta Jackson, *Mask of the Wolf Boy* (Minneapolis, MN: Bethany House, 1999), p. 139.
11 Harrison, *Giants of the Missionary Trail*, p. 190.
12 Goforth, *Goforth of China*, p. 119.

13 John Foxe, *The New Foxe's Book of Martyrs*, rewritten and updated by Harold J. Chadwick (North Brunswick, NJ: Bridge-Logos, 1997), p. 325.
14 For a detailed account of the Goforth family's escape, see Robert Coventry Forsyth (ed.), *The China Martyrs of 1900: A Complete Roll of the Christian Heroes Martyred in China in 1900, with Narratives of Survivors* (London: Religious Tract Society, 1904), pp. 202–18.
15 Goforth, *Climbing*, p. 101.
16 Goforth, *Goforth of China*, p. 187.
17 Harrison, *Giants of the Missionary Trail*, p. 194.
18 Harrison, *Giants of the Missionary Trail*, p. 194.
19 Harrison, *Giants of the Missionary Trail*, p. 194.
20 Harrison, *Giants of the Missionary Trail*, p. 197.
21 Jonathan Goforth, *By My Spirit* (Minneapolis, MN: Bethany House, 1942), pp. 74–5.
22 Goforth, *By My Spirit*, pp. 78–9.
23 Goforth, *By My Spirit*, p. 80.
24 J. Goforth, "The Revival in Honan," *China's Millions* (March 1909), p. 42.
25 Goforth, *By My Spirit*, p. 83.
26 Goforth, *By My Spirit*, p. 84.
27 Goforth, *By My Spirit*, pp. 93–4.
28 Stauffer, *The Christian Occupation of China*, p. x.
29 See Table 2: "Christians in Henan." There were 68 Three-Self churches in Anyang City alone in 2002, according to a TSPM prayer calendar.
30 Tucker, *From Jerusalem to Irian Jaya*, p. 193.
31 *Moody Monthly* (November 1936).
32 Harrison, *Giants of the Missionary Trail*, p. 180.
33 See Rosalind Goforth, *Chinese Diamonds for the King of Kings* (Toronto: Evangelical Publishers, 1945).
34 See Jonathan Goforth, *By My Spirit* (Minneapolis, MN: Bethany House, 1942); and Jonathan and Rosalind Goforth, *Miracle Lives of China* (New York, NY: Harper & Bros., 1932).
35 John D. Woodbridge (ed.), *Ambassadors for Christ: Distinguished Representatives of the Message throughout the World* (Chicago, IL: Moody Press, 1994), p. 181.

1910s

1 Mrs. Ford, "Mrs. Chu—an Answer to Prayer," *China's Millions* (August 1910), p. 127.
2 E. G. Bevis, "From Darkness to Light: Tidings of Blessing at Chenchowfu, Honan," *China's Millions* (November 1916), p. 133.

3 T. Ekeland, Albert Anderson, and Olive T. Christensen (eds), *White Unto Harvest: A Survey of the Lutheran United Mission* (Minneapolis, MN: Board of Foreign Missions, 1919), p. 203.
4 Ekeland, Anderson, and Christensen, *White Unto Harvest*, p. 204.
5 Ekeland, Anderson, and Christensen, *White Unto Harvest*, p. 204.
6 Milton T. Stauffer (ed.), *The Christian Occupation of China* (Shanghai: China Continuation Committee, 1922), p. x.
7 This figure consists of approximately 54,000 members of Three-Self churches and 92,000 members of Evangelical house churches. See Table 2: "Christians in Henan."
8 Jonathan Goforth, *By My Spirit* (Minneapolis, MN: Bethany House, 1942), p. 111.
9 Rosalind Goforth, *Chinese Diamonds for the King of Kings* (Toronto: Evangelical Publishers, 1945), p. 95.
10 "How the Good News Came to the K'ong Village," *China's Millions* (September 1917), p. 105.
11 Stauffer, *The Christian Occupation of China*, p. vi.
12 Myrrul Byler, "A Letter to Henry Brown, Mennonite Missionary to Puyang (1911–1947)," Amity News Service (June 1995).
13 See Table 2: "Christians in Henan."

1920s

1 Milton T. Stauffer (ed.), *The Christian Occupation of China* (Shanghai: China Continuation Committee, 1922), p. 83.
2 Quoted in Rosalind Goforth, *Chinese Diamonds for the King of Kings* (Toronto: Evangelical Publishers, 1945), p. 54.
3 Peter Stursberg, *The Golden Hope: Christians in China* (Toronto: The United Church Publishing House, 1987), p. 72.
4 Marshall Broomhall, *Marshal Feng: A Good Soldier of Christ Jesus* (London: China Inland Mission, 1924), pp. 20–1.
5 Goforth, *Chinese Diamonds*, p. 58.
6 Stursberg, *The Golden Hope*, p. 71.
7 R. H. Mathews, "Among General Feng Yu-Hsiang's Troops," *China's Millions* (August 1921), p. 92.
8 Rosalind Goforth, *Climbing: Memories of a Missionary's Wife* (Grand Rapids, MI: Zondervan, 1940), p. 98.
9 Daniel Nelson, *The Apostle to the Chinese Communists* (Minneapolis, MN: Board of Foreign Missions of the Norwegian Lutheran Church of America, 1935), p. 4.
10 Nelson, *The Apostle to the Chinese Communists*, pp. 4–5.

11 Nelson, *The Apostle to the Chinese Communists*, p. 7.
12 Nelson, *The Apostle to the Chinese Communists*, p. 8.
13 Nelson, *The Apostle to the Chinese Communists*, p. 21.
14 Nelson, *The Apostle to the Chinese Communists*, p. 21.
15 Mrs. Howard Taylor, *Guinness of Honan* (London: China Inland Mission, 1930), p. 100.
16 Geraldine and Howard Taylor were his sister and brother-in-law, and fellow missionaries in China.
17 Taylor, *Guinness of Honan*, p. 188.
18 Taylor, *Guinness of Honan*, p. 272.
19 Taylor, *Guinness of Honan*, p. 299.

Marie Monsen

1 Marie Monsen, *The Awakening: Revival in China, a Work of the Holy Spirit* (London: China Inland Mission, 1961), p. 25.
2 Marie Monsen, *A Wall of Fire*, trans. Joy Guinness (Minneapolis, MN: Bethany House, 1967), p. 15.
3 Deuteronomy 33:25 KJV.
4 Monsen, *A Wall of Fire*, p. 16.
5 Monsen, *The Awakening*, p. 27.
6 Monsen, *The Awakening*, p. 27.
7 Monsen, *The Awakening*, p. 28.
8 Monsen, *The Awakening*, p. 28.
9 Gustav Carlberg, *China in Revival* (Rock Island, IL: Augustana Book Concern, 1936), pp. 70–1.
10 Daniel Bays' biography of Marie Monsen, in Gerald H. Anderson (ed.), *Biographical Dictionary of Christian Missions* (Grand Rapids, MI: Eerdmans, 1999).
11 Brother Yun with Paul Hattaway, *The Heavenly Man: The Remarkable True Story of Chinese Christian Brother Yun* (London: Monarch, 2002), pp. 19–20.
12 Monsen, *The Awakening*, p. 39.
13 Monsen, *The Awakening*, p. 40.
14 Monsen, *The Awakening*, p. 43.
15 Monsen, *The Awakening*, pp. 122–3.
16 Monsen, *The Awakening*, p. 123.
17 Monsen, *The Awakening*, p. 123.
18 Monsen, *A Wall of Fire*, pp. 27–8.
19 Monsen, *A Wall of Fire*, p. 42.
20 Monsen, *A Wall of Fire*, p. 55.

21 Marie Monsen, *A Present Help*, trans. Joy Guinness (London: China Inland Mission, 1960), pp. 37–8.
22 Monsen, *A Wall of Fire*, p. 62.
23 Even today there is some dispute about the reason Monsen returned to Norway. While the official reason given was that she needed to take care of her mother, others claim her radical style of ministry was more than the Lutheran mission could handle, and they removed Monsen from the field despite being in the midst of powerful revival. Norwegian friends have told me the one thing that infuriated the Lutheran mission was Monsen's baptism as an adult, which effectively demonstrated her opposition to their practice of infant baptism. At the time, this subject was being fiercely debated in Norway and strongly defended by the Lutheran Church. Whatever the true reason for Monsen's missionary career coming to an end at the age of just 54, she never publicly contradicted the official line that she had left China to care for her mother. For years after Monsen's return to Norway, her ministry was largely rejected, but her books inspired so many people in Scandinavia and around the world that over time her legacy has been accepted by most Lutherans, and today she is held in great honor.
24 Monsen, *The Awakening*, p. 86.
25 Isaiah 60:22.
26 Milton T. Stauffer (ed.), *The Christian Occupation of China* (Shanghai: China Continuation Committee, 1922), p. xi.
27 This figure consists of just over 1 million members of Three-Self churches and 2.2 million members of Evangelical house churches. See Table 2: "Christians in Henan."
28 Yun with Hattaway, *The Heavenly Man*, p. 16.
29 Yun with Hattaway, *The Heavenly Man*, pp. 16–7.

1930s

1 Quoted in Gustav Carlberg, *China in Revival* (Rock Island, IL: Augustana Book Concern, 1936), p. 21.
2 Victor E. Swenson, *Parents of Many: Forty-Five Years as Missionaries in Old, New, and Divided China* (Rock Island, IL: Augustana Press, 1959), pp. 184–5.
3 J. Edwin Orr, *Evangelical Awakenings in Eastern Asia* (Minneapolis, MN: Bethany House, 1975), p. 79.
4 Henry Guinness, "Floods upon the Dry Ground," *China's Millions* (August 1933), p. 150.
5 Orr, *Evangelical Awakenings in Eastern Asia*, p. 78.

6 Carlberg, *China in Revival*, pp. 90–1.
7 Leslie T. Lyall, *A Biography of John Sung: Flame for God in the Far East* (London: China Inland Mission, 1954), p. 108.
8 Orr, *Evangelical Awakenings in Eastern Asia*, p. 78.
9 Chu Huaian, "The Footprints of an Evangelist," *Christian Life Quarterly* (December 1997).
10 Chu, "The Footprints of an Evangelist."
11 *China's Millions* (February 1930), p. 25.
12 China Inland Mission, *The Obstinate Horse and Other Stories* (London: China Inland Mission, 1955), p. 40.
13 Carlberg, *China in Revival*, pp. 134–6.
14 Swenson, *Parents of Many*, pp. 191–9.

1940s and 1950s

1 David Adeney, "An Earnest Spirit," *China's Millions* (March–April 1941), p. 27.
2 Gustav Carlberg, *China in Revival* (Rock Island, IL: Augustana Book Concern, 1936), p. 139.
3 Barbara Jurgensen, *All the Bandits of China: Adventures of a Missionary in a Land Savaged by Bandits and War Lords* (Minneapolis, MN: Augsburg, 1965), p. 177.
4 *China Study Journal* (August 1994).
5 Bertram Wolferstan, *The Catholic Church in China from 1860 to 1907* (St. Louis, MO: Sands & Co., 1909), p. 451.
6 Milton T. Stauffer (ed.), *The Christian Occupation of China* (Shanghai: China Continuation Committee, 1922), p. 84.
7 *China Study Journal* (August 1994).
8 Brother Yun with Paul Hattaway, *The Heavenly Man: The Remarkable True Story of Chinese Christian Brother Yun* (London: Monarch, 2002), pp. 20–1.
9 Victor E. Swenson, *Parents of Many: Forty-Five Years as Missionaries in Old, New, and Divided China* (Rock Island, IL: Augustana Press, 1959), p. 197.
10 "The Bitter Experiences of Rev. Dong Shaowu," *Bridge* (June 1992).
11 John Foxe, *The New Foxe's Book of Martyrs*, rewritten and updated by Harold J. Chadwick (North Brunswick, NJ: Bridge-Logos, 1997), pp. 348–9.

1960s and 1970s

1 Tony Lambert, *China's Christian Millions*, rev. edn (Oxford: Monarch, 2006), p. 249.

2 *China Study Journal* (August 1994).
3 "Where Two or Three Have Met Together," *Bridge* (September–October 1993), pp. 9–10.
4 Personal interview with Feng Jianguo, May 2001.
5 Personal interview with Peter Xu Yongze, October 2003.
6 These two testimonies were told to me by Zhang Rongliang, March 2002.
7 Danyun, *Lilies Amongst Thorns: Chinese Christians Tell Their Story through Blood and Tears* (Tonbridge, UK: Sovereign World, 1991), p. 298.
8 Personal interview with Peter Xu Yongze, October 2003.
9 The Red Guards were members of a student-led militia formed by Mao at the start of the Cultural Revolution in 1966. In their zeal and nationalistic fervor they were responsible for the deaths of millions of Chinese.
10 Paul Hattaway, *Back to Jerusalem: Three Chinese House Church Leaders Share Their Vision to Complete the Great Commission* (Carlisle: Piquant, 2003), p. 117.
11 Hattaway, *Back to Jerusalem*, p. 117.
12 Personal interview with Peter Xu Yongze, October 2003.
13 Danyun, *Lilies Amongst Thorns*, p. 243.
14 Personal interview with Zheng Shuqian, March 2001.

The Born-Again Movement

1 One of the few books highlighting this important church movement is Yalin Xin, *Inside China's House Church Network: The Word of Life Movement and Its Renewing Dynamic* (Lexington, KY: Emeth Press, 2009).
2 Confidential report from a mission leader, April 2000.
3 David Aikman, *Jesus in Beijing: How Christianity Is Transforming China and Changing the Global Balance of Power* (Washington, DC: Regnery, 2003), p. 88.
4 *China Prayer Letter and Ministry Report* (September–October 1997).
5 Personal interview with Peter Xu Yongze, October 2003.
6 *South China Morning Post* (April 24, 1988).
7 Alex Buchan, "God the Vandal" (March 1, 2002), at: <www.globalengage.org>. The web page may no longer be active.
8 Chinese Church Research Center (April 25, 1988).
9 Personal interview with Peter Xu Yongze, October 2003.
10 Personal interview with Peter Xu Yongze, October 2003.
11 Personal interview with Peter Xu Yongze, October 2003.
12 Personal interview with Peter Xu Yongze, October 2003.
13 Personal interview with Peter Xu Yongze, October 2003.

14 *Pingguo Ribao* (May 16, 1997).
15 Personal interview with Peter Xu Yongze, October 2003.
16 Personal interview with Peter Xu Yongze, October 2003.
17 "Persecution in China: A Party Member's View," *Compass Direct* (October 24, 1997).
18 Personal interview with Peter Xu Yongze, October 2003.
19 Personal interview with Peter Xu Yongze, October 2003.
20 Personal interview with Peter Xu Yongze, October 2003.
21 Personal interview with Peter Xu Yongze, October 2003.
22 Personal interview with Deborah Xu Yongling, July 2001.
23 *International Christian Concern* (August 19, 1997).
24 David Aikman, "A Church Grows in China," *The Weekly Standard* (September 28, 1998).
25 See 2 Samuel 24 and 1 Chronicles 21 for accounts of this incident.
26 Personal interview with Peter Xu Yongze, October 2003.
27 *Asian Report* (July–August 2006).
28 Aikman, *Jesus in Beijing*, p. 94.

1980s

1 Li Shixiong and Xiqiu (Bob) Fu (eds), "Religion and National Security in China: Secret Documents from China's Security Sector," unpublished report, 2002, p. 18.
2 Brother Yun with Paul Hattaway, *The Heavenly Man: The Remarkable True Story of Chinese Christian Brother Yun* (London: Monarch, 2002), pp. 49–50.
3 Chu, "The Protestant House Churches," *Pai Shing* (February 1, 1982).
4 Chu, "The Protestant House Churches."
5 More than 25 years later Brother David shared the full story in Brother David with Paul Hattaway, *Project Pearl: The One Million Smuggled Bibles That Changed China* (Oxford: Monarch, 2007).
6 Letter to Open Doors, August 10, 1981.
7 *Pray for China* (July–August 1982).
8 Stéphane Courtois et al., *The Black Book of Communism: Crimes, Terror, Repression* (Cambridge, MA: Harvard University Press, 1999), p. 542.
9 "Pastors Sentenced as Criminals," *Asian Report* (May–June 1984), p. 6.
10 *Asian Report* (September–October 1983).
11 Danyun, *Lilies Amongst Thorns: Chinese Christians Tell Their Story through Blood and Tears* (Tonbridge, UK: Sovereign World, 1991), p. 222.
12 Danyun, *Lilies Amongst Thorns*, p. 230.

13 Danyun, *Lilies Amongst Thorns*, pp. 234–5.
14 Danyun, *Lilies Amongst Thorns*, pp. 236–7.
15 Dan Wooding, "A Life Sentence for Sister Quan: The Moving Story of a Courageous Chinese House Church Leader," from a website that is no longer active.
16 Leslie T. Lyall, *God Reigns in China* (London: Hodder & Stoughton, 1985), p. 172.
17 Paul Estabrooks, *Secrets to Spiritual Success* (Tonbridge, UK: Sovereign World, 1996), p. 145.
18 Jonathan Chao, *Wise as Serpents, Harmless as Doves: Christians in China Tell Their Story* (Pasadena, CA: William Carey Library, 1988), p. 165.
19 Revival Chinese Ministries International, *The Challenge of China* (April 1988).
20 Open Doors, March 1982.
21 Brother David with Hattaway, *Project Pearl*, pp. 253–4.
22 *Asian Report* (April 1983).
23 *Pray for China* (May–June 1984).
24 *Pray for China* (July–August 1985).
25 *Pray for China* (August–September 1988).

The Nanyang Church

1 "Three-Self Preaching Team Sent to Henan," *China News and Church Report* (November 30, 1988).
2 Personal communication with an experienced missionary, November 2007.
3 Personal interview with Brother Timothy, March 2001.
4 Brother Yun with Paul Hattaway, *The Heavenly Man: The Remarkable True Story of Chinese Christian Brother Yun* (London: Monarch, 2002), pp. 37, 40–1.
5 Yun with Hattaway, *The Heavenly Man*, p. 164.
6 Yun with Hattaway, *The Heavenly Man*, p. 165.
7 During the interview, Elder Fu pulled a roll of paper out of his coat pocket which listed the 60 names of people he frequently prays for.
8 See Brother Yun with Paul Hattaway, *The Heavenly Man: The Remarkable True Story of Chinese Christian Brother Yun* (London: Monarch, 2002).
9 So extraordinary was this incident that every eyewitness I interviewed almost 20 years later was reduced to tears when he or she remembered the sight of Yun that day.
10 Matthew 16:24.

11 Personal interview with Brother Timothy, March 2001.
12 Personal interview with Brother Timothy, March 2001. This story was confirmed by several house church believers from the area.
13 See Table 2: "Christians in Henan."

The China Gospel Fellowship

1 Personal interview with Feng Jianguo, May 2001.
2 David Aikman, *Jesus in Beijing: How Christianity Is Transforming China and Changing the Global Balance of Power* (Washington, DC: Regnery, 2003, p. 81.
3 Aikman, *Jesus in Beijing*, p. 83.
4 Personal interview with Feng Jianguo, May 2001.
5 Aikman, *Jesus in Beijing*, p. 80.
6 Personal interview with Feng Jianguo, May 2001.
7 Personal interview with Feng Jianguo, May 2001.
8 Aikman, *Jesus in Beijing*, p. 84.
9 Aikman, *Jesus in Beijing*, pp. 85–6.
10 Personal interview with Feng Jianguo, May 2001.
11 Personal interview with Feng Jianguo, May 2001.
12 Luke Wesley, *The Church in China: Persecuted, Pentecostal, and Powerful* (Baguio, Philippines: AJPS Books, 2004), pp. 42–3.
13 Personal interview with Feng Jianguo, May 2001.
14 Shen Xianfeng, "House Churches Reply: Are We Truly a Cult?" *China Prayer Letter* (September–October 1998).
15 Shen, "House Churches Reply: Are We Truly a Cult?"
16 David Aikman, "A Church Grows in China," *The Weekly Standard* (September 28, 1998).
17 Aikman, "A Church Grows in China."
18 *Asian Report* (September–October 2000).
19 OMF International, "House Church Networks—an Overview," *Global Chinese Ministries* (April 2006).
20 The kidnapping of the CGF leaders was particularly shocking to the author, who had enjoyed rich fellowship with many of the abducted leaders just weeks earlier in China.
21 From Part 7 of a report written by the leaders of the CGF at: <www.chinaforjesus.com>. The web page may no longer be active.
22 "Testimony of Younger Shen: The Kidnapping," at: <www.chinaforjesus.com>.
23 From Part 16 of a report at: <www.chinaforjesus.com>. The web page may no longer be active.

24 "Testimony of Younger Shen: The Kidnapping," at: <www.chinaforjesus.com>.

25 "SWAT Team Raids Christian Dinner," *China Aid* (January 19, 2019).

1990s

1 *China Prayer Letter and Ministry Report* (May–June 1992).

2 "House Church Raided," *Pray for China* (January–February 1994).

3 "108 Christians Remain in Detention after House Church Raid," *China News and Church Report* (November 6, 1992).

4 *China Prayer Letter and Ministry Report* (May 1993).

5 *China Prayer Letter and Ministry Report* (May 1993).

6 Personal interview with Brother Joseph, June 2001.

7 Personal interview with Peter Xu Yongze, October 2003.

8 David Aikman, "A Church Grows in China," *The Weekly Standard* (September 28, 1998).

9 *DAWN Friday Fax* (no. 31, 1995).

10 Revival Chinese Ministries International, *The Challenge of China* (no. 2, 1995).

11 Revival Chinese Ministries International, *The Challenge of China* (no. 2, 1995).

12 "Extensive Persecution of Christians in Henan Province," *China News and Church Report* (July 14, 1995).

13 *DAWN Friday Fax* (no. 31, 1995).

14 *Global Chinese Ministries* (December 1999–January 2000).

15 See Table 2: "Christians in Henan."

16 See "Religious Deceiver Drowns Twenty Believers," *China News and Church Report* (August 31, 1990); "Wolves Scatter China's Sheep," *Asian Report* (July–September 1992), p. 19.

17 "Inability to Disciple the Vast Number of New Converts to Christianity Provides Fertile Ground for Heresy," *China News and Church Report* (August 7, 1992).

18 Dennis Balcombe, *China's Opening Doors: Incredible Stories of the Holy Spirit at Work in One of the Greatest Revivals in Christianity* (Lake Mary, FL: Charisma House, 2014), p. 5.

19 See Table 2: "Christians in Henan."

20 *Christianity Today* (March 11, 2002), p. 41.

21 *China News and Church Report* (August 9, 1996).

22 Cited in "Henan Province: Ripe for Harvest (Part Three)," *Asia Harvest* (July 2002).

23 "Christians Rounded Up," *Open Doors* (February 1999).

24 "Continued Persecution of Protestants," *Media Work Press Releases and Statements* (November 24, 1998).
25 Personal interview with a missionary, January 2000.
26 "Christians Beaten in New Blitz on Worship," *South China Morning Post* (November 11, 1998).
27 See Amity News Service, December 1998.
28 Tony Lambert, *China's Christian Millions*, rev. edn (Oxford: Monarch, 2006), p. 198.
29 Tony Lambert, *The Resurrection of the Chinese Church* (Wheaton, IL: Harold Shaw, 1994), p. 310.
30 Patrick Johnstone and Jason Mandryk, *Operation World: 21st Century Edition* (Carlisle: Paternoster Lifestyle, 2001), p. 172.
31 The Local Church is a large Christian denomination in China, founded by Watchman Nee; it is also known as "the Little Flock."
32 Far East Broadcasting, August 1992.
33 Far East Broadcasting, June 1992.
34 Far East Broadcasting, March 1993.
35 Far East Broadcasting, June 1993.
36 Far East Broadcasting, February 1994.
37 Far East Broadcasting, June 1995.
38 Far East Broadcasting, May 1996.
39 Far East Broadcasting, August 1996.
40 Far East Broadcasting, April 1997.
41 Far East Broadcasting, August 1998.
42 Far East Broadcasting, August 1999.

The Fangcheng Church

1 Milton T. Stauffer (ed.), *The Christian Occupation of China* (Shanghai: China Continuation Committee, 1922), p. ix.
2 David H. Adeney, *China: The Church's Long March* (Ventura, CA: Regal, 1985), p. 141.
3 Adeney, *China: The Church's Long March*, p. 25.
4 Jonathan Chao, *Wise as Serpents, Harmless as Doves: Christians in China Tell Their Story* (Pasadena, CA: William Carey Library, 1988), p. 189.
5 David Aikman, *Jesus in Beijing: How Christianity Is Transforming China and Changing the Global Balance of Power* (Washington, DC: Regnery, 2003), p. 75.
6 Aikman, *Jesus in Beijing*, pp. 75–6.
7 Personal interview with Zhang Rongliang, August 2002.
8 Aikman, *Jesus in Beijing*, p. 77.

9 Personal interview with Zhang Rongliang, August 2002.
10 Aikman, *Jesus in Beijing*, p. 104.
11 Personal interview with Zheng Shuqian, March 2001.
12 Personal interview with Zhang Rongliang, August 2002.
13 Chao, *Wise as Serpents*, pp. 189–92.
14 Dennis Balcombe, *China's Opening Doors: Incredible Stories of the Holy Spirit at Work in One of the Greatest Revivals in Christianity* (Lake Mary, FL: Charisma House, 2014), pp. 126–7.
15 Revival Chinese Ministries International, *The Challenge of China* (September 1997).
16 Personal interview with Zhang Rongliang, August 2002.
17 Personal interview with Zhang Rongliang, August 2002.
18 Personal interview with Zhang Rongliang, August 2002.
19 Personal interview with Zhang Rongliang, August 2002.
20 Personal interview with Zhang Rongliang, August 2002.
21 Personal interview with Sister Mei, August 2002.
22 Mark O'Keefe, "China Widens Crackdown on Faithful," *The Oregonian* (September 18, 1999).
23 O'Keefe, "China Widens Crackdown on Faithful."
24 *The Voice of the Martyrs* (June 2005).
25 "China Sentences Underground Pastor to 7.5 Years in Prison," *China Aid* (July 8, 2005).
26 See "CAA Released Prosecution Paper of Zhang Rongliang," *China Aid* (July 8, 2006).
27 *Christian Solidarity Worldwide* (July 10, 2006).
28 *Compass Direct* (July 6, 2006).
29 Aikman, *Jesus in Beijing*, p. 80.
30 Aikman, *Jesus in Beijing*, p. 99.
31 Personal interview with Ding Hei, March 2001.
32 *Asian Report* (September–October 2005).
33 Balcombe, *China's Opening Doors*, p. 130.
34 *Asian Report* (March–April 2004).
35 Aikman, *Jesus in Beijing*, p. 78.
36 O'Keefe, "China Widens Crackdown on Faithful"; and David Aikman, "A Church Grows in China," *The Weekly Standard* (September 28, 1998).

2000s

1 Amity News Service, March 1996. Three-Self figures typically only include adult baptized church members.

2 "Where Have All the Evangelists Gone?" Amity News Service (January–February 2000).
3 "Growing Christian Community Short of Pastoral Workers, Buildings, Bibles," Amity News Service (March 1996).
4 "Three Plentifuls and One Shortage: Churches in Henan Province," Amity News Service (December 2001).
5 See "Three Plentifuls and One Shortage."
6 *China Daily* (November 19, 2005), cited in *The Washington Times* (November 28, 2005).
7 Stefan J. Bos, "American Evangelist Palau Apologizes for China Remarks," *BosNewsLife* (December 4, 2005).
8 *The Times* (October 24, 2006).
9 This list led to the establishment by Asia Harvest of the Living Martyrs' Fund, providing support to those who were incapacitated by persecution, and aid to the families of those in prison. The fund continues to the present time. See <www.asiaharvest.org> for details.
10 Intercessors for China, *The Persecuted, the Poor and the Pioneer Missionaries* (2001 prayer calendar).
11 Xiao Ruozhi, "A Martyr at the Turn of the Century," *Christian Life Quarterly* (December 2000).
12 "Brother Liu Haitao's Martyrdom in Henan, China," *The Mandate Christian News* (February 3, 2001).
13 "Brother Liu Haitao's Martyrdom in Henan."
14 Brother Yun with Paul Hattaway, *The Heavenly Man: The Remarkable True Story of Chinese Christian Brother Yun* (London: Monarch, 2002), p. 70.
15 The Committee for the Investigation of Persecution of Religion in China (CIPRC), "People's Police: Enforcing the Law," undated.
16 International Mission Board, *The Commission* (June 2002).
17 Far East Broadcasting, January 2001.
18 *Global Chinese Ministries* (March 2001).
19 *Compass Direct* (February 8, 2003).
20 Letter to Asia Harvest, October 2006.
21 Letter to Asia Harvest, April 2007.
22 Letter to Asia Harvest, February 2008.

2010s

1 "Church Leader's Wife Dead after Buried Alive during Church Demolition," *China Aid* (April 18, 2016).
2 Brent Fulton, "China Reveals What It Wants to Do with Christianity," *Christianity Today* (April 28, 2016).

3 "Henan Removed More Than 4,500 Crosses," *China Aid* (March 12, 2019).
4 "Henan Church to Be Converted to Hotel," *China Aid* (May 29, 2019).
5 Jiang Tao, "New Testimonies Help to Sort Out the Mystery of Pastor's Suicide," *Bitter Winter* (September 6, 2019).
6 "Henan Officials Bomb Church," *China Aid* (December 6, 2018).
7 "Pastor Disappears," *China Aid* (October 10, 2019).
8 "Government Removes First of Ten Commandments from Church," *China Aid* (January 7, 2019).
9 "Henan Bureau Calls Christianity an 'Enormous Harm' to Chinese Society," *China Aid* (May 2, 2019).
10 "Pastor Imprisoned for Eight Months," *China Aid* (October 22, 2019).
11 "Pastor Force-Fed Medicine," *China Aid* (December 20, 2019).
12 Letter to Asia Harvest, September 2010.
13 Letter to Asia Harvest, June 2014.

Selected bibliography

Adeney, David H., *China: The Church's Long March* (Ventura, CA: Regal, 1985).

Aikman, David, *Jesus in Beijing: How Christianity Is Transforming China and Changing the Global Balance of Power* (Washington, DC: Regnery, 2003).

Anderson, Palmer A., *In the Crucible: Being Incidents Showing the Power of the Gospel in China* (Saskatoon, Canada: The Canada District Young People's Luther League, no date).

Augustana Synod, *Our First Decade in China, 1905–1915: The Augustana Mission in the Province of Honan* (Rock Island, IL: Board of Foreign Missions of the Augustana Synod, 1915).

——, *Our Second Decade in China, 1915–1925: Sketches and Reminiscences by Missionaries of the Augustana Mission in the Province of Honan* (Rock Island, IL: Board of Foreign Missions of the Augustana Synod, 1925).

Austin, Alvyn J., *Saving China: Canadian Missionaries in the Middle Kingdom* (Toronto: University of Toronto Press, 1986).

——, et al., *China's Millions: The China Inland Mission and Late Qing Society, 1832–1905*, Studies in the History of Christian Missions (Grand Rapids, MI: Eerdmans, 2007).

Balcombe, Dennis, *China's Opening Doors: Incredible Stories of the Holy Spirit at Work in One of the Greatest Revivals in Christianity* (Lake Mary, FL: Charisma House, 2014).

Bartel, H. C., *A Short Review of the First Mennonite Mission in China* (Tsaohsien, China: Truth Publishing House, 1913).

Bays, Daniel H. (ed.), *Christianity in China: From the Eighteenth Century to the Present* (Stanford, CA: Stanford University Press, 1996).

Benge, Janet and Geoff, *Jonathan Goforth: An Open Door in China* (Seattle, WA: YWAM Publishing, 2001).

Bitton, Nelson, *Griffith John: The Apostle of Central China* (London: National Sunday School Union, 1920).

Broomhall, A. J., *Hudson Taylor and China's Open Century, Book Six: Assault on the Nine* (London: Overseas Missionary Fellowship, 1988).

——, *The Shaping of Modern China: Hudson Taylor's Life and Legacy, Vol. 1: Early to 1867* (Carlisle: Piquant, 2005).

Broomhall, Marshall, *The Bible in China* (London: China Inland Mission, 1934).
——, *The Jubilee Story of the China Inland Mission* (London: China Inland Mission, 1915).
——, *Marshal Feng: A Good Soldier of Christ Jesus* (London: China Inland Mission, 1924).
—— (ed.), *The Chinese Empire: A General and Missionary Survey* (London: Morgan & Scott, 1907).
—— (ed.), *Martyred Missionaries of the China Inland Mission: With a Record of the Perils and Sufferings of Some Who Escaped* (London: Morgan & Scott, 1901).
Carlberg, Gustav, *China in Revival* (Rock Island, IL: Augustana Book Concern, 1936).
—— (ed.), *Thirty Years in China, 1905–1935: The Story of the Augustana Synod Mission in the Province of Honan as Told by the Missionaries* (Rock Island, IL: Board of Foreign Missions of the Augustana Synod, 1937).
Chao, Jonathan (ed.), *The China Mission Handbook: A Portrait of China and Its Church* (Hong Kong: Chinese Church Research Center, 1989).
——, *Wise as Serpents, Harmless as Doves: Christians in China Tell Their Story* (Pasadena, CA: William Carey Library, 1988).
China Inland Mission, *The Obstinate Horse and Other Stories* (London: China Inland Mission, 1955).
——, *Through Fire: The Story of 1938* (London: China Inland Mission, 1939).
Christensen, Erleen J., *In War and Famine: Missionaries in China's Honan Province in the 1940s* (Montreal: McGill-Queen's University Press, 2005).
Companjen, Anneke, *Hidden Sorrow, Lasting Joy: The Forgotten Women of the Persecuted Church* (Wheaton, IL: Tyndale House, 2001).
Cronin, Vincent, *The Wise Man from the West* (New York, NY: E. P. Dutton, 1955).
Danyun, *Lilies Amongst Thorns: Chinese Christians Tell Their Story through Blood and Tears* (Tonbridge, UK: Sovereign World, 1991).
David, Brother, with Paul Hattaway, *Project Pearl: The One Million Smuggled Bibles That Changed China* (Oxford: Monarch, 2007).
Davis, George T. B., *China's Christian Army: A Story of Marshal Feng and His Soldiers* (New York, NY: Christian Alliance, 1925).
Doyle, G. Wright, *Builders of the Chinese Church: Pioneer Protestant Missionaries and Chinese Church Leaders*, Studies in Chinese Christianity (Eugene, OR: Pickwick, 2015).
Ekeland, T., Albert Anderson, and Olive T. Christensen (eds), *White Unto*

Harvest: A Survey of the Lutheran United Mission (Minneapolis, MN: Board of Foreign Missions, 1919).

Engelsviken, Tormod, et al., *A Passion for China: Norwegian Mission to China until 1949* (Eugene, OR: Wipf & Stock, 2015).

Flynt, Wayne, and Gerald W. Berkley, *Taking Christianity to China: Alabama Missionaries in the Middle Kingdom, 1850–1950* (Tuscaloosa, AL: University of Alabama Press, 1997).

Foote, Paulina, *God's Hand over My Nineteen Years in China* (Hillsboro, KS: M. B. Publishing, 1962).

Forsyth, Robert Coventry (ed.), *The China Martyrs of 1900: A Complete Roll of the Christian Heroes Martyred in China in 1900, with Narratives of Survivors* (London: Religious Tract Society, 1904).

Gih, Andrew, *Launch Out into the Deep: Tales of Revival through China's Famous Bethel Evangelistic Band and Further Messages* (London: Marshall, Morgan & Scott, 1938).

Goforth, Jonathan, *By My Spirit* (Minneapolis, MN: Bethany House, 1942).

——, and Rosalind Goforth, *Miracle Lives of China* (Elkhart, IN: Bethel, 1988).

Goforth, Rosalind, *Chinese Diamonds for the King of Kings* (Toronto: Evangelical Publishers, 1945).

——, *Climbing: Memories of a Missionary's Wife* (Grand Rapids, MI: Zondervan, 1940).

——, *Goforth of China* (Grand Rapids, MI: Zondervan, 1937).

Griffiths, Valerie, *Not Less Than Everything: The Courageous Women Who Carried the Christian Gospel to China* (Oxford: Monarch, 2004).

Guinness, Geraldine, *In the Far East: Letters from China* (London: Morgan & Scott, 1890).

——, *Letters from Geraldine Guinness (Mrs. F. Howard Taylor) in China* (New York, NY: Fleming H. Revell, 1889).

Guinness, M. Geraldine, *The Story of the China Inland Mission* (2 vols) (London: Morgan & Scott, 1893).

Harrison, Eugene Myers, *Giants of the Missionary Trail: The Life Stories of Eight Men Who Defied Death and Demons* (Three Hills, Canada: Prairie Bible Institute, 1973).

Hattaway, Paul, *Back to Jerusalem: Three Chinese House Church Leaders Share Their Vision to Complete the Great Commission* (Carlisle: Piquant, 2003).

——, *China's Christian Martyrs: 1300 years of Christians in China Who Have Died for Their Faith* (Oxford: Monarch, 2007).

——, *China's Unreached Cities, Vol. 1* (Chiang Mai, Thailand: Asia Harvest, 1999).

——, *China's Unreached Cities, Vol. 2* (Chiang Mai, Thailand: Asia Harvest, 2003).
——, *Fire and Blood, Vol. 1: China's Book of Martyrs* (Carlisle: Piquant, 2007).
——, *Fire and Blood, Vol. 2: Henan: The Galilee of China* (Carlisle: Piquant, 2009).
——, *Operation China: Introducing All the Peoples of China* (Carlisle: Piquant, 2000).
Hefley, James and Marti, *By Their Blood: Christian Martyrs of the Twentieth Century* (Milford, MI: Mott Media, 1979).
Jackson, Dave and Neta, *Mask of the Wolf Boy* (Minneapolis, MN: Bethany House, 1999).
Jiang Wen-Han, *Ancient Chinese Christianity and the Jews of Kaifeng* (Shanghai: Zhi Shi Press, 1982).
Jurgensen, Barbara, *All the Bandits of China: Adventures of a Missionary in a Land Savaged by Bandits and War Lords* (Minneapolis, MN: Augsburg, 1965).
Kreider, Robert (ed.), *James Liu and Stephen Wang: Christians True in China* (Newton, KS: Faith and Life Press, 1988).
Lack, C. N., *Farmer Wu: The Man Who Baptized Himself* (London: China Inland Mission, 1927).
Lambert, Tony, *China's Christian Millions*, rev. edn (Oxford: Monarch, 2006).
——, *The Resurrection of the Chinese Church* (Wheaton, IL: Harold Shaw, 1994).
Latourette, Kenneth Scott, *A History of Christian Missions in China* (New York, NY: Macmillan, 1929).
Lawrence, Carl, *The Church in China* (Minneapolis, MN: Bethany House, 1985).
——, with David Wang, *The Coming Influence of China* (Sisters, OR: Multnomah, 1996).
Leslie, Donald Daniel, *The Survival of the Chinese Jews: The Jewish Community of Kaifeng* (Leiden: Brill, 1972).
Lodwick, Kathleen L., *Crusaders Against Opium: Protestant Missionaries in China, 1874–1917* (Lexington, KY: University of Kentucky Press, 1996).
Lovett, Richard, *The History of the London Missionary Society, 1795–1895* (2 vols) (London: Henry Frowde, 1899).
Lowrie, Walter M., *The Land of Sinim, or, An Exposition of Isaiah XLIX, 12 Together with a Brief Account of the Jews and Christians in China* (Philadelphia, PA: W. S. Martin, 1850).
Lyall, Leslie T., *Come Wind, Come Weather: The Present Experience of the Church in China* (London: Hodder & Stoughton, 1961).

——, *Flame for God: John Sung and Revival in the Far East* (London: Overseas Missionary Fellowship, 1954).

——, *God Reigns in China* (London: Hodder & Stoughton, 1985).

——, *A Passion for the Impossible: The China Inland Mission, 1865–1965* (London: Hodder & Stoughton, 1965).

——, *The Phoenix Rises: The Phenomenal Growth of Eight Chinese Churches* (Singapore: Overseas Missionary Fellowship, 1992).

MacGillivray, D. (ed.), *A Century of Protestant Missions in China (1807–1907)* (Shanghai: American Presbyterian Mission Press, 1907).

Mackenzie, Murdoch, *Twenty-Five Years in Honan* (Toronto: Board of Foreign Missions, Presbyterian Church in Canada, 1913).

Miner, Luella, *China's Book of Martyrs: A Record of Heroic Martyrdoms and Marvelous Deliverances of Chinese Christians during the Summer of 1900* (Philadelphia, PA: Westminster Press, 1903).

Moffett, Samuel Hugh, *A History of Christianity in Asia, Vol. 2: 1500 to 1900* (Maryknoll, NY: Orbis, 2005).

Monsen, Marie, *The Awakening: Revival in China, a Work of the Holy Spirit* (London: China Inland Mission, 1961).

——, *A Present Help*, trans. Joy Guinness (London: China Inland Mission, 1960).

——, *A Wall of Fire*, trans. Joy Guinness (Minneapolis, MN: Bethany House, 1967).

Nelson, Daniel, *The Apostle to the Chinese Communists* (Minneapolis, MN: Board of Foreign Missions of the Norwegian Lutheran Church of America, 1935).

Orr, J. Edwin, *Evangelical Awakenings in Eastern Asia* (Minneapolis, MN: Bethany House, 1975).

——, *Through Blood and Fire in China* (London: Marshall, Morgan & Scott, 1939).

Paper, Jordan, and Alex Bender (eds), *The Chinese Jews of Kaifeng: A Millennium of Adaptation and Endurance* (Lanham, MD: Lexington Books, 2017).

Paterson, Ross, *The Continuing Heartcry for China* (Tonbridge, UK: Sovereign World, 1999).

Pollock, J. C., *Hudson Taylor and Maria: Pioneers in China* (New York, NY: Overseas Missionary Fellowship, 1952).

Ramseyer, R., *Mennonites in China* (Winnipeg, Canada: China Educational Exchange, 1988).

Rees, Charlotte Harris, *Courage, Endurance, Sacrifice: The Lives and Faith of Three Generations of Missionaries* (Durham, NC: Torchflame Books, 2016).

Royal, Robert, *The Catholic Martyrs of the Twentieth Century: A Comprehensive History* (New York, NY: Crossroad, 2000).

Sam, Georgina, and David Wang, *Still Red* (Hong Kong: Asian Outreach, 2007).

Saunders, Alexander R., *A God of Deliverances: The Story of the Marvellous Deliverances through the Sovereign Power of God of a Party of Missionaries, when Compelled by the Boxer Rising to Flee from Shan-si, North China* (London: Morgan & Scott, 1901).

Scherer, Frances, *George and Mary Schlosser: Ambassadors for Christ in China* (Winona Lake, IN: Light and Life Press, 1976).

Sellew, Walter A., *Clara Leffingwell: A Missionary* (Chicago, IL: Free Methodist Publishing House, 1907).

Skinsnes, Casper C., *Scalpel and Cross in Honan* (Minneapolis, MN: Augsburg, 1952).

Stauffer, Milton T. (ed.), *The Christian Occupation of China* (Shanghai: China Continuation Committee, 1922).

Stock, Eugene, *The History of the Church Missionary Society: Its Environment, Its Men, and Its Work* (3 vols) (London: Church Missionary Society, 1899).

Stursberg, Peter, *The Golden Hope: Christians in China* (Toronto: The United Church Publishing House, 1987).

Swenson, Victor E., *Parents of Many: Forty-Five Years as Missionaries in Old, New, and Divided China* (Rock Island, IL: Augustana Press, 1959).

Taylor, Dr. and Mrs. Howard, *Hudson Taylor and the China Inland Mission: The Growth of a Work of God* (London: China Inland Mission, 1919).

Taylor, Mrs. Howard, *Guinness of Honan* (London: China Inland Mission, 1930).

Taylor, J. Hudson, *After Thirty Years: Three Decades of the China Inland Mission, 1865–1895* (London: China Inland Mission, 1896).

Thompson, R. Wardlaw, *Griffith John: The Story of Fifty Years in China* (London: Religious Tract Society, 1908).

Walmsley, Lewis C., *Bishop in Honan: Mission and Museum in the Life of William C. White* (Toronto: University of Toronto Press, 1974).

Waugh, Geoff, *Flashpoints of Revival: History's Mighty Revival* (Shippensberg, PA: Revival Press, 1998).

Wesley, Luke, *The Church in China: Persecuted, Pentecostal, and Powerful* (Baguio, Philippines: AJPS Books, 2004).

White, Theodore H., and Annalee Jacoby, *Thunder Out of China* (New York, NY: William Sloane, 1946).

White, William, *Chinese Jews: A Compilation of Matters Relating to the Jews of Kai'-feng Fu* (Toronto: University of Toronto Press, 1966).

Williamson, Glen, *Geneva: The Fascinating Story of Geneva Sayre, Missionary to the Chinese* (Winona Lake, IN: Light and Life Press, 1974).
Winebrenner, Jane, *Steel in His Soul: The Dick Hillis Story* (Mukilteo, WA: Overseas Crusaders, 1985).
Wolf, Sister Ann Colette, *Against All Odds: Sisters of Providence Mission to the Chinese, 1920–1990* (St Mary-of-the-Woods, IN: Sisters of Providence, 1990).
Woodbridge, John (ed.), *More Than Conquerors: Portraits of Believers from All Walks of Life* (Chicago, IL: Moody Press, 1992).
Yalin Xin, *Inside China's House Church Network: The Word of Life Movement and Its Renewing Dynamic* (Lexington, KY: Emeth Press, 2009).
Yun, Brother, with Paul Hattaway, *The Heavenly Man: The Remarkable True Story of Chinese Christian Brother Yun* (London: Monarch, 2002).
——, *Living Water: Powerful Teachings from Brother Yun* (Grand Rapids, MI: Zondervan, 2008).
Zambon, Mariagrazia, *Crimson Seeds: Eighteen PIME Martyrs* (Detroit, MI: PIME World Press, 1997).
Zhang Rongliang, with Eugene Bach, *I Stand with Christ: The Courageous Life of a Chinese Christian* (New Kensington, PA: Whitaker House, 2015).

Contact details

Paul Hattaway is the founder and director of Asia Harvest, a non-denominational ministry which serves the Church in Asia through various strategic initiatives, including Bible printing and supporting Asian missionaries who share the gospel among unreached peoples.

The author can be reached by email at <**paul@asiaharvest.org**>, or by writing to him via any of the addresses listed below.

For more than 30 years Asia Harvest has served the Church in Asia through strategic projects that equip the local churches. At the time of going to print, Asia Harvest has successfully distributed just over one million Bibles to house church Christians in Henan Province, in addition to supporting many evangelists and providing aid to hundreds of persecuted church leaders and their families.

If you would like to receive the free Asia Harvest newsletter or to order other volumes in the China Chronicles series or Paul's other books, please visit <**www.asiaharvest.org**> or write to the address below nearest you:

Asia Harvest USA and Canada
353 Jonestown Rd #320
Winston-Salem, NC 27104
USA

Asia Harvest Australia
36 Nelson Street
Stepney, SA 5069
Australia

Asia Harvest New Zealand
PO Box 1757
Queenstown, 9348
New Zealand

Asia Harvest UK and Ireland
c/o AsiaLink
31A Main Street
Ballyclare
Co. Antrim BT39 9AA
United Kingdom

Asia Harvest Europe
c/o Stiftung SALZ
Moehringer Landstr. 98
70563 Stuttgart
Germany